Contributions to Economics

For further volumes:
http://www.springer.com/series/1262

Juan Felipe Mejía

Export Diversification and Economic Growth

An Analysis of Colombia's Export Competitiveness in the European Union's Market

Physica-Verlag
A Springer Company

Juan Felipe Mejía Ph.D.
School of Business Administration
EAFIT University
Carrera 49, No 7 Sur-50
Medellín
Colombia
jfmejia@eafit.edu.co

ISSN 1431-1933
ISBN 978-3-7908-2741-5 e-ISBN 978-3-7908-2742-2
DOI 10.1007/978-3-7908-2742-2
Springer Heidelberg Dordrecht London New York

Library of Congress Control Number: 2011935048

Printed on acid-free paper

Physica-Verlag is a brand of Springer-Verlag Berlin Heidelberg
Springer-Verlag is a part of Springer Science+Business Media (www.springer.com)

Acknowledgements

These years dedicated to my dissertation represent a very valuable, enriching, and important experience that I will always remember and cherish. Undertaking Doctoral studies in Germany allowed me to significantly broaden my academic vision and knowledge. It also offered me the possibility of interacting with very dedicated Professors and Doctoral students that I will never forget.

This academic undertaking could not have been accomplished without the help and support of many people that contributed in a very important manner. First of all, I am deeply grateful to Professor Dr. Harald Hagemann, who believed in my skills and capacities and generously accepted to be my First Supervisor. His insights, comments, and guidance have been of the utmost importance for accomplishing the research objectives formulated. I also appreciate very much his interest in the economic and political situation of my home country, Colombia, as well as his permanent disposition and kindness at the moment of providing orientation.

The dissertation benefited immensely from the feedback, comments, and suggestions from Professor Dr. Ansgar Belke, who in a very enthusiastic manner accepted to be my Second Supervisor. I owe much thanks to him for his guidance, which has been of paramount importance within the research project. I am very grateful for his attention, time, and extremely important feedback. I would also like to thank Professor Dr. Peter Spahn, for his comments within the framework of the Ph.D. Students Seminar, and for accepting to be included within the examination committee.

The DAAD – *Deutscher Akademischer Austausch Dienst* played a crucial role for making this project possible, both in economic and human terms. It is a great pleasure to acknowledge here the support of Mr. Arpe Caspary, former Director of the DAAD in Colombia, who provided me with important orientation about the possibilities of undertaking Doctoral studies in Germany. I am also thankful to Dr. Eckhard Schmidt, and to Mrs. Elke Massa-Miranda.

EAFIT University, where I will continue to pursue my academic career in Colombia, deserves special mention. His President, Mr. Juan Luis Mejía Arango, as well as the Dean of the School of Business Administration, Dr. Francisco López

Gallego, wholeheartedly supported my objective of studying abroad. The support of EAFIT during these four years was not just financial, but also personal, offering me the time and part of the resources to conduct studies in Europe.

I am deeply indebted to Julian Christ, Research and Teaching Assistant and Doctoral Student in Economics at the University of Hohenheim. His comments and feedback motivated me to think harder and deeper about my research questions, and it was always a pleasure to have very motivating academic conversations with him. I am also thankful to Andreja Benkovic, Constanze Dobler, Patricia Hoffmann, Arash Molavi and Ralf Rukwid, Doctoral Students in Economics at the University of Hohenheim. Dr. Julia Spies (*Institut für Angewandte Wirtschaftsforschung e.V.*) and Mr. Jan Hogrefe (ZEW Mannheim) also provided very important feedback. I am also indebted to Mrs. Christine Eisenbraun, Secretary of the Chair of Economic Theory, for her kindness and collaboration.

My loving wife Sandra has been my company, personal support, and very important ally in this academic and personal experience. I owe much thanks to her for her patience and affection. Last but not least, I owe a debt of gratitude to my family in Colombia, 9,089 kilometers away from Stuttgart, who also encouraged me to pursue my academic goals and constantly sent me their best wishes.

Contents

List of Abbreviations

ACP	African, Caribbean, and Pacific Group of States
AM	Amemiya MaCurdy Estimator
ASEAN	Association of Southeast Asian Nations
BANCOLDEX	Banco de Comercio Exterior de Colombia
BRIC	Brazil, Russia, India, and China
CARICOM	Caribbean Community and Common Market
CEPAL	Comisión Económica para América Latina
CES	Constant Elasticity of Substitution
COMIFAL	Colombian Technical Support Committee for the Facilitation of Trade, Logistics, and Transport
CSTI	Commodity-Specific Traditionality Index
CTPA	Colombia Trade Promotion Agreement
CU	Customs Union
DANE	National Administrative Department of Statistics
EBA	Everything but Arms Initiative of the European Union
ECLA	United Nations Economic Commission for Latin America and the Caribbean
ECLA	United Nations' Economic Commission for Latin America
EFTA	European Free Trade Association
EP	Export Promotion
ESCAP	United Nations Economic and Social Commission for Asia and the Pacific
EU	European Union
EUROSTAT	Statistical Office of the European Union
FDI	Foreign Direct Investment
FE	Fixed Effects Estimation
FTA	Free Trade Agreement
GCI	Global Competitiveness Index
GDP	Gross domestic product
GSP	Generalyzed System of Preferences

GSPEU	Generalized System of Preferences of the European Union
GSP PLUS	Generalyzed System of Preferences Plus
HD	Harrod-Domar
HHI	Herfindahl-Hirschmann Index
HT	Hausman-Taylor estimator
ICT	Information and Communication Technologies
IIT	Intra-Industry Trade
IMD	International Institute for Management Development
IMF	International Monetary Fund
INSEAD	Institut Européen d'Administration des Affaires
IS	Import Substitution
ISI	Import-Substitution Industrialization
IT	Information Technology
ITC	International Trade Centre
IV	Instrumental Variable
LAC	Latin American and Caribbean Countries
LDC	Less Developed Countries
LM	Lagrange Multiplier
LPI	Logistics Performance Index
MERCOSUR	Mercado Común del Sur
MFN	Most Favored Nation
MNC	Multinational Corporations
NAFTA	North American Free Trade Agreement
NBER	National Bureau of Economic Research
NICs	Newly Industrialized Countries of Asia
NRI	Networked Readiness Index
OAS	Organization of American States
OAS	Organization of American States
OECD	Organisation for Economic Cooperation and Development
OECD	Organization of Economic Cooperation and Development
OLS	Ordinary Least Squares
PISA	Program for International Student Assessment
POLS	Pooled Ordinary Least Squares
PPA	Partial Preferential Agreements
PPI	Public Private Partnerships
PROEXPO	Export Promotion Agency
PROEXPORT	Colombian national business support organization
R&D	Research and development
RCA	Revealed Comparative Advantage Index
RE	Random Effects
RoO	Rules of Origin
RTA	Regional Trade Agreement
TFP	Total Factor Productivity
TRQs	Tariff-Rate Quotas

UN COMTRADE	United Nations Commodity Trade Statistics Database
UNCTAD	United Nations Conference on Trade and Development
UNESCO	United Nations Educational, Scientific and Cultural Organization
US-CTPA	US-Colombia Trade Promotion Agreement
USD	United States Dollar
WEF	World Economic Forum
WIPO	World Intellectual Property Organization
WTO	World Trade Organization

List of Figures

List of Tables

List of Tables in the Appendix

Chapter 1
Introduction

From a failed state, Colombia is turning now to be an attractive nation. . .Much of our national territory was ungovernable, and we lived in an internal confrontation with terrorist groups that terrorized our citizens. . .We hope that in a couple of generations we remain as a case study of a country that has finally overcome its adversities.

(Own Translation: Speech at the United Nations of Colombian President Juan Manuel Santos, September 22, 2010).

1.1 Motivation and Scope

Within the World Bank's classification, Colombia is at present considered as an upper-middle-income economy. The country's growth performance for almost 50 years, its sound macroeconomic management, and its democratic tradition, are some factors that have been recognized by leading international economic institutions. Other recent positive developments that have been praised are, among others, its accelerating economic growth between 2002 and 2007—mainly due to advancements in domestic security, to rising commodity prices, and to the current administration's pro-market economic policies. Moreover, investor friendly reforms to the hydrocarbon sector and the US-Colombia Trade Promotion Agreement (CTPA) negotiations have attracted record levels of foreign investment during the last years. Taking into account that at the end of the 1990s this nation stood on the brink of a social and economic collapse, the above mentioned accomplishments appear particularly impressive. As stated by the World Bank (2010a), while other Latin American and Caribbean nations have been fighting against inequality, poverty or violence, Colombia has been facing all three at the same time.

In contrast, it has also been remarked how Colombia's science and technological capacities are staying behind, its infrastructure is poor and a sense of insecurity remains, despite of the recent government successes. While it is true that the country's resource-based economy has accomplished to relatively diversify from the export of its traditional commodities, it should also be noted how the levels of

J.F. Mejía, *Export Diversification and Economic Growth*, Contributions to Economics, DOI 10.1007/978-3-7908-2742-2_1, investment have not been sufficient to bring widespread technological modernization or commensurate infrastructure development. Poverty remains one of Colombia's main challenges, alongside inequality, which continues to be one of the highest in Latin America. Underemployment and narcotrafficking, notwithstanding the unquestionable advances of the last 7 years, still pose significant challenges. An unemployment rate of 12%, coupled with a percentage of approximately 49.2% of the population living below the poverty line, the urgent need of employment generation, and a staggering 60% of its people working in the informal economy, are all reasons for considering the need of spurring economic growth and development in that nation.

Another concerning trend not just of Colombia, but of Latin America as a whole, is represented by the concentration of exports. A study conducted by the World Bank reports that 52% of the region's exports were composed of commodities in the past decade. In contrast, commodity exports in dynamic developing regions—East Asia and the Pacific—just represented a share of 30% (The Economist 2010). In the particular case of Colombia, the mining sector (e.g. petroleum, natural gas, and coal) has become increasingly important: it accounts for 8% of the GDP, and since 2008 the sector's annual growth exceeds the economy's overall growth by far. Employment originated in these activities has been growing, and the income taxes payed by the sector represented a share of 23% of the total government revenues in 2009 (Caballero 2010). Moreover, in the past 8 years exports of mining products have significantly increased, and FDI levels in the sector are booming, especially since 2009 (Caballero 2010). But, as a recent report of The Economist (2010) was rightfully titled, "commodities alone are not enough to sustain flourishing economies". Both the literature and the empirical evidence provide evidence of different problematic aspects linked to export concentration, like the vulnerability to sharp declines in terms of trade, the risks associated to foreign earnings volatility, and the fact that export concentration, be it on commodities, industrial products, or services, is indeed detrimental for growth.

The main research problem addressed by the current dissertation project is the one regarding the possible role that export diversification, both in terms of new products and new geographic markets, could play for enhancing economic growth in Colombia. The underlying motivations for centering the analysis on the European Union's market are manifold, reaching from the evident concentration of exports – both in terms of composition and markets- that Colombia still shows, to the small amount of empirical studies analyzing the current status and potentialities of the commercial relations between Colombia and the European Union.

As stated by Brenton, Newfarmer, Shaw, and Walkenhorst (2009), export diversification is playing again an important role for development concerns. It is considered by different scholars as a channel trough which trade boosts economic growth, by promoting productivity, by capturing economies of scale, and by controlling volatility. Consequently, export diversification has been proposed as a policy mechanism seeking to stabilize export earnings, which would be especially required in those developing countries where the share of commodities in its export basket is particularly pronounced. As stated by Ali et al. (1991), export diversification entails changing the composition of a country's export mix, being it "directly related to the structure of the economy and how it changes as development proceeds". A broader exports base, coupled with a special promotion of those commodities with positive price trends, should be beneficial for growth. A country's degree of diversification is usually considered as dependent upon the number of commodities within its export mix, as well as on the distribution of their individual shares. At this point, a very important clarification to be made is that export diversification does not necessarily imply the export of manufactured goods. As stated by Agosin (2006), this process may also be carried out in the form of primary commodities that evolve into natural-resource-based industries, rather than into manufactures. Indeed, commodity exports should not be literally associated with export concentration. Additionally, diversification has usually been related to the production and export of goods with higher skill and knowledge intensity (Agosin 2006).

1.2 Outline of the Dissertation

Within the literature review section, some specific research questions are addressed from a theoretical perspective. Before shifting the analysis towards the export diversification topic, the chapter discusses, in an introductory fashion, if international trade effectively might enhance economic growth in a developing country such as Colombia. The relationship between trade and economic growth is discussed, both from the international trade theory and the growth theory stances. Starting with the Smithian perspective, and continuing with David Ricardo's model, the Specific Factors Model, the standard Heckscher-Ohlin model, the *New Trade Theory* and ultimately, the so-called *New New Trade Theory,* the static and dynamic gains from trade are analyzed. As far as the growth theory is concerned, scholarly contributions of authors such as Rivera-Batiz, Romer, Grossman, Helpman, Barro and Sala-i-Martin are analyzed, as well as the Harrod-Domar and Solow models. The role of trade as the principal channel that allows knowledge to be transmitted internationally – as proposed by endogenous growth theories-is also discussed. Relevant empirical studies dealing with the relationship between trade and growth are analyzed – multy-country qualitative studies, simultaneous equations "channels" models, cross-country regressions (growth on trade), simple correlation analyses, and "robust studies" (sensitivity analyses).

Later on, the chapter focuses on the paramount theoretical and empirical issue considered within the dissertation, namely, how a process of export diversification may contribute to economic growth in developing countries. This section reviews and analyzes relevant scholarly contributions that would allow understanding if there is a causal relationship between export diversification and economic growth. Also, it evaluates if export diversification is an outcome derived from the growth process. The main definition and implications of export diversification are discussed, taking into account different contributions such as the one provided by the product-cycle literature (Vernon 1966; Krugman 1979a; Dollar 1986;

Segerstrom et al. 1990; Grossman and Helpman 1991), which has suggested a link between export diversification and growth. Another strand of the literature analyzed is the one concerned with those determinants that would be needed for diversification to be successful. Among these factors, the level of income of an economy, its investment and productive capacity levels, the role of industrial policy, and its technology absorption capability, are examined.

Relatively new contributions on endogenous growth, placing a special emphasis on the importance of diversification, are also explained. This chapter finalizes by conducting a review of different econometric and statistical studies that explore the relationship between export diversification and growth, which can be classified into sectoral regressions, cross-country growth regressions, causality tests, instrumental variables specifications, and the analysis of concentration and diversification indexes.

Based on the examination of different concentration and diversification indexes, Chap. 3 explores the evolution of Colombian exports over the period 1990–2008. The analysis is concentrated on this lapse of time, considering that the country embarked on an active outward-oriented trade policy in February 1990. In that year, the Colombian government officially announced its decision of reforming the country's economic development model, launching the so-called *Program for the Modernization and Industrialization*. In an introductory manner, it starts analyzing some macroeconomic trends of this period, such as the evolution of GDP growth, inflation, and unemployment rates. An important distinction is then introduced, namely, the one concerning the distinction between the notions of "traditional exports" and "non-traditional exports".

On first instance, the main research question tackled in this chapter is if a process of export diversification can be identified in Colombia since the year 1990. Coupled with that, this section analyzes if the growth of exports in Colombia has been due to the so-called "intensive margin of export diversification", or to the so-called "extensive margin of export diversification". Different indicators are calculated and analyzed for answering to those questions: in first instance, cumulative export experience functions and industry-specific traditionality indexes—based on the approach of Amin Gutiérrez de Piñeres and Ferrantino (1997a)—are calculated, with the objective of capturing the degree of "traditionality" of the Colombian export industries. In addition to that, the analysis is conducted based on the country's performance in the Herfindahl-Hirschman index (HHI) of export concentration, the Export Diversification Index, the Intensive and Extensive Margin of Exports Indexes—the latter based on the methodology of Evenett and Venables (2002)—, the Diversification of Markets Index, and the trade performance of Colombian export sectors.

Another interesting perspective of Colombia's trade pattern is obtained from applying the Grubel & Lloyd index of trade overlap to the Colombian industrial exports. Colombia's trade specialization is evaluated based on the Revealed Comparative Advantage (RCA) index. Finally, an analysis of the behavior of Colombian exports with some selected market is conducted (NAFTA, European Union, Andean Community of Nations, Mercosur, and the Central American Common Market), with the objective of exploring if a process of geographical diversification of exports has taken place.

Among different conclusions drawn in the chapter, it is reported that a number of Colombian industries have been benefited by greater markets and the implementation of economies of scale in the period of time analyzed. The processed food, apparel and clothing, petro-chemical, and the metal-mechanic industries are some examples of economies of scale that have been taking profit from larger markets. Trade between Colombia and developed counterparts, in line with the classical theory and most of the empirical evidence, remains strongly based on comparative advantage and an inter-industry pattern. In the same line of argumentation of Moreno and Posada (2006), it is reported how Colombia's specialization in the world's marketplace remains heavily dependent upon comparative advantage, centered on the production of goods abundant in natural resources and low-skilled labor. The latter, taking into account the scarcity in terms of qualified human capital, as well as the technological gap, which in turn seriously undermines the productivity of Colombian industrial exports.

The statistics and figures analyzed in this section document that Colombia, especially since 2002, has been reaping the benefits derived from the implementation of an outward-oriented policy: GDP rates of growth and the total value of exports have remarkably increased. But, on the other hand, the average participation of Colombian industrial exports has not been augmented over the period 1990–2008. An important challenge is related to fostering their productivity and therefore, its capacity to compete in the world's marketplace.

At the light of the gravity model and the gravity equation, Chap. 4 seeks to analyze the Colombian pattern of exports in the period 1990–2008. The underlying motivation of this empirical analysis has been to explore, from an econometrical perspective, to which extent the trade preferences offered by the European Union have exerted an effect upon Colombia's exports. It is also intended to analyze how well the gravity model, and specifically the gravity equation, explain the Colombian pattern of exports. The main variable of interest is related therefore to the European *GSP Plus*, a unilateral set of preferences granted by the European Union to Colombia and the other three members of the Andean Community of Nations. In the first section of the chapter, the theoretical foundations of the gravity model are discussed, conducting a brief review of the academic literature related to the gravity model. After that, the testable log-linearized gravity equation used to address the above mentioned research questions is exposed, taking the following specification:

$$\ln EXP_{ijt} = \beta 0 + \beta 1 \ln GDP_{it} + \beta 2 \ln GDP_{jt} + \beta 3 \ln D_{ij} + \beta 4 \ln re_{ijt} + \beta 5 Border_{ij} + \beta 6 Landl_{ij} + \beta 7 Island_{ij} + \beta 8 Lang_{ij} + \beta 9 GSPEU_{it} + \beta 10 RTA_{ijt} + \varepsilon_{ijt} \tag{1.1}$$

where i and j denote countries, and t denotes time. (EXP_{ijt}) is the value of Colombian exports to country j at time t, GDP_{it} is Colombia's GDP, GDP_{jt} is the partner country's GDP, accounting respectively for export supply and demand conditions. D_{ij} is the great-circle distance between Colombia and the capital city of its trade partner, which is a proxy for the transportation costs. As mentioned before, re_{ijt} seeks to capture the influence of the bilateral real exchange rate upon trade between both partners. The set of binary dummy variables capturing geographical factors is composed by $Border_{ij}$, which is unity if the countries share a land border, $Landl_{ij}$, which is unity if one of the countries is a landlocked territory, and $Island_{ij}$, which is unity if one of the trade partners is an island. $Lang_{ij}$ takes the value of one if both countries share the same language.

Finally, two binary dummy variables represent institutional factors exerting an influence upon Colombia's exports: $GSPEU_{it}$, which takes the value of one if the exports have been covered by the European Union's GSP, and RTA_{ijt}, *which* is unity if both countries make part of any regional trade agreement, or if Colombia receives any other preferences from the trade partner.

The estimations are based on a panel data set including 45 countries which together account for more than 80% of the total amount of Colombian exports, over the period 1990–2008. The main sources of the data are the International Monetary Fund's Direction of Trade Statistics (DOT) CD-Rom, the United Nations National Accounts Main Aggregates Database, and the World Bank's World Development Indicators Database. Information concerning Colombia's membership to the different regional trade agreements, as well as regarding the unilateral preferences obtained, has been obtained from the Organization of American States' Foreign Trade Information System.

The so-called "standard features of the gravity model" – GDP and distance variables, as Rose, Lockwood, and Quah (2000) calls them – show the expected signs and coefficients. Both Colombia's GDP and the trade partner's GDP exert a positive and significant influence on Colombian exports. In what relates to distance, its expected sign according to the literature and previous empirical studies is negative: the further away trade partners are from each other, the less they are expected to conduct trade relations. Traditionally, the effect of distance is interpreted as a proxy for transport costs, an indicator of time elapsed during shipment, synchronization costs, transaction costs or cultural distance (Correia 2008). The distance variable showed the expected negative coefficient, and was also statistically significant.

From the four variables capturing geographical and cultural factors that affect trade, only *island* showed to be statistically significant. Moreover, the results obtained from the regression analysis provided evidence showing that the European Union's GSP exerted a positive influence upon Colombian exports over the period of time analyzed. This suggests that Colombian exports have positively benefitted from the unilateral scheme of preferences offered by the European Union, and that this trade mechanism had a large and positive effect on Colombian exports within the period of time analyzed.

Next, Chap. 5 is intended to evaluate if Colombia is, indeed, prepared to reap the benefits of export diversification. As has been suggested by Cramer (1999), while it is commonly believed that greater benefits could be expected from export diversification – like more stable and less "biased" price behavior-, this positive outcome should not be taken for granted: domestic conditions are also required, along with the diversification process. In brief, increasing levels of export diversification do not guarantee, by themselves, higher levels of growth (Bebczuk and Berrettoni 2006, p. 2). If there are, for instance, shortage of inputs, bad management practices or weak infrastructure in a country, such conditions could outweigh the possible benefits from diversifying away from primary production (Love 1983). Hence, the current section evaluates the current status of factors of paramount importance for a successful process of diversification in the world's marketplace, such as the support for national innovation and technology adoption, the access to finance, the quality and level of the infrastructure, the status quo of the human capital in the country, and the role of trade-related institutions. In summary, this chapter explores the degree of "export competitiveness" of Colombia, placing a special emphasis on the commercial relations with the European Union. At this point, the analysis focuses on the trade mechanisms offered by the latter regional block of integration and the potentialities offered.

The analysis is undertaken based on time-series analysis of different indicators, such as the World Economic Forum's Global Competitiveness Index (GCI), which is intended to capture the microeconomic and macroeconomic foundations of national competitiveness (Sala-i-Martin et al. 2009). The most relevant indicators associated to the so-called "12 pillars of competitiveness" (institutions, infrastructure, macroeconomic stability, health and primary education, higher education and training, goods market efficiency, labor market efficiency, financial market sophistication, technological readiness, market size, business sophistication, and innovation) are analyzed. The study of the behavior of these indexes is complemented with the evaluation of other statistics relevant to the field of competitiveness, such as the macroeconomic environment (GDP rates of growth, exchange rates, inflation, among others) and human capital indicators (public expenditure on education as a percentage of the GDP, literacy rates, enrollment rates). Finally, this chapter conducts brief study about the competitiveness strategy implemented by Colombian policymakers, as well as the so-called "National Competitiveness System", integrated by different branches of the Colombian government, like the Presidential Council for Competitiveness, the National Planning Department, and some Colombian Ministries (Finance, International Relations, Trade, Energy and Mining, among others).

Within the 2009–2010 Global Competitiveness Report, Colombia is included in the list of *efficiency-driven* countries, according to its stage of development. Developing more efficient production processes and increasing product quality is, at this phase, crucial for enhancing competitiveness. Among the different findings of this chapter, it is argued that some of the greatest problems that still need to be tackled in that country are related to the poor levels of infrastructure, the scarce coverage in terms of education – especially at the secondary and tertiary levels-, and the technological gap that needs to be surpassed. The poor institutional environment, as well as the rather inefficient factor markets, are also cited as factors that impose serious limitations.

Taking into account the positive approach of the previous sections, Chap. 5 seeks to provide a normative approximation to the topic of the evolution of the export diversification in Colombia, placing special emphasis on the European Union's market. For accomplishing that objective, a critical evaluation of the opportunities and challenges derived from an increased level of trade with the European Union is introduced. In addition to the opportunities currently offered by the European GSP, an evaluation of the different conditions requested by the European Union to Colombia is conducted. Finally, the chapter makes reference to different policies focusing on export diversification that have proved to be successful in other nations, and that could be considered by Colombian policymakers for overcoming market failures (such as the incentives regime, or the necessity of reducing the costs of doing business in the country in terms of infrastructure, logistics, or security, among different factors).

Chapter 2
Export Diversification, International Trade, and Economic Growth: A Survey of the Literature

As it is by treaty, by barter, and by purchase, that we obtain from one another the greater part of those mutual good offices which we stand in need of, so it is this same trucking disposition which originally gives occasion to the division of labour.

(Adam Smith, *The Wealth of Nations*, 1776).

Without continual growth and progress, such words as improvement, achievement, and success have no meaning.

(Benjamin Franklin, 1706–1790)

Since the very beginning of the 1990s, Colombian policy-makers introduced a new approach towards the national economic development: As stated by Ocampo and Villar (1992), the so-called "Modernization and Internationalization Program" was officially launched, encouraging national industries to face competition in the international markets. Just in the same direction of other developing nations, this initiative has been vigorously defended ever since, based on an expected positive correlation between economic growth and an increased openness of the country to foreign trade.

At first, the current chapter discusses in an introductory fashion the relationship between trade and economic growth, from the international trade theory and the growth theory perspectives. In Sect. 2.1, a survey of the academic literature and a number of relevant empirical studies is conducted. Section 2.2 focuses on the paramount theoretical issue considered within the whole dissertation, namely, how a process of export diversification may contribute to economic growth in a developing country like Colombia. The main theoretical and empirical approaches dealing with export diversification are analyzed here. Finally, conclusions are drawn, related to the possible impact that both international trade and export diversification could exert upon Colombia's economic growth.

J.F. Mejía, *Export Diversification and Economic Growth*, Contributions to Economics,
DOI 10.1007/978-3-7908-2742-2_2, © Springer-Verlag Berlin Heidelberg 2011

2.1 The Static and Dynamic Gains from Trade

2.1.1 Trade and Economic Growth, from the Perspective of the International Trade Theory and the Growth Theory

The relation between trade and economic growth has been thoroughly and extensively analyzed. As pointed out by Van den Berg and Lewer (2007), since Adam Smith's explanation of the concept of absolute advantage in the late eighteenth century, over the past 200 years the economic literature has built strong arguments to justify free trade policies. In the first place, the current section analyzes the relationship between trade and economic growth, at the light of the international trade theory.

Smith stated that increasing specialization and the division of labor, coupled with international exchange, would contribute to raise welfare and growth of a nation. It can be deduced that Smith saw international trade as a welfare-enhancing mechanism: the division of labor required people exchanging goods and services. Higher levels of trade would imply more specialization – division of labor- and by these means, economic growth would be enhanced. Specialization is considered by Smith both as a source of efficiency gains and continued technological progress, since it implies the development of new tools and mechanisms for undertaking the specialized tasks. When specialization is promoted, new gains from exchange could be expected, as countries exploit the gains from that specialization (Van den Berg and Lewer 2007). More specialization, induced by free trade, would reinforce the economy's growth path.

For Smith, as suggested by Van den Berg and Lewer (2007):

> International trade has a very positive effect on economic growth. A sudden shift in trade policy that opens up new trade provides an immediate gain in real per capita income, which, in turn, accelerates technological progress and increases the rate of economic growth permanently. (p. 76)

Subsequently, it can be affirmed that the Smithian perspective associated trade both to gains in per capita output and increases in the rate of economic growth. An increase in productivity, derived from the lifting of restrictions on foreign trade, would generate a greater output for the given level of capital (Barkai 1969).

David Ricardo's two countries-two goods-one factor of production example proposes gains from trade and specialization for the countries involved, even when one of the countries is more efficient in the production of both goods. The Ricardian model explains trade as a sort of "win-win situation", where the two countries engaged are benefited, despite of their differences in terms of technology or wages. International trade originates in international differences in the productivity of labor. The pattern of trade, being determined by comparative advantage, increases welfare in both nations by means of improvements in production and consumption efficiency. Specialization turns out to be beneficial for the countries involved. Wages and incomes are also better off, after trade takes place. As stated by Sen (2005), free trade was proposed by Smith and Ricardo as a route to achieve production efficiency at a global level.

Within the Ricardian model, trade welfare effects are considered from two different perspectives. The first one is associated to the rise in real wages for the workers in the two countries engaged in trade, as compared to their situation in autarky. A situation is depicted where, if both countries specialize in their comparative advantage goods and engage in free trade, then both countries could experience gains from trade (Suranovic 2009).

The second perspective is linked to the aggregate welfare effects of free trade, originated in increased production and consumption efficiency. Specialization and comparative advantage allow countries to achieve higher levels of aggregate utility, implying a rise in their national welfare. Trade allows consumers to reach a higher indifference curve and hence, a higher welfare level, than under autarky.

Producers and consumers are benefitted by free trade, since it increases the ranges of choice in both countries involved. World output can be augmented, if each country specializes in producing the good in which it has comparative advantage (Krugman and Obstfeld 2006).

Until this point, trade has been considered as a clearly beneficial process for all the parties involved. This is why the Specific Factors Model introduces an innovative idea: there are factors specific to particular industries, allowing to understand how trade affects income distribution. Feenstra and Taylor (2008) point out how the change in relative prices, due to the opening of trade, generates winners and losers. Some factors of production gain in real terms while other factors of production lose.

The standard Heckscher-Ohlin model proposes that trade enhances welfare for the nations engaged in trade, considering that countries realize higher levels of aggregated utility as compared to autarky. Countries resort to trade because of differences in terms of the availability of their factors of production. Aggregate welfare gains from free trade are classified into two distinct effects; namely, production efficiency gains and consumption efficiency gains (Suranovic 2009). But it is also clear that the shift from autarky to free trade entails some redistributive effects: the country's relatively abundant factor gains from trade, while the country's relatively scarce factor loses from it (Suranovic 2009). This is a noticeable difference with respect to former approaches: it is now shown that the benefits from trade will not necessarily be received by all individuals.

The increase in aggregate welfare leads to a situation where the gains will surpass the losses, but this does not imply that every single individual will gain from trade. Hence, the approach is oriented towards the gains derived from the country's abundant factor and the losses associated to the scarce factor, after it opens to trade. Krugman and Obstfeld (2006) highlight how in the short run, factors that are specific to industries that must compete with imports lose from trade. In the long run, a country's scarce factors lose from trade. As a consequence of that, a clear effect on income distribution can be expected. But in the end, the gains clearly outweigh the losses, and "overall" gains from trade should be expected.

Later on, an important shift in the international trade theory takes place. From models based on comparative advantage in terms of differences in endowment of production factors, and sector-specific input requirements under perfect competition, a new theory explaining intra-industry trade -accompanied by product differentiation under monopolistic competition- is proposed (Tomiura 2006).

Based on a general equilibrium model with one single factor of production (labor) and economies of scale internal to the firm – imperfect competition, assuming *n* different goods and consumers' taste for variety- the so-called *New Trade Theory* shows trade as beneficial, since it increases market size (Krugman and Obstfeld 2006). Gains from trade could be expected, even when production takes place in imperfectly competitive industries with increasing returns to scale. As a result of specialization, an opportunity for mutual gain arises, even if countries are similar in terms of economic development or capital-labor ratios. A larger market leads to both lower average prices and the availability of a greater variety of goods. Welfare would be, therefore, increased: consumers get now bigger consumption possibilities.

Krugman and Obstfeld (2006) also state that:

> In these circumstances the income distribution effects of trade will be small and there will be substantial extra gains from intra-industry trade. The result may be that despite the effects of trade in income distribution, everyone gains from trade. (p. 129)

Consequently, it is proposed that the resulting gains would be larger than the ones associated to comparative advantage. Gains from trade will arise "even between countries with identical tastes, technology, and factor endowments" (Krugman 1979b, p. 469). In brief, opening up to trade derives in a larger number of goods, the exploitation of economies of scale, and lower unit costs.

Further support to the notion of additional gains from trade has also been lent by other authors. Leibenstein (1966) proposes that the level of efficiency in the economy is influenced by the level of competition. This would imply that, holding all other factors equal, international trade reinforces competition and thus, a country's managerial and productive effort. It has also been proposed that the traditional trade models do not account for the costs of "rent seeking behavior by special interests seeking to influence trade policy" (Van den Berg and Lewer 2007, p. 19).

The most recent shift in the international trade theory is based on an extension of Krugman's model, which has been stimulated by the positive increase in data availability at the firm level (Neary 2009). The so-called *New New Trade Theory*, led by Melitz and Antras, differs in the sense that the unit of analysis is now transferred from the industry, to the firm (Tomiura 2006). Melitz (2003) brings forward a new gain from trade not accounted for by the trade theory so far. Within the framework of a dynamic industry model with heterogeneous firms, he shows how opening up to trade induces "only the more productive firms to enter the export market (while some less productive firms continue to produce only for the domestic market), simultaneously forcing the least productive to exit" (p. 1695). The aggregate industry productivity growth, proceeding from the reallocations, would contribute to a welfare gain. Hence, the exit of the least productive firms and the additional sales of the more productive ones, lead to a reallocation of market shares towards the more productive firms, enhancing aggregate productivity (Melitz 2003, p. 1695). The existence of export market entry costs strongly influences the impact of trade across different types of firms. But despite of those costs, the welfare-enhancing nature of trade is highlighted. What exports costs do is to adjust the distribution of the gains from trade across firms (Melitz 2003). Nevertheless, it is also suggested that this reallocation process also entails some short-run costs. Further lines of research dealing with the possible impact of trade policy on inter-firm reallocations are suggested, for compensating these transitional costs.

As will be explained in a next section, the idea of additional or new sources of gains from trade has both advocates and opponents. At the first side of the debate, one interesting perspective concerning the welfare effects from trade is the one defended by Van den Berg and Lewer (2007). For them, the gains from trade cannot be merely linked to the static ones derived from comparative advantage. They suggest that the largest benefits are derived from long-term dynamic gains proceeding from the positive effect of trade on economic growth, trough different channels such as technology transfer. They conclude by affirming that "combining trade theory and growth theory potentially leads to a strong case for free trade" (p. 253). On the other side of the discussion, authors like (Arkolakis, Costinot, and Rodríguez-Clare 2010) – as will be more clearly explained hereinafter – contest this proposal, affirming that "richer trade models do not entail larger gains from trade" (p. 1). They suggest that the new sources of gains from trade may change their composition, but not their total size.

At this point, a number of benefits associated to trade have been mentioned, all of them proposed by the international trade theory. The welfare-enhancing nature of trade has been stated by the different schools of thought, taking into account aspects such as production and consumption efficiency gains, productivity increases, greater output, and the rise of real wages. Besides that, the most recent contributions emphasize how trade increases market size, allowing for a larger variety of goods and lower prices. Finally, it has been proposed that trade could lead to an increased aggregate productivity growth at the industry level.

But the cause for free trade is not unanimously accepted. The debate has mainly developed along the arguments of the so-called "trade optimists" – supporters of free trade, and outward-looking development- and of the "trade pessimists" – advocates of greater protection, and inward-looking development (Todaro and Smith 2006). However, before addressing this discussion, it is important to analyze the possible linkages between trade and economic growth.

Establishing the linkage between trade and economic growth is not an easy task: this is certainly one of the most interesting and rich debates present in the economic literature. In addition to the different trade theories and models, a wide number of empirical and statistical studies are frequently cited, when supporting or countering the case for free trade. On the one hand, since the times of Adam Smith in the late eighteenth century, different schools of thought have advocated for free trade, placing a special emphasis on the gains derived from it. On the other hand, counter-arguments in the economic literature, and possible shortcomings of the empirical estimations, are frequently exposed by the sceptics of the free trade cause, as will be analyzed later.

As Van den Berg and Lewer (2007) observe, one important clarification in advance is that causality between trade and growth seems to have a bi-directional nature: at one side of the relationship, trade seems to enhance growth. On the other side, it is apparent that higher levels of development and better technologies lead to a larger degree of trade among economies. Another interesting aspect that should be considered within the debate is the one concerning the complexity of this relation, taking into account that many other variables- such as economic, social, and political factors- seem to exert an influence both on trade and growth.

Furthermore, it is important to recall the distinction between the static and dynamic gains from trade. The former result from the reallocation of resources from one sector to another -as increased specialization, based on comparative advantage, takes place. Dynamic gains from trade constantly shift outwards the production possibility frontier, provided that trade is associated with more investment and faster productivity growth based on scale economies, learning by doing and the acquisition of new knowledge from abroad, particularly through foreign direct investment (Thirlwall 2000, p. 6). And as stated before, different authors have suggested how understanding the possible linkage between exports and growth is possible by not only analyzing the international trade theory, but also the growth theory. This is why the focus of the analysis is now shifted to the approach offered by the principal schools of thought and theories related to the field of economic growth.

Exports have been considered as growth-enhancing within the traditional development literature, based on the suggested positive productivity spillovers from the tradable to the non-tradable sector (Madsen 2009; Edwards 1993). Its role of encouraging more efficient investment projects has also been proposed.

Due to Levine and Renelt (1992), the theoretical linkages between trade and growth have been formalized by prominent scholars such as Rivera-Batiz, Romer, Grossman, and Helpman. An interesting argument brought by the former two authors is that even though theoretical discussions frequently focus on the relationship between international trade and growth, empirical studies have traditionally only examined the relationship between exports and growth.

Coming back again to Adam Smith, this time from the economic growth perspective, it can be highlighted that this process is considered by him as welfare-enhancing, driven both by investment in capital and innovation. Afterwards, David Ricardo's theory of comparative advantage showed that under perfect competition and the full employment of resources, countries engaged in trade can obtain gains by specializing in the production of those goods with the lowest opportunity cost, and trading the surplus of production over domestic demand (Thirlwall 2000). These would essentially be static gains derived from the reallocation of resources from one sector to another, as increased specialization takes place (Thirlwall 2000). The classical school of thought has also considered technology as the mechanism that would help to solve the problem of diminishing returns, raising the production function. Following this line of reasoning, it is stated that an increased international trade would lead to an improved efficiency, aspect that would in turn spur technological progress.

Later on, within the Harrod-Domar (HD) model, an economy's growth rate is explained in terms of capital's level of saving and productivity. Economic growth is, therefore, attributed exclusively to capital accumulation. While it must be acknowledged that trade does not play an obvious role within the Harrod-Domar perspective, it does indeed enter in a subtle way, as stated by Van den Berg and Lewer (2007): it can influence how savings are invested. Some studies have found, for instance, that domestic prices in developing countries show to be distorted by trade restrictions, leading to a misallocation of resources. In contrary, in an open economy prices are supposed to be more accurate and to truly reflect opportunity costs, improving the allocation of resources.

Based on the Solow model, Baldwin (1992) analyzes the gains from trade: the economy's efficiency is augmented, by shifting the production function and hence, generating economic growth while the economy moves up to a higher steady state equilibrium level of capital and output (Van den Berg and Lewer 2007, p. 95). If the Solow model is extended (by including a variable for technology for given rates of savings and depreciation, as well as population growth), continuous economic growth can now be explained. A constant rate of technological progress continually raises the production function and thus, constantly increases the economy's steady state capital-labor ratio and per capita real output at the same rate (Van den Berg and Lewer 2007, p. 92). Hence, trade would encourage permanent growth as long as it is intertwined with technological progress. Taking into account the characteristics of technological progress, an open economy is likely to enjoy a faster rate of technological advance than a closed economy. The role of international trade as a promoter of technological transfer is, therefore, crucial.

The effect of trade on economic growth has also been extensively analyzed from the point of view of the foreign exchange generation. It has been affirmed that an increase of exports could be advantageous in terms of alleviating the foreign exchange constraint, ultimately exerting a positive effect on growth. As explained by Edwards (1993, p. 1385), an increase in imports of intermediate products permits to overcome bottlenecks, exerting an influence on output growth. Esfahani (1991, cited in Edwards 1993) points out that export-oriented policies would positively affect growth by supplying foreign exchange, alleviating import shortages, and supporting output expansion.

Moreover, endogenous growth theories place special emphasis on trade as the principal channel that allows knowledge to be transmitted internationally (Grossman and Helpman 1991). As stated by Madsen (2009, p. 398), the early endogenous growth models have been developed within the first generation endogenous growth framework, in which the level of research and development (R&D) activity and growth vary proportionally.

At this point, it is interesting to mention how the former argument has been quite recently moved from the export to the import perspective. As stated by Madsen (2009 p. 399), the recent endogenous growth literature focuses on the way that imports of knowledge enhance economic growth (Romer 1990a, 1992; Grossman and Helpman 1991; Rivera-Batiz and Romer 1991; Baldwin and Forslid 2000). By the same token, it has been suggested that imports give domestic producers access to a wider variety of capital goods, thus enlarging the efficiency of production (Barro and Sala-i-Martin 1995).

Madsen (2009), citing Grossman and Helpman (1991), argues that the quality of intermediate goods positively influences the efficiency of production. The new technology incorporated in foreign intermediate goods makes imported products more productive, increasing labor productivity and total factor productivity (TFP). An interesting remark of Madsen is that trade will enhance growth only to the extent that a country trades with research-intensive economies. Developing economies trading with advanced economies would have a potential for catching up, considering that the costs of imitation are lower than the costs of innovation (Barro and Sala-i-Martin, 1995, cited in Madsen 2009). Studies conducted would provide support to the hypothesis that knowledge spillovers through imports exert a positive influence on growth. Madsen further states that "R&D intensity has permanent growth effects, in consistency with the predictions of Schumpeterian growth theories" (p. 411).

In his work, Edwards (1993) undertakes a thorough review of the modern literature on trade policy in developing countries: the underlying objective is to analyze if the results of empirical studies do support the policy view that the performance of open economies has surpassed the one of restrictive economies. Two types of investigations are examined, namely, multi-country studies of protectionist practices and liberalization episodes -such as the influential ones elaborated by Balassa (1971), Krueger (1978) and Bhagwati (1978) and Michaely et al. (1991)- and cross-country regression analyses on the relationship between exports growth and economic performance- e.g. Balassa (1985), Ram (1985, 1987), Gray and Singer (1988) and Esfahani (1991).

After asserting that many of the cross-country regressions "have been plagued by empirical and conceptual shortcomings" (p. 1389), and that the multi-country studies have not been successful at providing a fully convincing theoretical framework, Edwards (1993) proposes that the theory of endogenous growth provides a stringent answer to the question of how trade policy might influence economic growth. Different to the traditional neoclassical models where in long-run equilibrium the steady-state rate of growth is totally independent of national policies, within these new models it would be possible to establish a long-run equilibrium relationship between openness and economic growth (Edwards 1993). For instance, in Romer's model of endogenous growth, an increased amount of resources assigned to research and development (R&D) would imply a larger availability of intermediate inputs, as well as a higher marginal product of capital. Open economies would have the opportunity to specialize in the production of some intermediate inputs, according to their comparative advantage (Edwards 1993). It is then suggested that openness would make it possible for a larger number of inputs to be available at lower cost, which in turn would result in a higher equilibrium growth. Openness would allow countries to overcome bottlenecks and to grow faster (Quah and Rauch 1990, cited in Edwards 1993).

The role of trade in the generation and diffusion of technological progress is also frequently analyzed. It has been proposed that more open regimes allow small economies to absorb technology originated in the advanced nations at a quicker pace, permitting them to attain higher rates of growth. Openness, under certain conditions, would lead to faster growth even in the long run (Grossman and Helpman 1991; Edwards 1992, as cited in Edwards 1993).Edwards further states that microeconomic analysis, by means of studying aspects like the use of multiple intermediate inputs, the invention of designs, and the absorption of technological progress, could be helpful to get a better comprehension on the specific linkages between trade policy and growth.

As indicated by Van den Berg and Lewer (2007), not just international trade, but also accompanying activities such as international marketing, market research, product planning, and international travel contribute to the transfer of knowledge and technology. Hence, globalization would allow trade, under certain circumstances, to expand knowledge and ideas and by this means, to enhance economic growth. Logically, these "special circumstances" are related to an even spread of the benefits of innovation. It has also been argued that international trade can hasten the economic growth of small economies by facilitating the movement of technology, frequently embodied in products. Adopting existing technologies, rather than creating new ones, should be an easier process for countries. But this is, in turn, determined by other factors such as a country's institutions (Lucas 2000).

Based on neoclassical production functions, some scholars propose that exports may contribute to economic growth by means of generating positive externalities on non-trading sectors, through more efficient management styles and better production techniques (Edwards 1993). Besides that, a productivity differential in favor of the exports sector would imply its expansion relative to the non-trading sector, leading to a positive effect on aggregate output. This phenomenon would also encourage the allocation of resources to more efficient investment projects. Feder (1983) divides the economy into an export sector and a non-export sector. The production function of the export sector is specified as:

$$X = g(K, L) \tag{2.1}$$

Where X is output in the export sector, K is the capital stock, and L is the labor force in the export sector. Feder's proposition is that the export sector generates positive externalities for the rest of the economy (Feder 1983). He also explains the non-export sector production function as:

$$N = f(K, L, X) \tag{2.2}$$

As shown in Feder's equation, here output in the non-export sector N is determined by the externalities generated from production X in the export sector as well as by the capital stock and the labor force (Feder 1983).

Feder also came up with the following regression equation:

$$G_Y = \alpha(I/Y) + \beta G_L + \delta(X/Y)G_x + \theta G_x \tag{2.3}$$

Where the coefficient δ represents the growth effect of the export sector's higher relative productivity, while θ captures the externalities of export production on the rest of the economy (Feder 1983). Average coefficients for the "trade" variable in a growth equation, from 99 cross-section and 116 time-series regressions using the Feder regression model, reported values of over 0.40, similar to those found by Feder in his own study (Van den Berg and Lewer 2007). These estimates would support the hypothesis of trade's positive effect on economic growth based on the positive externalities generated on the export sector, and transmitted to other parts of the economy, leading to an aggregated higher output. Based on the argument of substantial differences in marginal factor productivities between the export and non-export sectors, Feder suggests that economies which shift resources into exports will gain more than inward-oriented economies Feder (1983).

One interesting term that can also be found when the relationship between trade and growth is analyzed, is the one of "learning-by-trading". Besides Feder's arguments, it has been suggested that trade can potentially reduce the cost of capital goods, stimulating investment in an economy and hence, creating potential investment externalities (Lee 1995; Mazumdar 1996, as cited in Van den Berg and Lewer 2007). This gain of learning-by-trading is also supposed to be realized when an economy faces international competition.

In a seminal contribution, Frankel and Romer (1999) analyze the impact of international trade on income. They report that trade seems to raise income by stimulating the physical and human capital accumulation, and by increasing output (p. 394). The authors further remark that their results "bolster the case for the importance of trade and trade-promoting policies" (p. 395). As stated by Van den Berg and Lewer (2007), their results also suggest that international trade has a larger impact on productivity.

Furthermore, international trade seems to encourage the process of technology diffusion from the North to the South. Other leader-follower models propose that in the long run, countries will tend to grow at similar rates, provided that technology diffusion takes place. Lucas (2000) proposes, for instance, that if the liberalization of international trade or an improved capability of technology absorption in developing countries is accomplished, then a faster diffusion of technology would give the latter the opportunity to imitate rather than create new technologies.

Within the endogenous growth theory, policies which embrace openness, competition, change and innovation are thought to encourage economic growth. Structural diversification may be considered by the interplay of innovation in developed countries and imitation in developing ones.

Hitherto, the possible linkage between trade and economic growth has been analyzed, taking into account a number of scholarly contributions in the fields of international trade and economic growth. In the next section the same relationship is evaluated, now from an empirical standpoint.

2.1.2 *The Empirical Assessment*

A vast number of empirical studies support the hypothesis that, all other things equal, countries open to international trade benefit their residents with higher incomes and higher rates of economic growth. But even though some of these studies have been confronted because of their apparent lack of stringent theoretical background, methodological shortcomings or omitted variable problems, the evidence is even clearer in its rejection of the alternative hypothesis that there could be a negative correlation between trade and economic growth (Van den Berg and Lewer 2007). As depicted in Fig. 2.1, different econometric and statistical methods have been applied by the authors of these studies, trying to capture the nexus between trade and economic growth. Likewise, Table A.1 in the appendix includes a classification of the same studies, based on the methodologies and data utilized.

As frequently reported in the scientific literature, early empirical studies testing the linkage between trade and growth were mostly based on correlation analysis, being the ones of Michaely (1977) and Balassa (1978b) two of the most known, where in both cases a positive relationship was founded. These studies testing the hypothesis that trade does exert an influence on growth were mostly based on linear econometric models derived from the neoclassical production function, like:

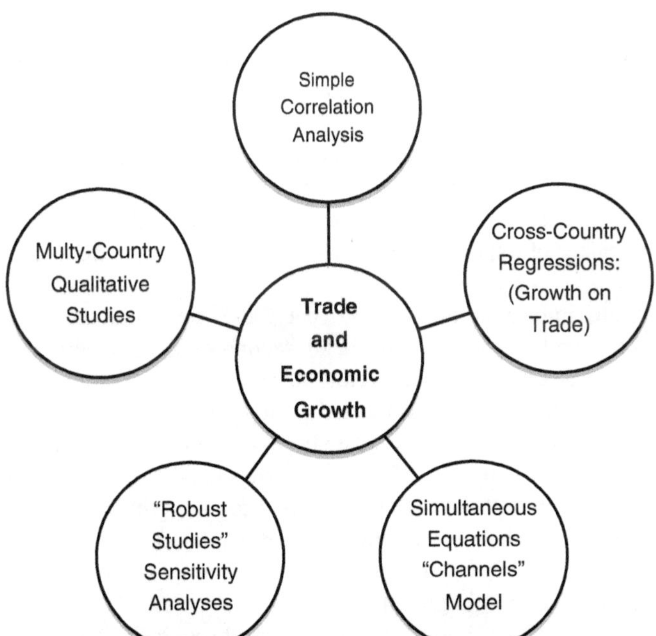

Fig. 2.1 Radial diagram – empirical studies dealing with the trade and growth linkage (Source: own illustration, based on Levine and Renelt [1992])

$$G_{GDP} = a_0 + a_1 G_k + a_2 G_L + a_3 TRADE + a_4 Z + u \tag{2.4}$$

Being G_{GDP}, G_k, and G_L the growth rates of real gross domestic product, capital stock, and labor force, respectively, *TRADE* the growth of trade, Z a set of other variables that are considered to explain economic growth, and u the standard error term (Van den Berg and Lewer 2007, p. 35). It is further supposed that output follows the Cobb-Douglas production function,

$$Y = AK^{\alpha}L^{1-\alpha}, \text{in which } 0 < \alpha < 1. \tag{2.5}$$

Authors such as Feder (1983), Rivera-Batiz and Romer (1991), MacDonald (1994), Edwards (1998), Clerides et al. (1998), Bernard and Bradford Jensen (1999) and others have based their studies on this type of regression models. While these early empirical studies did encourage the discussion and were indeed influential upon policy-makers, many of them have been criticized on the grounds of different methodological limitations. It has been commonly argued that problems such as omitted variable bias, simultaneity or measurement errors were not properly considered. And these methodological limitations have precisely been one of the most important foundations for the arguments of the so-called "trade sceptical" strand of the literature.

In their work, Levine and Renelt (1992) conduct an extensive analysis of empirical studies concerning the relationship between long-run growth rates and a variety of economic policy, political, and institutional indicators. After clarifying that very few economic variables showed to be robustly correlated with cross-country growth rates or the ratio of investment expenditures to GDP, they report a positive and robust correlation between average growth rates and the average share of investment in GDP, as well as between the share of investment in GDP and the average share of trade in GDP. In their sample of 119 countries over the 1960–1989 period, they found that those economies that grew faster than average tended to have a higher share of exports in GDP, as well as a higher share of investment in GDP.

It is, though, important to mention that these were not the only common characteristics found: larger primary- and secondary-school enrolment rates, a lower black-market exchange-rate premium, and lower inflation rates were also evident. Consequently, Levine and Renelt's study (1992) highlights two important arguments: first of all, that the relationship between trade and economic growth is a complex one, and that many other factors – besides exports or trade policy- should be also taken into account, not merely exports. Secondly, that the channel through which trade seems to enhance economic growth is related to investments. In other words, that an increased level of exports alone or a more outward oriented policy per se do not cause economic growth.

Due to Madsen (2009), knowledge spillovers through the channel of imports exert a positive influence on growth. He investigates if openness exerts an influence on total factor productivity (TFP) growth and per capita growth. Utilizing an annual data set for a panel of 16 Organisation for Economic Cooperation and Development (OECD) countries over the 1870–2006 period, he examines the productivity growth and productivity level effects of trade barriers and import penetration. An important contribution of his study is that the proposition of openness influencing growth -by means of enabling countries to import knowledge produced in other countries- is tested. The latter argument has been suggested by the endogenous growth theory (Romer 1990a, 1992; Grossman and Helpman 1991; Rivera-Batiz and Romer 1991; Aghion and Howitt 1998; Baldwin and Forslid 2000). The empirical studies of Madsen provide evidence regarding a positive effect of knowledge spillovers for growth in all periods considered, which were accomplished through the channel of imports. Moreover, his empirical evidence provides support to the hypothesis that R&D intensity has permanent growth effects, "in consistency with the predictions of Schumpeterian growth theories" (p. 411).

The so called "learning-by-exporting hypothesis" has been also subject of analysis within the literature, when analyzing the relationship between trade and growth. The assumption has been carefully tested by Clerides et al. (1998), using data on individual exporting firms in Colombia, Mexico, and Morocco. This study reported a fall in the costs for exporting industries, which eventually took place through a self selection process, where high-cost firms stopped exporting and low-cost firms increased their exports. This argument is exposed as evidence showing that international trade could contribute in a positive manner to economic growth, by spurring a process where inefficient firms are forced out while the efficient ones are rewarded. This type of micro-level studies is mainly oriented toward the analysis of the differences in productivity and economic behavior between exporting and non-exporting firms, hoping to resolve the issue of trade-growth causality issue in a more convincing manner (Wälde and Wood 2004).

Wacziarg (2001) considers six links between trade policy and economic growth, with the intention of identifying dynamic gains -or possible losses- from trade. The underlying assumption is that together, "these six channels adequately capture most of the effect of trade policy on growth" (p. 395). He further groups these channels in three broad categories, namely: government policy (macroeconomic policies, size of government), allocation and distribution (price distortion, factor accumulation), and technological transmissions (technology transmissions, foreign direct investment). In summary, Wacziarg provides evidence supporting the argument that there is a positive total effect of trade policy on growth, being investment apparently the most important channel, and government consumption the only negative channel. Technology transmission and macroeconomic policy quality are also suggested as significant channels of the effect of trade policy on growth.

The study carried by Wacziarg and Welch (2003) reports how countries that liberalized their trade regimes in the period 1950–1998 benefitted, on average, from an increase in their annual rate of growth of approximately 1.5% points, compared to pre-liberalization times. A link between the liberalization episodes and a post-liberalization increase in investment is also reported, suggesting a possible effect of liberalization on physical capital accumulation. Countries that showed negative or no effects of liberalization of growth were those were other constraining factors were present, such as political instability, contractionary macroeconomic policies, or the protection of domestic sectors from necessary adjustments.

Despite of the different methodologies approached, the possible shortcomings associated to them and the different positions present in the literature, what does indeed appear to be clear is that trade's effect on economic growth is linked with many other influences on growth. In other words, that policy recommendations only addressing trade policies as a possible mechanism for enhancing growth should be very carefully considered, as the experience of many developing nations that have resorted to more "open" regimes has shown. Trade seems to positively influence growth, but if accompanied with other policies and mechanisms which are also of crucial importance for spurring economic development.

Until this point, the empirical studies surveyed providence evidence in favor of a positive relationship between trade and growth, which would take place through different channels, such as an increased level of investment or technology transmission. Moreover, different benefits associated to trade have been highlighted, such as the attainment of higher incomes and higher rates of growth, the increase of investments, and larger knowledge spillovers. But not all of the studies unanimously support this argument: as will be explained next, many of them have been criticized on the grounds of supposed methodological shortcomings, as well as the possible omission of variables that could eventually me more relevant for growth than trade by itself.

Wälde and Wood (2004) conduct a profound survey of the empirical and theoretical literature, in order to find out if it "unambiguously supports, from an efficiency perspective, the case for liberalization" (p. 276). They categorize the empirical studies surveyed according to the methodology used: cross-country OLS growth regressions, simultaneous equations, instrumental variables, and panel data models, Granger causality tests, and micro-studies. As far as OLS growth regressions are concerned, they suggest that these studies suffer from lack of robustness, and that the issue of causality between exports and growth is not straightforward. Regarding the other three methodologies, robustness concerns, as well as the lack of inclusion of policy variables as explanatory variables, are mentioned as important elements that seriously undermine the explanatory power of these studies.

Their most important conclusion remark is that the literature is "surprisingly quiet on the link between trade policy instruments and economic growth" (Wälde and Wood 2004, p. 289). Causality is also found to be a major issue to be defined, since it is not clear whether there is more growth because of more trade, or more trade because of more growth (causality may run in either direction). Taking into account the "lack of convincing evidence that trade or export policies can be used to generate higher growth rates" (Wälde and Wood 2004, p. 277); the authors affirm that no trade policy recommendations can be formulated.

One of the most important lines of the debate associated to the relationship between trade and economic growth is, for sure, the one related with causality, as defined by Edwards (1993):

> Do countries with rapidly growing exports have a higher rate of aggregate growth, or is it that faster growing countries have a more dynamic export sector? Most studies have tended to ignore this issue, assuming that it is exports that drive aggregate GDP. There are, however, some nontrivial reasons why more rapid GDP growth could, in principle, result in faster growth of exports. Just dismissing the issue as being irrelevant, as a number of authors have done, does not seem to be fully justified. (p. 1388)

The first position defends the argument that increased trade enhances growth and industrialization. Other scholars believe that it is economic growth that permits the increase of trade. This is a very relevant question for developing countries since, as stated by Wälde and Wood, it goes in the direction of "whether the major sources of growth and industrialization are external -i.e. learning through trade- or internal -i.e., through human and physical capital investment and increased research and development-" (p. 276). Proponents of the first site of the debate suggest that East Asia's impressive exports performance since the 1960s can be identified as the source of its industrialization and convergence. The contrary position refutes this argument, citing that some interventionist mechanisms of these nations (e.g. industrial, technology and human development policies) are the factors that truly explain their development path (Wälde and Wood 2004, p. 276).

The latter claim is quite near to the so-called "infant industry" argument, frequently defended by developing countries governments, who stress the necessity of temporarily protecting local firms until they move up their learning curves, realize production efficiency improvements, and finally "grow up" to compete in international markets. The answer to this question is of paramount importance for policy makers in developing nations: should these countries open themselves to trade and start this "engine of growth"? Or should they better focus on measures related to physical capital investment and human resource development?

Another line of the debate deals with the issue of export-led growth as a possible developmental strategy. Sachs (1987) has placed in doubt the idea that trade liberalization is a necessary component of a successful outward-oriented strategy. For the particular case of the East Asian nations, he underscores how these countries implemented different policies and mechanisms -such as the promotion of exports, macroeconomic stability or avoiding a complete liberalization of imports- that strongly contributed to their development path. Interventionist governmental policies were decisive, and not just merely the opening up to foreign trade. He has argued that the success of the East Asian countries was to a large extent due to an active role of government in promoting exports in an environment where imports had not been fully liberalized, and where macroeconomic (and especially fiscal) equilibrium was fostered.

Rodrik, Subramanian, and Trebbi (2004) also suggest that trade actually becomes an insignificant variable in a growth equation that includes explicit variables representing a number of institutional characteristics. Factors such as the rule of law, property rights, a consistent legal system, and many other institutions seem to be more relevant for growth than export-oriented policies. Within the same line of argumentation, Rigobon and Rodrik (2004) use an econometric method to offset the simultaneous effects of some variables, called identification through heteroskedasticity. As cited by Van den Berg and Lewer (2007), their main finding is that when other institutional variables are present, the openness variable has a negative impact upon income levels. Lee et al. (2004) resort to the same method, finding that trade's influence on growth although still positive, is well below earlier estimates.

The position defended by Rodríguez and Rodrik (1999) and Rodrik, Subramanian, and Trebbi (2004) is, therefore, that the effects of trade policy on growth appear to be intertwined with the effects of other policies that usually are implemented simultaneously. Thus, it would be very difficult to determine which are exactly the effects of trade policy upon economic growth. It is also suggested that the empirical methods cannot exactly distinguish between trade's effects on economic growth and the effects of other variables and policies on growth (Van den Berg and Lewer 2007).

Rodríguez and Rodrik (1999) question the judgement based on empirical methods that find a positive relationship between openness and growth, such as the ones conducted by Dollar (1992), Ben-David (1993), Sachs et al. (1995), and Edwards (1998). Their basic argument is that this correlation is not robust to various measures of openness and important control variables. Additionally, Rodriguez and Rodrik express their concern that empirical analyses of trade and growth have been biased by omitting institutional variables correlated with international trade. One of the most important arguments brought by them is that many of the missing institutional variables are correlated with trade. As a result of that, omitted variable bias would cause in many studies the estimated coefficient of the "trade" variable to overstate trade's influence on growth. The experience of the East Asian "Tigers" would show how other factors such as macroeconomic stability, the rule of law, education, and the absence of social conflict have positively influenced their economic growth. Taking that into account, if just the "trade" variable is considered and other crucial variables are omitted, an improvement in total factor productivity would be incorrectly explained by trade, according to the standard empirical methods.

International trade policy, according to this position, is extremely intertwined with other economic policies, making it impossible to differentiate between the trade's effect on growth and the growth effects of those other policies. Rodriguez and Rodrik's proposal is therefore, that economic growth eventually depends more on "those other policies" than trade policy by itself. It is, though, important to clarify that Rodriguez and Rodrik's position does not support trade protection. The authors rather warn about "the tendency to greatly overstate the systematic evidence in favor of trade openness", that "has had a substantial influence on policy around the world", leading to high expectations and "crowding out" other institutional reforms with "potentially greater payoffs" Rodriguez and Rodrik, 1999, p. 62.

Trade liberalization, on "standard comparative advantage grounds", is not put into question. What Rodriguez and Rodrik effectively controvert is that integration to the global economy could substitute a development strategy. The idea behind this argument is not that trade is inimical to growth: the argument is rather that trade, by itself, should not be considered as the unique source of economic growth. There are many other variables that do exert an influence, when it comes to raising the living standards of a society. In this same line of argumentation, human capital and institutions have increasingly drawn the attention of recent research, aspects considered of critical importance for a successful technology adoption.

Other scholars have proposed that the effect of trade on growth is relative, being also determined by the country's trade partners. Vamvakidis (1998) provides empirical evidence supporting the hypothesis that countries engaging in trade with "open, large, and more developed neighboring economies grow faster than those with closed, smaller, and less developed neighboring economies" (p. 251). Other authors likeSchiff and Wang (2003), Keller (2000a, b), Schiff et al. (2002), and Venables (2003) have contributed with additional evidence showing that it would be more beneficial for developing countries to more actively engage in international trade with developed economies, taking into account the possible technology inflows that could be associated.

Several authors have examined whether inflows of foreign technology depend on who the country's trade partners are. Vamvakidis (1998) concluded that developing countries that trade freely with larger, more developed neighbors grow faster, all other things equal, than countries that trade more with other developing countries. Specifically, he notes that countries that joined regional trade blocks consisting only of other developing economies do not, on average, experience any acceleration of economic growth as a result of their regional economic integration. Schiff and Wang (2003) found that Mexico achieved a permanent rise in its total factor productivity after joining Canada and the United States in the North American Free Trade Area. Keller (2000a, b), Schiff et al. (2002), and Venables (2003) provide further evidence that developing countries gain more technology inflows by trading with developed countries than they do through trade with other developing countries.

Grossman and Helpman (1991) and Matsuyama (1992) also refer to other situations where trade could eventually not lead to the desired positive outcome of strengthening the development process: countries sufficiently far behind the technological frontier may, through imports, be driven toward production of traditional goods. This would lead to lower growth rates. In a similar manner, Howitt (2000) affirms that the host country needs a sufficiently high capacity to absorb the technology developed in the technologically more advanced countries.

Another interesting field of controversy is related to the extent of the gains derived from trade. (Arkolakis, Costinot, and Rodríguez-Clare 2010) examine the different reasons advocated by the theory, concerning the benefits of international trade. From a novel perspective, the authors pose the question if "new sources of gains from trade necessarily lead to larger gains from trade" (p. 1). Their most relevant finding is that within the different models analyzed, the total size of the gains is the same. What might actually change, according to the authors, is the composition of these gains. "Richer trade models", as they call them, would not imply additional gains from trade.

This is a position contrary to the one defended by Krugman and Obstfeld (2006), who suggests that when monopolistic competition and economies of scale are considered, trade will be beneficial since it increases market size. As a result of specialization, an opportunity for mutual gains arises, even if countries are similar in terms of economic development or capital-labor ratios. A larger market leads to both lower average prices and the availability of a greater variety of goods. Welfare is increased: consumers may count now with bigger consumption possibilities. Krugman also states that "the income distribution effects of trade will be small and there will be substantial extra gains from intra-industry trade. The result may be that despite the effects of trade in income distribution, everyone gains from trade" (p. 129). The associated gains would, therefore, be above the ones associated to comparative advantage. Besides the increase in product variety, Melitz (2003, p. 1695), in turn, states that his model "shows how the aggregate industry productivity growth generated by the (inter-firm) reallocations, contributes to a welfare gain", not addressed by the theory before. The reallocation of market shares toward more productive firms would generate an "aggregate productivity gain and an increase in welfare" (Melitz 2003, p. 1717).

Taylor (1988) bases his critique on a structuralist approach to development macroeconomics. It is interesting to notice that, as well as in the case of Rodriguez and Rodrik, he defends the idea that it is pointless to think about openness in general terms: each country's (and the world's) institutional and historical context should be considered, in order to take a stance. Based on the analysis of average trade proportions of GDP for a sample of 50 developing countries in the period 1980–1982 (with growth rates over the period 1964–1982), he suggests that "in contrast to mainstream assertions, export-led growth does not stand out", and that "the ratio of industrial to primary exports is not correlated with growth rates, nor are overall export ratios higher in the high performance economies" (Taylor 1988, p. 8). He argues further that trade "does not seem to be closely related to the way economies perform", and that "fast-growing countries are more or less open, have diverse patterns of specialization, and their success is not obviously led by exports" (Taylor 1988, p. 10).

The South Korean experience, according to Taylor, does not fit into a plausible explanation of openness as a source of economic growth: as other scholars already cited, Taylor underscores the influence of the interventionist policies implemented by the government of that nation, and that productivity growth is rather a result of those interventionist policies, as well as of a long history of industrialization and rigorous work norms. He finally comes to the conclusion that "the case for a positive association between trade liberalization and economic performance as measured by growth is *primie facie* difficult to make, and is not supported by cross-sectional or time-series evidence" (Taylor 1988, p. 32).

Taylor's (1988) main concern is if trade liberalization is an optimal development strategy. He suggests that for developing nations, there were no great benefits in undertaking open trade and capital market strategies even in the well-favored decades of the 1960s and 1970s. It is therefore proposed that internal development strategies "may be a wise choice toward the century's end". However, such a path is not easy to follow (Taylor 1988, p. 66). He concludes by saying that in the mid-1980s the trade liberalization strategy "is intellectually moribund", kept alive by life support from the World Bank and International Monetary Fund.

Another line of discussion is related to the wide spectrum of development stages: are all developing countries, indistinctively speaking, going to profit from a more open trade regime? Or will the benefits mostly be realized by those economies with specific characteristics and possibilities? – e.g., the so-called "middle-income nations"? Arguments in favor of the first position can be found in studies such as the one conducted by Michaely (1977), who analyzed a sample of 41 countries for the 1950–1973 period and applied the Spearman rank coefficient to determine if the rate of growth of exports was associated with GDP growth. While the coefficient was significantly positive (0.308) for the whole sample, it was larger (0.523), for a subsample of 23 middle income countries. As Edwards (1993) points out, also Helleiner (1986) advocates that without a minimum level of development, the benefits of exports promotion will not be realized. Kavoussi (1984) and Ram (1985), cited in Edwards (1993), have also reported larger coefficients for middle-income economies.

As highlighted by Edwards (1993), the "homogeneity question" has also been addressed from a different perspective: instead of somehow arbitrarily classifying countries according to their income per capita, studies such as the one conducted by Kohli and Singh (1989) divide the sample according to a "minimum critical threshold" related to the trade structure itself. According to their typology of "outward oriented" and "non-outward-oriented" economies, they find that the coefficient of exports growth was significantly positive for both groups of countries. Nevertheless, it was significantly larger for the former group.

In summary, as Edwards points out:

> Most studies have found that in GDP growth regressions the importance and significance of the exports growth coefficient varies across groups of countries, casting some doubt on the desirability of pooling all these nations together in the econometric analysis. (p. 1383)

The role of world market conditions has also been frequently considered. As reported by Edwards (1993), Balassa found clear "advantages of outward oriented policies for export performance and for economic growth in the face of external shocks," and also, that the "reliance on export promotion in response to external shocks under an outward-oriented strategy favorably affected economic growth" (Balassa 1981, p. 189). Another perspective is the one offered by scholars that have classified countries between those who face "favorable" and "unfavorable" world demand. For the former group of economies, a positive correlation between exports growth and GDP growth has been reported. This would not be the case for countries confronting "below normal world demand" (Edwards 1993, p. 1384). Based on this argument, it would not be possible to establish a general policy recommendation for all developing economies.

It has also been stated that growth models do not properly address the issue of how international trade exerts different effects on different sectors of the economy, and how this process could affect the overall rate of growth (Van den Berg and Lewer 2007). According to this position, based on comparative advantage some industries will grow and others would be displaced a result of free trade. Some of these contractions would negatively influence the economy's welfare. Situations like this could be present if the industries that expand generate few technology spillovers to the rest of the economy, or if the industries that grow face a declining world demand. The counterargument to this position is that international trade could indeed enhance growth, as long as it promotes the transfer of technology across borders.

Bhagwati (1958a, b) rejected the hypothesis that trade enhances growth, suggesting the possibility of immiserizing growth. He made reference to a situation where an open economy that experiences an expansion in its productive capacity - caused either by economic growth or technological progress- could become worse off if its terms of trade deteriorate sufficiently and offset the beneficial effects of economic growth. Chacholiades (1990, cited in Van den Berg and Lewer 2007) specifically suggested six conditions that would make immiserizing growth possible: (1) the exporting country's growth in productive capacity is concentrated in the sectors of the economy that export, (2) the price elasticity of demand for the export product is inelastic, (3) exports account for a large share of the country's GDP, (4) technological progress is minimal, (5) the export country supplies a large portion of total world output, and (6) the export country does not restrict trade (p. 210).

As pointed out by Krugman and Obstfeld (2006), the conditions that could make possible immiserizing growth to occur are extreme. Taking that into account, this situation is nowadays considered more as a theoretical standpoint, than a real-world situation (p. 103). Furthermore, as Van den Berg and Lewer point out, its occurrence would require another condition to be present: investment in factors of production used intensively in the export industry must go on, despite of the deterioration of the terms of trade, implying a decline in the returns to these factors (2007, p. 211). Such a situation is rare to be found.

Regarding the first two topics often defended by the "trade pessimists", the Prebisch-Singer hypothesis stated that there was a secular decline in the terms of trade of primary-commodity exporters, which could be explained by a combination of low income and price elasticities of demand (Todaro and Smith 2006). This transfer of income from developing to developed countries, according to this approach, could only be countered by protecting domestic manufacturing industries (through import-substitution industrialization – ISI). It would be the interest of developing countries to impose protective tariffs, so that they could industrialize. In the long run, ISI strategies were supposed to lead to greater domestic industrial diversification.

The experience of the ISI demonstrated to be largely unsuccessful, due to a number of undesirable results: as Todaro and Smith (2006) affirm, these were mainly related to the inefficiency of the protected industries, the fact that many of the most important beneficiaries were foreign companies that operated behind the tariff walls, and the negative impacts on the balance of payments. By contrast, the successful experience of some developing countries that promptly resorted to export-oriented industrialization and their impressive performances, – the Asian

Tigers -provided support to the case for outward-oriented trade policies. The evidence demonstrating that ISI just temporarily spurred growth, which was then followed by stagnation, also caused it to lose favor (Van den Berg and Lewer 2007). As Edwards (1993) explains:

> The poor performance of the Latin American countries, most of which had followed with almost religious zeal the dictates of import substitution, offered a dramatic contrast to the rapidly growing East Asian countries that had aggressively implemented outward oriented strategies. Suddenly, this difference in performance which had been documented by the academic literature on trade orientation, became a fundamental topic in the public policy debate. (p. 1359)

It is also interesting to mention that the so-called "industrialization strategy approach" has appeared since the 1980s as another strand of the literature analyzing the relationship between trade and development. While it stands for outward-oriented and export-led development, it still proposes an active role for the government, by "influencing the type and sequencing of exports, as a country strives to produce more advanced products, adding higher value" (Todaro and Smith 2006, p. 641). The "industrialization strategy approach" argues that, in a large extent, the success of the export-oriented East Asian economies would be unthinkable without an active government intervention and the associated industrial policies. Besides, it is proposed that market failures in the transfer of technology from developed to developing countries would provide a justification for a governmental industrialization strategy that places special emphasis on technology absorption from abroad (Todaro and Smith 2006).

Nevertheless, it should also be mentioned that the so-called process of "picking winners" has been strongly criticized, putting in doubt the capacity of the government to get unbiased information about the future (Van den Berg and Lewer 2007). Another relevant aspect to be considered is the one of the World Trade Organization (WTO) legislation, since this type of policies could clearly violate internationally recognized commercial principles and legislations, implying the possibility of retaliation.

From a political economy perspective, Kohli (2009) defends "a prudent and effective state intervention and selective integration with the global economy" (p. 212). He argues that well constructed "developmental states", like the ones of East Asia, contributed to a process of rapid industrialization. He further proposes that it is of the utmost importance to improve the quality of the state and other institutions, for accomplishing economic growth in many developing countries. He conveys the central message that "success or failure at economic development is associated more with the kind and less with the degree of state intervention" (p. 223).

Reservations have also been expressed regarding the possible productivity-export correlation. Based on micro-studies where the performance of firms both within the export and non-export sector is analyzed, some authors have come to the conclusion that firms "are first productive and then start exporting, rather than the other way around" (Wälde and Wood 2004, p. 285). This "self-selection" process would be the explanation for the increase of efficiency in the economy.

After having conducted the review of a number of influential and recognized empirical studies, it is now important to take a stance on the controversy concerning the relationship between trade and growth, and to critically appraise these arguments.

First of all, it should be noted that the empirical works and studies do not seem to be so opposite to each other, in the sense that it has not been demonstrated that trade could exert a negative influence on growth. Rather, it has been stated that the possible effects have been either overstated, or not properly measured. Despite of the observations made concerning the methodological shortcomings and the not straightforward causality issue, this does not imply that there is not a relationship between trade and growth. What is needed, as pointed out by different authors, are more sophisticated econometrical studies and techniques that would allow to fully estimate the extent of this relationship.

One very important aspect brought by the studies which are sceptical of the relationship between trade and growth, is the issue of the "omitted variables" problem. Certainly, both the theoretical framework and a number of influential works provide support to the argument that trade alone does not cause growth: besides trade, developing countries have to place special emphasis on other crucial factors, like physical and human capital formation. This is a reasoning of paramount importance, leading to the conclusion that trade policies should be coupled with other developmental strategies.

Additionally, it should be noted that not just the trade theory, but also the growth theory, allow to fully capture the extent of the linkage between trade and growth. As has been previously mentioned, the relationship between trade and growth seems to be developed through different channels, like investments and knowledge spillovers. Of the utmost importance is also the consideration that trade could be beneficial for a country, provided that some requirements have been realized: e.g. a good technology absorption capacity, a sound macroeconomic environment, political stability, and the required human capital formation, among others. Trade seems to positively influence growth, but coupled with other factors and characteristics of crucial importance.

Finally, a chief observation founded in some works is the one concerning the *relativity* of the gains derived from trade. In other words, for a developing country its trade basket, as well as its trade partners, could be of great relevance for reaping the desired gains from trade. As stated by Thirlwall (2000):

> Given the predictions of trade theory and the facts, the important point to make in this introduction is that the issue for developing countries in general, and Africa in particular, is not so much whether to trade but in what to trade, and the terms on which trade should take place with the developed countries of the world (or between themselves). There can be no doubt that there are both static and dynamic gains from trade, and that trade provides a vent for surplus production (as stressed by Adam Smith). What is in dispute is whether the overall gains to developing countries could be greater if the pattern of trade was different from its present structure, and if the developed countries modified their policies towards the developing world. (p. 7)

All in all, this section has discussed the linkage between trade and economic growth from an empirical perspective. At this point, it is important now to address the paramount question formulated within the whole research project: does export diversification contribute to economic growth? And if yes, how could this process be beneficial for a developing nation, such as Colombia?

2.2 Export Diversification and Economic Growth

The dependence on primary-product exports has been frequently mentioned as one of the main features of developing nations. As stated by Todaro and Smith (2006), less developed countries (LDCs) tend to specialize in the production of primary products, instead of secondary and tertiary activities. Consequently, exports of primary products play a very significant role in terms of foreign exchange generation in these countries, traditionally representing a significant share of their gross national product. Specially in the case of the non-mineral primary products exports, markets and prices are frequently unstable, leading to a high degree of exposure to risk and uncertainty for the countries that rely on them (Todaro and Smith 2006). Primary-products exports have been characterized by relatively low income elasticity of demand and inelastic price elasticity, being fuels, certain raw materials, and manufactured goods, some exceptions that exhibit relatively high income elasticity (Todaro and Smith 2006).

Taking these arguments into account, the cause for export diversification has been commonly supported based on the so-called "export instability argument". Consequently, export diversification has been proposed as a policy mechanism seeking to stabilize export earnings, which would be especially required in those developing countries where the share of commodities in its export basket is particularly pronounced. This situation is additionally complicated by the fact that many of the LDCs have incurred in deficits on their balance of payments, due to their import demands of capital goods, intermediate goods, and consumer products that their industrial expansion requires. Furthermore, LDCs are usually more dependent on trade than developed nations, in terms of its share in national income.

In their work, Prebisch and Singer suggested the trend of prices of primary products to decline, which has been the matter of different discussions, concerning their secular or cyclical trend (Todaro and Smith 2006). Taking all these arguments into consideration, the problems of export earnings instability and terms of trade worsening for developing countries where primary products account for the bulk of their foreign sales, has been frequently discussed, as well as their negative effect on growth. This has led developing countries to consider the need of diversification of their export mix, based on a structural transformation of their economies, process that has been especially visible in the East Asian economies, China, and India (Todaro and Smith 2006). But it should be noted that despite of the diversification efforts, different empirical studies have also shown a declining trend for the prices of labor-intensive basic manufactures increasingly produced by some LDCs, contrary to the rising tendency for the prices of the knowledge-intensive products exported by developed countries.

As stated by Ali et al. (1991), export diversification entails changing the composition of a country's export mix, being it "directly related to the structure of the economy and how it changes as development proceeds" (1991, p. 6). The underlying consideration behind export diversification as a possible developmental strategy is related to the expectation of achieving stability-oriented and growth-oriented policy objectives (Ali et al. 1991). A broader exports base, coupled with a special promotion of those commodities with positive price trends, should be beneficial for growth. Hence, the value-added export commodities would be stimulated, by means of additional processing and marketing activities (Ali et al. 1991). A country's degree of diversification is usually considered as dependent upon the number of commodities within its export mix, as well as on the distribution of their individual shares.

The United Nations Economic and Social Commission for Asia and the Pacific (ESCAP) has stated that for small, low-income economies such as the least developed countries (LDCs), reasonable development goals cannot be limited to primary products exports. Diversification, both in terms of "non-traditional" and "traditional" commodities, is considered as an element of utmost importance for growth and development (ESCAP 2004). It has also been frequently stated that growth and export diversification may be linked. Besides structural changes of an economy, as Al-Marhubi (2000) points out, traditional development models propose that economic growth also implies a shift from dependence on primary exports towards diversified manufactured exports. Another interesting concept is linked to the so-called "graduation concept" addressed by empirical studies such as the ones conducted by Michaely (1977) and Moschos (1989). It suggests that the process of "graduation" from developing to developed status should be joined by a structural change of exports toward diversity (Amin Gutiérrez de Piñeres and Ferrantino 1997a, p. 376). This would suggest that the connection between exports and growth enters, when a certain level of development is attained.

At this point, a very important clarification to be made is that export diversification does not necessarily imply the export of manufactured goods. As stated by Agosin (2006), this process may also be carried out in the form of primary commodities that evolve into natural-resource-based industries, rather than into manufactures. Indeed, commodity exports should not be literally associated with export concentration. Additionally, diversification has usually been related to the production and export of goods with higher skill and knowledge intensity (Agosin 2006). As stated by Lederman and Maloney (2003):

> Clearly, dependence on any one export, be it copper in Chile or potentially micro-chips in Costa Rica, can leave a country vulnerable to sharp declines in terms of trade. The presence of a single, very visible export may also give rise to a variety of political economy effects deleterious to growth. (p. 4)

The distinction between vertical and horizontal diversification is also of chief importance. The first category is related to the move between different categories of goods – e.g. the shift from primary commodities to manufactures-, trough value-added mechanisms. The second category implies expanding the export basket, by "diversifying into goods within the same broad category of goods" (Agosin 2006, p. 7). The latter would be the case of shifting, for example, from coffee for the mass market to gourmet coffee (Agosin 2006). Additionally, export diversification may be accomplished either by adjusting shares of commodities in the existing export mix, or by adding new commodities to it (Ali et al. 1991). It is important to mention that a number of measures have been constructed for calculating an economy's export concentration, such as the ogive index, the entropy index, and the Gini-Hirschman index, among others (Ali et al. 1991).

Having said that, it is important to observe how export diversification might take different forms and relate to varied experiences. For the particular case of Latin America, Gutiérrez et al. (1997b) state that countries like Chile and Argentina have shifted from exporting a single primary product (such as copper, or beef) to a broadened export mix, being in Chile the emphasis placed on "non-traditional" agricultural products. On the other side, Mexico (with machinery, motor vehicles, and *maquiladoras*) and Brazil (with machinery, iron and steel, and transport equipment) opted for a type of diversification expressed in evolving from primary to manufactured goods. The Colombian case would be a mixture between the Chilean agricultural-based pattern, with an Asian-type increase in light manufactures. Finally, Venezuela has remained immersed in a pattern of export concentration, overwhelmingly dependent on the oil revenues (Amin Gutiérrez de Piñeres and Ferrantino 1997b).

Similar to the previously cited argument of Feder (1983), it has also been proposed that exports diversification could positively influence growth by means of generating positive externalities on non-trading sectors. These externalities would be associated to more efficient management styles and improved production techniques. Thus, economies with a diversified export structure would benefit from these externalities and the incentives for capital formation, leading to higher growth.

2.2.1 The Gains and Losses Derived from Export Diversification: A Theoretical Analysis

In addition to the hypothesis that openness leads to growth, the postulation that the pattern of economic development is linked to a structural change in exports and increased exports diversification has also been proposed. Nevertheless, as clarified by Amin Gutiérrez de Piñeres and Ferrantino (1997a), it should be said that the hypothesis of encouraging development through diversification is not exclusively associated with outward-orientation arguments. The infant industry argument, for instance, also defends the need of temporarily protecting some industries, which would eventually lead to a more diversified economic structure and thus, to diversification in exports.

As stated by Ben Hammouda et al. (2006), the starting works related to diversification focused on different elements considered essential for reinforcing the productive structure of developing economies, such as the need of channelling resources for investment, with the objective of diversifying economic structures and encouraging structural change. While some scholars defended the idea of balanced growth, others placed a very specific emphasis on some sectors that could imply a "cumulative role" for the whole economy. Some kind of consensus emerged, related to the need of "industrial development, and on its place on the transformation of traditional economies and the modernization of productive structures of developing countries" (Ben Hammouda et al. 2006, p. 21).

Within the economic development field, diversification has occupied an important position: a number of development strategies undertaken in the 1960s and the 1970s, considered it. Later on, the crisis that started at the end of the 1970s and the failure of import-substitution strategies in a number of developing countries brought about a dramatic change in the debate. Now export-led growth, macroeconomic stabilization, and international specialization would become the paramount topics (Ben Hammouda et al. 2006, p. 21). Accompanying the outward-oriented model, since the 1980s hypotheses related to structural changes in exports and augmented diversification of exports became more popular in the literature, since it was believed that they could lead to faster growth (ESCAP 2004).

The product-cycle literature (Vernon 1966; Krugman 1979a; Dollar 1986; Segerstrom et al. 1990; Grossman and Helpman 1991), has also suggested a link between export diversification and growth as cited by Amin Gutiérrez de Piñeres and Ferrantino (1997a). The process would operate in the following manner: innovation in developed economies would result in a larger variety of products. At the other side, imitation in the developing countries would also imply a larger diversity of products being produced and exported from these low-wage nations (Amin Gutiérrez de Piñeres and Ferrantino 1997a, p. 376). Within the new trade theory, the large volume of trade between similarly endowed developed countries has been explained in terms of product differentiation, usually associated with manufacturing (Amin Gutiérrez de Piñeres and Ferrantino 1997a, p. 376).

In recent times, export diversification has gained renewed importance in the economic literature. As Ben Hammouda et al. (2006) explain, reasons for that are the disappointing economic performances of a number of developing economies, as well as the fact that poor countries – especially in Africa- have not received the expected benefits from schemes of preferences granted by developed economies and groups of integration. Another strand of the literature is chiefly concerned with those determinants that would be needed for diversification to be successful. Among these factors, the level of income of an economy, its investment and productive capacity levels, the role of industrial policy, and its technology absorption capability, have been examined. As Ben Hammouda et al. (2006) point out:

> Indeed, the countries which have succeeded in improving their position are those that maintained during the last three decades a high investment rate particularly in the industrial sector. This investment enabled them to access new technologies and improve productivity and competitiveness of their economies. These links have enabled these countries to increase their exports and improve their international integration. (p. 24)

Furthermore, Bebczuk and Berrettoni (2006) state that:

> Richer economies tend to be economically and institutionally more stable, and such environment mitigates the business risks perceived by domestic producers, thus making diversification less imperative. Nevertheless, as these economies are characterized by higher total factor productivity and a better business climate, entrepreneurs may find it more appealing to broaden their productive mix. The access to credit, the quality of infrastructure, the gross investment ratio and the level of foreign direct investment are indicators of macroeconomic efficiency and strength that may likely enhance the growth prospects of firms, even though the implications for export diversification remain an open theoretical question. (p. 10)

Relatively new contributions on endogenous growth have placed a special emphasis on the importance of diversification. As stated by Ben Hammouda et al. (2006), the Romer model suggests a beneficial effect of diversification consistent of the availability of inputs within an economy, which could enhance labor productivity and human capital. Besides that, Romer (1990a) and Grossman and Helpman (1991) have suggested that productivity is boosted by increases in product variety (Feenstra et al. 1998).

In their work, Acemoglu and Zilibotti (1997) refer to a positive effect derived from increasing the number of sectors and therefore, augmenting investment opportunities and reducing investors' risks. Besides these observations, the possible effect of enhancing stabilization of export revenues has also been considered, situation that would lead to more stable paths of growth. A very interesting finding is the one suggested by Imbs and Wacziarg (2003), concerning a U-shaped pattern of sectoral concentration along the development path. As the authors state:

> We provide new and robust evidence that economies grow through two stages of diversification. At first, sectoral diversification increases, but there exists a level of per capita income beyond which the sectoral distribution of economic activity starts concentrating again. In other words, sectoral concentration follows a U-shaped pattern in relation to per capita income. (p. 63)

The empirical investigation carried by Imbs and Wacziarg uses sectoral data to analyze the evolution of sectoral concentration over time and in relation to the development level, in a wide set of developed and developing countries. The evidence provides support to the hypothesis that "poor countries tend to diversify, and it is not until they have grown to relatively high levels of per capita income that incentives to specialize take over as the dominant economic force" (Imbs and Wacziarg 2003, p. 83). The reallocation of resources, according to the authors, seems to be motivated by the relation between economic growth and openness to trade. Bebczuk and Berrettoni (2006) examine if the macroeconomic environment fosters or inhibits export diversification. The results of their regressions for 56 countries over the 1970–2002 period support the hypothesis that "richer, more efficient, more stable and more open countries tend to focus rather than to diversify exports" (p. 11). This finding goes in line with the U-shaped pattern of sectoral concentration suggested by Imbs and Wacziarg.

At this point, it is important to observe how export diversification may initially seem to go against the comparative advantage concept (Ali et al. 1991). As is widely known, specialization can imply greater efficiency, and countries engaging in international trade are expected to become specialized. But at the same time, it has been suggested that export earnings instability may result from export concentration. Taking that into account, export diversification would favor a country by stabilizing and/or increasing its foreign earnings. Arguments such as the ones provided by Imbs and Wacziarg (2003) have come to mediate in the discussion, proposing that specialization and diversification occur at different points in development.

The potential benefits of export diversification have been explained by Harding and Javorcik (2007):

> Export diversification may be an important issue for developing countries for several reasons. First, a diversified bundle of export products provides a hedge towards price variations and shocks in specific product markets (Bertinelli et al. 2006; Levchenko and di Giovanni 2006). Second, the type of products exported might affect economic growth and the potential for structural change (Hausmann, Hwang, and Rodrik 2007). Third, export diversification in the direction of more sophisticated products may be beneficial for economic development. Given these potential benefits of export diversification, an important policy question is what a country can do to diversify its exports. (p. 1)

The first of the above mentioned benefits, namely that diversification would provide a hedge towards price variations, is defined in the literature as the "portfolio effect" (Agosin 2006). In the same manner that single company stock portfolios are linked to higher risk, an economy which is "over-dependent" in one or a few export products is considered to be vulnerable. Diversification is, therefore, considered as a possibility of lessening the earnings variance of the country's "export portfolio" (Stanley and Bunnag 2001).

The underlying idea is that diversified economies are benefitted by a greater stability of export earnings, which is likely to be linked to lower variance of GDP growth (Agosin 2006). Especially for developing countries with imperfect access to international financial markets, diversification would be advantageous. It has also been suggested that countries where the trade basket is highly dependent upon a few products tend to show more volatile exchange rates than countries with diversified export structures. Volatility in the real exchange rate hinders investment in tradable goods or services. (Agosin 2006, p. 2) Foreign exchange earnings instability would also imply negative effects in terms of economic planning, import capacity, and foreign debt repayment (Stanley and Bunnag 2001). In this line of thought, it has for instance been proposed that the secular concentration of Latin American countries in primary products has been an obstacle for its development potential. Volatile terms of trade, sluggish productivity growth and low value added have been highlighted as some of the troubles derived from the region's export mix (Bebczuk and Berrettoni 2006).

Concerning an evolution to more sophisticated export products-, the literature also refers to some dynamic benefits of diversification (Agosin 2006). The underlying idea is that countries that successfully experience a structural change and that accomplish to spur diversification of their economic structure, will acquire a comparative advantage in a larger number of goods. The increase of labor productivity and human capital (Berthélemy and Söderling 1999), as well as the enlargement of investment opportunities and reduction of investors' risks (Acemoglu and Zilibotti 1997), have also been highlighted as possible benefits derived from diversification.

On the contrary, those countries with a comparative advantage in a limited number of goods, where a scarcity of skills or lack of complementary inputs is evident, would be affected by their inability to absorb foreign technologies. According to this hypothesis, as pointed out by Agosin (2006), those economies that successfully undertake a diversification process are then in a position of expanding their range of comparative advantage. A country's capability to absorb or adapt foreign technologies, is of paramount importance for that goal to be accomplished. It should be observed that diversification – both of output and exports- is a result of different factors associated to development, which have been addressed by the endogenous growth literature. Aspects such as "the accumulation of skills, learning by doing, positive pecuniary externalities that stem from the production of key non-traded inputs - e.g., infrastructure services-, positive technological externalities associated with skill creation, and technological innovation" are crucial for that diversification to take place. (Agosin 2006, p. 2).

When it comes to primary products exports, it is possible to find in the literature different approaches referring to issues such as the "natural resources curse", the Dutch disease, and poverty traps. As stated by Lederman and Maloney (2003), different scholars have referred to the issue of how natural resource abundance – and more specifically, their dominant participation within a country's trade basket- could be inimical for growth. Some scholars suggest that Adam Smith made an association between natural resources and lower human and physical capital accumulation, lower productivity growth, and lesser spillovers. In a study conducted by the United Nations Economic Commission for Latin America (CEPAL), Prebisch (1950) argued that natural resources' terms of trade tended to show a secular decline over time. Sachs et al. (1995) stated that the Dutch disease conduces to concentration in resource exports, implying fewer possibilities for productivity growth. In this same line of argumentation, other claims have been exposed dealing with issues such as the institutional failures derived from the rents resulting from resource extraction (Easterly and Levine 2002, cited in Lederman and Maloney 2003) and over-borrowing in those countries experiencing commodity – price booms (Manzano and Rigobon 2001, cited in Lederman and Maloney 2003).

By comparison, other contributions and works highlight the positive contribution that primary products exports and resource abundance has had for growth, citing some successful experiences. Martin and Mitra (2001), as cited by Lederman and Maloney (2003), reported total factor productivity growth to be larger in agriculture than in manufactures in a large sample of advanced and developing countries. Mining has been suggested by Wright (2001) and Irwin (2000), cited in Lederman and Maloney (2003), as a crucial industry for the US, taking into account its dynamic and knowledge-intensive character. The same argument has been exposed for forestry in Scandinavia (Lederman and Maloney 2003; Blomstrom and Kokko 2001). The so-called "resource curse" view (Bebczuk and Berrettoni

2006), namely the negative linkage between natural resource abundance and growth, has also been challenged by Ng and Yeats (2005). Besides that, Blomstrom and Kokko (2001) propose that Sweden and Finland accomplished a more diversified economic structure by introducing technology into their natural resource-based production. The Chilean case has been invoked by Herzer and Nowak-Lehmann (2004) as an example of an export diversification based on natural resources that positively affected growth. It has also been stated how, nowadays, natural resources exhibit higher technology content, having the possibility to generate upstream and downstream activities (Bonaglia and Fukasaku 2003, Bebczuk and Berrettoni 2006).

Likewise, Maloney (2002) considers the issue of resource-based industries, drawing a comparison between some successful experiences – like the American, Australian, Canadian or the Scandinavian cases- and the so-called "mineral underachievers" (natural resource abundant Latin American nations, according to Wright 2001). Some successful cases can be, though, also found in that region: Monterrey (Mexico), Medellín (Colombia), and Sao Paulo (Brazil) are presented as dynamic industrial centers based on mining and in the later two cases, coffee (Maloney, p. 2). Maloney's main statement is that the poor performance of that region can be explained by the barriers to technological adoption and innovation, with deep historical roots, which could even be traced back to the times of the Spanish colonization. Deficient national "learning capacities", coupled with faulty inward-looking development policies, also appear to be the main "culprits". On the contrary, successful experiences such as the mining industry in the US, of the forest industry in Sweden, have strongly relied on learning dynamics boosted by alliances among world class universities, private and public think tanks, and the government.

One interesting line of the debate concerning export diversification is linked to its possible "spontaneous" or "deliberated" nature. As Agosin (2006) points out, in the particular case of some developing countries that experienced an important diversification in the post-war period – e-g. South Korea and Taiwan-, the process has been linked to different interventionist policies supporting rapid industrialization. The Chilean case, notwithstanding the belief that its success on export diversification was based on market-oriented reforms, partially resulted from intentional policies directed toward the production of new goods for international markets (Agosin 1999). On the other side, cases such as the one of the Scandinavian countries – that evolved from natural resource exporters, to producers and exporters of a wide array of manufactures- are considered to be driven mainly by market forces.

Equally important, the debate between import substitution industrialization (ISI) and export promotion (EP) developmental strategies is also related to export diversification. On one hand, advocates of the infant industry argument propose that the successful experience of some of the East Asian countries – e.g., South Korea- would be unthinkable without the temporary shelter offered to some of its industries, before entering international markets. In contrast, proponents of the EP strategy cite for instance the Chinese experience -where previous industrialization does not explain the successful export diversification- while FDI – either in the form of multinational corporations (MNCs) or joint ventures- has played a very important role. The Chilean case is also considered here: while it is true that the government played a relevant role in supporting the country's diversification, this process has also been undertaken, as stated by Agosin (2006) "directly by exporting, especially when the first firms are fully or partly foreign-owned" (p. 4).

Finally, it is interesting to observe how the different nature of the response to crises has led to different experiences in terms of diversification: while East Asian nations encouraged accelerated investment and strengthened diversification, in Africa the response to the same crisis has been much less dynamic, resorting to concentration on a few commodity exports (UNECA 2007).

On the other side of the debate, findings like the ones of Stanley and Bunnag (2001) show that while diversification is supposed to stabilize export earnings and reduce the dependence on "volatile" primary products, in some cases, – e.g. Central America within the 1974–1995 period- precisely those countries that decided to specialize in established primary products and a few manufactures, outperformed the others. This is an interesting strand of the discussion, leading to the consideration that diversification by itself should not necessarily be beneficial for an economy. Of the utmost importance is that the "new" products, besides its novelty, should also offer lower instability levels. The "right mix" is found, as Stanley and Bunnag argue, only if the new products show low instability or negatively covariate with existing exports, lessening the variance. This does not necessarily imply a shift from natural resources to manufactures: some light manufactures, such as apparel, are also thought to be affected by volatility (Stanley and Bunnag 2001). The Latin American experience is also noteworthy: while most countries in the region diversified their export mix between the mid-1960s and the end of the 1990s, yet they did not accomplish considerable levels of GDP expansion. (Bebczuk and Berrettoni 2006, p. 2).

Furthermore, it has been stated that evaluating export diversification at the level of aggregated commodities does not permit to fully capture the extent of diversification within, as well as outside, the commodity sector (UNCTAD 1995). In other words, only an examination of the shift from commodities to manufactures would be possible under that approach. Thus, it has been proposed that the possibilities of export diversification should not be limited to the movement from primary products to manufactured goods: export diversification may also be the result of a "more vibrant" commodity sector (UNCTAD 1995). Besides that, export diversification into manufactures can be coupled with a diversification of the commodity sector.

Another important aspect addressed in the literature has been suggested by Cramer (1999): while it is commonly believed that greater benefits could be expected from diversifying into manufactures – like more stable and less "biased" price behavior-, this positive outcome should not be taken for granted: domestic conditions are also required, along with the diversification process. In brief, increasing levels of export diversification do not guarantee, by themselves, higher levels of growth (Bebczuk and Berrettoni 2006, p. 2). If there are, for instance, shortages of inputs, bad management practices or weak infrastructure in a country, such conditions could outweigh the possible benefits from diversifying away from primary production (Love 1983).

Based on this type of consideration, the potential advantages of diversification in some African countries have been disputed. The relevance of domestic macroeconomic and general country conditions is also supported by the experience of those developing countries that, besides diversification, showed a good performance in these internal aspects (UNCTAD 1995). Summing up, different "determinants" of diversification – as Ben Hammouda et al. (2006) call them- have to be considered along with export diversification: the level of income, investment, technology absorption capability and even the possible role of trade and industrial policies, have been for instance proposed. Equally important is the analysis of different experiences in export diversification, which as Cramer (1999) proposes, could also be explained by the differences "in policy and technological progress, with a strong role for research and development and for close public/private cooperation in industrial upgrading" (p. 1252).

2.2.2 Export Diversification and Growth: The Empirical Evidence

Similar to the case of trade and economic growth, the relation between export diversification and economic growth has been analyzed in a wide number of empirical studies. Figure 2.2 depicts a diagram including different econometric and statistical methods that have been used for evaluating this possible linkage. Likewise, the most relevant methodologies and data used in these studies are briefly described in Table A.1.

Al-Marhubi (2000) conducts an empirical study of 91 countries, in the 1961–1988 period, to test the hypothesis of a possible link between export diversification and growth. He finds out that those economies with a larger number of export products experienced faster growth. Besides that, he argues that greater export diversification and lower export concentration is associated with faster growth. The relationship between export diversification and growth proved to be economically large. He also concludes that when export diversification occurs, growth in developing countries is positively influenced by stimulating the accumulation of capital.

Gutiérrez et al. (1997b) evaluate the experience of six Latin American countries – Argentina, Brazil, Chile, Colombia, Mexico, and Venezuela- in terms of export diversification and structural change in exports in the 1980s and the 1990s. They state that export diversification has been attempted both at times of import substitution (IS) and export promotion (EP) developmental models. Nevertheless, the export-oriented policy reforms introduced reinforced the export diversification process. Their most relevant findings are related to the fact that export diversification in the region – with the exception of Venezuela – is a long-run phenomenon. In general, the debt crisis of the 1980s was a factor that triggered export diversification in all countries. But in the case of Brazil, some of its diversification is attributed to

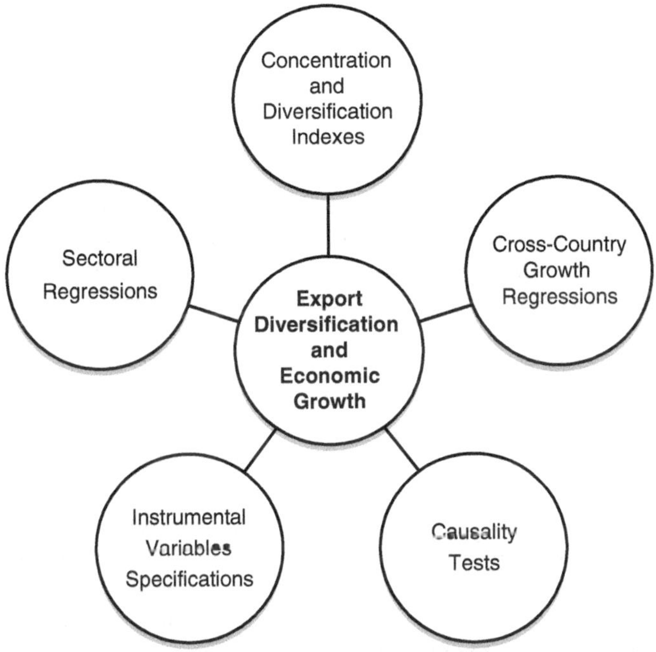

Fig. 2.2 Radial diagram – empirical studies dealing with the trade and growth linkage (Source: own illustration, based on the list of studies surveyed, [see Table A.1])

the remnants of the IS strategies, and as the authors state, it is questioned whether some of its manufacturing exports "are the fruits of technological experience gained under import substitution, or are mere by-products of inefficient policy-induced resource allocation" (p. 476).

Hausmann et al. (2007) develop a general-equilibrium model with a modern sector producing a variety of goods and a traditional sector producing a single homogenous good, being labor the only factor of production. The model is used to analyze the determination of the production structure of an economy "in which the standard forces of comparative advantage play some role, but not the exclusive role" (p. 5). According to the authors, the underlying cost structure of the economy contributes to what a country will produce and ultimately, to its level of wealth. Afterwards, empirical estimations are conducted for a sample of countries, covering over 5.000 products for the years 1992–2003. One interesting contribution of their work is the suggestion that an economy may produce and export goods determined not only by its "fundamentals" (physical and human capital endowments, labor, natural resources, and the quality of its institutions, as the authors call them). The basket of goods could also be influenced by stimulating "the number of entrepreneurs to engage in cost discovery in the modern sectors of the economy" (Hausmann et al. 2006, p. 3).

Hence, the crucial issue to be considered by policy-makers would be that because of knowledge externalities, investment levels in cost discovery are sub-optimal. Consequently, it would be necessary for the government or the industry to intervene. The joint role of the so-called "fundamentals" of the economy, and the stimulus that could be offered to the entrepreneurs to engage in cost discovery in the modern sectors of the economy, would determine the goods that a country produces. For Hausmann et al., economies exporting goods associated with higher productivity levels experience higher rates of growth. Growth "is the result of transferring resources from lower-productivity activities to the higher-productivity goods identified by the entrepreneurial cost-discovery process" (Hausmann et al. 2006, p. 17).

The linkage between changes in export variety and the growth in total factor productivity (TFP) at a disaggregated level is examined by Feenstra et al. (1998) in 16 sectors, over the 1975–1991 period, for the cases of South Korea and Taiwan. Based on input–output tables, the sample is divided between primary industries – that basically rely on natural resources as inputs, and show weak upstream linkages to manufacturing – and secondary industries – with stronger upstream linkages, generally purchasing more from other supplying industries than from themselves- (Feenstra et al. 1998, p. 13). The empirical evidence lends strong support to the argument that secondary industries would better fit the hypothesis of endogenous growth, taking into account both their differentiated inputs and outputs. The authors report that seven out of the nine industries in this group hint at a positive and significant impact of export variety on productivity. Likewise, five of these industries indicated a positive and significant impact of upstream export variety on productivity.

One relevant argument proposed by Hausmann et al., is that an economy's specialization is crucial for its development path, and that this specialization can be influenced or "pushed up" the product scale. Countries have the possibility to overcome the limitations imposed by their cost discovery and go further than what their "fundamentals" allow them to. Again, the stimulus given to the entrepreneurs is of the utmost importance. As the authors indicate:

> There are economically meaningful differences in the specialization patterns of otherwise similar countries. We have captured these differences by developing an index that measures the "quality" of countries' export baskets. We provided evidence that shows that countries that latch on to a set of goods that are placed higher on this quality spectrum tend to perform better. The clear implication is that the gains from globalization depend on the ability of countries to appropriately position themselves along this spectrum. (p. 13)

Other studies, such as the one conducted by Lederman and Maloney (2003), analyze the empirical relationship between trade structure and economic growth, focusing on the influence of natural resource abundance, export concentration and intra-industry trade. The authors utilize panel data of 5 year periods going from 1975 to 1999, being the core data set that of Summers and Heston (1991), updated to 2000. The *Herfindahl* index, as well as the share of natural resources exports in total exports, are used to determine the degree of concentration. Furthermore, the *Grubel-Lloyd* (1975) index of intra-industry trade is calculated. One of the most interesting findings reported is that the assertion of resource abundance adversely affecting growth (e.g. Sachs and Warner 1995), is not found to be robust. Thus, it is suggested that the common belief about natural resources being inimical to growth should be reevaluated, and further research is advised "on the channels through which they may have a positive effect, possibly, through introducing higher productivity growth" (Lederman and Maloney 2003, p. 15). Furthermore, the study concludes that export concentration per se is detrimental for growth, be it on natural resources or manufactures. As the authors argue:

> In contrast to much of the recent literature, natural resource abundance appears to have a positive effect on growth whereas export concentration hampers growth, even after controlling for physical and human capital accumulation, among other factors (Lederman and Maloney, p. 1).

Finally, intra-industry trade provides evidence of beneficial impacts on growth.

Agosin (2006) refers to some stylized facts derived from a cross-country comparison of the Hirschmann-Herfindahl (HH) index between Asian countries and Latin American and Caribbean countries. The author notes how the former countries have been approaching HH indexes similar to those of developed economies. For the latter countries, it is evident that some of them – e.g. Mexico, Colombia, and Chile – have been partially successful in diversifying their exports. However, exports are still much more concentrated than those of the Asian countries.

In addition to this, Agosin's study (2006) further investigates whether export diversification has any explanatory power in a standard empirical model of growth. Cross-sectional data in the 1980–2003 period is considered, for a sample of Asian and Latin American countries. It is suggested that export growth by itself does not appear to be relevant for growth, while *export growth together with diversification* appears to be relevant. This argument is supported by the fact that the interactive variable (measuring diversification and export growth) showed the expected sign and was highly significant, providing the strongest explanatory power. Export diversification is supposed to contribute to growth through two different channels, namely, the "portfolio effect" – less export volatility- and the widening of comparative advantages, as a result of a more diversified economy.

As mentioned before, Stanley and Bunnag (2001) analyze the performance of four Central American countries – Costa Rica, El Salvador, Guatemala, and Honduras- that underwent diversification processes. Based on panel data for the 1974–1995 period, they analyze how diversification has impacted the countries' earnings instability. The study comes to the conclusion that diversification by itself is not the answer to any country's problems associated to foreign earnings volatility. Besides their novel character, these products should also be characterized by low instability or negatively covariate with existing exports, lessening the variance. Consequently, support is given to the argument that besides diversification, other accompanying factors are needed for stabilizing foreign earnings, like political and economic stability. It is also suggested that even though "manufacturing products offer the greatest opportunity to reduce instability" (p. 1380), the stabilization of some important traditional sectors of the economy – such as coffee in El Salvador-should be considered as important as diversification.

The possible influence of export diversification on growth is also examined by Amin Gutiérrez de Piñeres and Ferrantino (1997a), by analyzing the Chilean experience within the period 1962–1991. They study the possible link between diversification, export growth and aggregate development, by constructing different measures of diversification and structural change in exports. These measures are afterward used to test different relationships among the structure of exports and export growth. Two different interesting findings are reported: first of all, a link between the domestic economic performance and diversification is reported, suggesting that diversification in Chile has taken place mostly during times of internal crisis or external shock. Secondly, that the new products most successfully introduced in that country were mainly primary products (such as tobacco, coffee and tea, and dairy products) while a number of manufactures (like plastics, manufactured fertilizers, electrical and non-electrical machinery) have shown less dynamism. As highlighted by the authors, "the most striking source of diversification has been the emergence of new agricultural exports under the stimulus of real exchange rate depreciation" (Amin Gutiérrez de Piñeres and Ferrantino 1997a, p. 389). It is also proposed that export diversification, in the long run, has boosted Chilean growth performance. As mentioned in a previous section of this chapter, export diversification should not automatically be associated with value-added manufactures, as the Chilean and other experiences show. In addition, these empirical studies lend further support to the argument that natural resources and primary products exports can also enhance growth.

For Krishna and Levchenko (2009), the focus of the analysis is placed on analyzing the sources of higher output volatility in less developed countries, which could be related to their pattern of specialization. By examining industry-level data of 459 manufacturing sectors for the period 1970–1997, they suggest that openness to international trade leads to specialization in more volatile sectors in poorer countries. Less developed countries have relatively higher export shares in goods with low product complexity -being complexity measured as the number of intermediates required for production in each sector (Levchenko 2007). On the contrary, wealthier and more developed economies tend to specialize in more complex goods (Krishna and Levchenko 2009). Empirical evidence is provided, supporting the hypothesis that less complex goods are characterized by greater volatility. A strong negative relationship between complexity and volatility is founded. "Comparative advantage in less complex goods, that could arise from institutional quality or productivity differences, drives specialization in more volatile industries by developing countries" (Krishna and Levchenko 2009, p. 17).

As far as developmental strategies are concerned, Ben Hammouda et al. (2006) conduct statistical and econometric estimations, with the aim of examining if diversification can be envisioned as a framework to formulate strategies in Africa. Analyzing a panel data sample of 18 African countries in the 1996–2001 period, the authors report that investment shows to be determinant for a country to diversify. Furthermore, the income level shows a positive and significant link with diversification: as income per capita increases, countries tend to become more diversified, result that lends further support to Imbs and Wacziarg's (2003) empirical evidence. Furthermore, macroeconomic stability is found to be one of the most important explanatory factors of diversification. On the contrary, trade openness does not show to necessarily lead to diversification: this quite surprising finding is explained suggesting that, at a specific stage in the diversification process, "the portfolio motive for diversification ceases to dominate the comparative advantage considerations" (Ben Hammouda et al. 2006, p. 72). This finding would go in line with the Ricardian trade theory, which predicts that open economies become more specialized and produce a specific array of goods. Finally, institutions are reported to show a significant and positive relation with diversification.

An investigation carried out by the ESCAP (2004), dealing with the empirical estimation of the relationship between GDP growth rates and exports and export diversification, tested the so -called "export-led growth hypothesis" in three Asian LDCs (Bangladesh, Nepal and Myanmar). Comparisons are drawn with the diversification experience of Malaysia. The analysis of diversification and structural changes in exports is carried out based on different measures, namely: the commodity-specific cumulative export experience function, commodity-specific traditionality index (CSTI), the variance of CSTI, the concentration ratio of export earnings, and the aggregate specialization index. The analysis of these measures is done for the above mentioned countries along the period 1972–2000. Besides that, econometric estimations of the impact of the export diversification on export growth, as well as of the impact of total exports on growth, are performed.

The empirical results obtained provide support to the hypothesis that export growth could accelerate the development process of the three countries analyzed. But it is also stated that to accomplish higher rates of export growth, both horizontal and vertical diversification should be pursued, as shown by the Malaysian experience (ESCAP 2004). The experience of this country is cited as a successful case: for enhancing economic growth, Malaysia undertook both a vertical diversification of its "non-traditional" commodities – producing goods with some value-added, like electric appliances- and simultaneously diversified its "traditional" exports (horizontal diversification) toward commodities such as palm oil, rubber and tin (ESCAP 2004, p. 55).

On the contrary, some studies conducted reject the idea of the possible beneficial effects that export diversification could have upon economic growth. Among the opponents, Love's (1983) position is important to be taken into account. In his work, he states that moving from primary products into manufactures should not be always considered as the best developmental strategy for developing economies. Some characteristics, like recurring shortages of raw materials, capital equipment, spare parts and skilled labor, would seriously limit the capacity of many developing countries to efficiently produce manufactures. Coupled with that, Love refers to empirical evidence demonstrating that some manufactured goods actually experience more volatility and price variations than some "traditional" exports. In some cases, "increased shares of non-traditional exports have been accompanied by relatively greater increases in their instability" (Love 1983, p. 791). According to this evidence, policies leading to export diversification would not necessarily result in a positive effect for growth in some developing countries.

Following the same line of thinking, Ali et al. (1991) provide empirical evidence contrary to the argument that an increased level of export diversification would lead to more stable export earnings. The authors warn about the risk of considering diversification as a "panacea", because of the trade-offs between growth and stability of export earnings. They conduct statistical estimations for three African countries that have been seriously affected by instability and downward trend in export earnings, namely Malawi, Tanzania and Zimbabwe, over the period 1961–1987. For the particular case of these countries, despite of the fall in international prices of some of their most important commodities, it is proposed that augmenting and stabilizing the agricultural production would be the best way to accomplish export earnings growth and/or stability (Ali et al. 1991, p. 33). It is also reported that no clear relationship between the degree of export diversification and export performance could be established, when considering the experience of these three countries. Finally, it is also stated that export diversification is difficult in these economies, considering the lack of technological expertise, infrastructure and support services (Ali et al. 1991, p. 36). Tackling the issue of unstable domestic production, in turn explained by elements such as political disruptions and poor macroeconomic measures, is suggested as a factor of paramount importance before thinking about diversification.

2.3 Concluding Remarks

The relationship between trade and economic growth is, for sure, one of the richest and more interesting intellectual puzzles present in the economic literature. This question has been tackled several times, based on an ample number of theoretical models and empirical studies. While it is true that the debate is still open, and that the controversy is far from being resolved, it has not been demonstrated that trade could exert a negative influence on growth. Rather, the possible effects have been either overstated, or not properly measured. As pointed out by different scholars, the possible effects of trade upon economic growth seem to take place through different channels. Coupled with that, more sophisticated econometrical studies and techniques are needed, that would allow to appraise the extent of this linkage. Finally, not just the static gains from trade, but also the long-term dynamic ones should be considered, when analyzing the benefits derived from trade for a country's economic growth.

Export diversification has been proposed as a possible instrument that could enhance economic growth. Similarly to the relation between trade and economic growth, this argument has both advocates and opponents. The first group bases its position on the expectation of achieving stability-oriented and growth-oriented policy objectives, the possible linkage between economic growth and structural change, the modernization of productive structures, the augmentation of investment opportunities, and the reduction of investors' risks, among other claims. The endogenous growth literature highlights how diversification – both of output and exports- is a result of different factors associated to development. In contrast, skeptics argue that diversification *by itself* should not necessarily be beneficial for an economy, since the "new" products, could also be affected by volatility. Furthermore, aspects such as the futility of promoting export diversification without meeting the required previous conditions for it to be successful, have also been discussed.

As well as in the case of the nexus between trade and economic growth, the proposal of this chapter is that there is no clear or stringent evidence of possible detrimental effects of export diversification per se on economic growth. Both the theoretical framework and the empirical studies surveyed mostly converge on the hypothesis that export diversification may contribute to economic growth. Greater export diversification and lower export concentration has been associated with faster growth. As has been reported, export expansion coupled with diversification has shown in empirical studies to be relevant for economic growth. Plausibly, this instrument should be coupled with other initiatives: finding the right "export mix", and guaranteeing the required domestic conditions – such as the availability of the infrastructure, inputs, or skills needed-, are other factors of paramount importance. In a next chapter, an analysis of the current situation and perspectives in Colombia is carried out, trying precisely to determine if the country is prepared to successfully embark on a process of a structural change of exports towards diversity.

Finally, one interesting lesson derived from the survey is that export diversification should be decoupled from the notion that just industrial products and services should be promoted for a country to successfully evolve in economic terms. As in the case of positive experiences like the Chilean, Canadian, American, and the Scandinavian ones, natural resources exports could continue playing an important role for Colombia's economic development. The promotion of natural resource-based industries should therefore continue to be encouraged, but taking into account the necessary introduction of larger skills and knowledge intensities. Hence export diversification, considered on the whole as the evolution towards more sophisticated products, seems to exert a positive effect upon economic growth.

Chapter 3
Structural Change in Exports and Export Diversification: A Look at Colombia over the Period 1990–2008

Based on the examination of different concentration and diversification indexes, the current chapter explores the evolution of Colombian exports over the period 1990–2008. The analysis is concentrated on this lapse of time, considering that the country embarked on an active outward-oriented trade policy in February 1990, as mentioned previously. It begins by discussing the historical background of the shift from an import substitution to an export promotion model in Latin America as a whole, and in Colombia in particular. Next, there is a brief description of Colombia's trade policy since the 1990s, as well as a short review of some macroeconomic trends within the period of time analyzed.

Section 3.3 considers the distinction between the notions of "traditional" and "non-traditional" exports in Colombia, in the light of some international definitions. Section 3.4 aims to provide an answer to the main research question tackled in this chapter, namely, if a process of export diversification can be identified in Colombia since the year 1990. The analysis is based on different measures for export diversification, specialization, and structural change of exports. Finally, an analysis of the behavior of Colombian exports with some selected market is conducted, with the objective of exploring if a process of geographical diversification of exports has taken place.

3.1 From an Import Substitution to an Export Promotion Model

3.1.1 The Policy Shift in Latin America

The import substitution (IS) model, as explained by Amin Gutiérrez de Piñeres and Ferrantino (1997), is quite a recent development in Latin American economic history. Citing Maddison (1991), who used data for 1913 and showed that the region was much more integrated into the global economy than the Asian countries

J.F. Mejía, *Export Diversification and Economic Growth*, Contributions to Economics,
DOI 10.1007/978-3-7908-2742-2_3, © Springer-Verlag Berlin Heidelberg 2011

at that time, they emphasize that Latin America "has a long tradition of economic liberalism dating back to the nineteenth century, punctuated by periodic experiments with import substitution" (Amin Gutiérrez de Piñeres and Ferrantino 1997b, p. 466). Latin America was rather open to international trade, exporting primary products and importing capital goods and consumer durables (Hofman 2001). But changes associated to the international economic scenario, such as the Great Depression of 1929 and the associated capital and trade restrictions, made Latin American countries take a turn towards protectionism. Furthermore, the fact that the openness of these economies intensified the effects of the global recession, as well as the evident decrease in their volume of trade, were undoubtedly factors that contributed to this shift in the political and economic policy approach.

Mahon (1992) explains how by 1945 a number of commonalities were present among the different Latin American economies: the exhaustion of the foreign exchange reserves, the inflation-driven wage disputes, and the consolidation of the IS model (supported on trade protection and state subsidies as its main instruments) were some of the problems shared by those nations.

Two key driving forces, related to the initial allocation of factors in the region and the import substitution process itself, were crucial for the expansion of manufacturing exports in Latin America. For one group of products, this driving force was related to the exploitation of comparative advantages associated with the transformation of natural resources and the intensive use of – mostly unskilled – labor, both abundant factors in the region. This type of goods was mostly exported to non-Latin American countries with a scarcer endowment of these factors. For the other group of products, this initial engine was associated with the protection granted by the state, in order to satisfy the internal demand of goods intensive in capital and skilled labor, scarce factors in the region (GRECO 2002, p. 5). The exports of the latter products have been traditionally destined for the regional market, where these goods have been competitive due to the preferential duties received and lower transport costs (Greco 2002, p. 5).

As stated by Mahon (1992, p. 244), different factors explain why the process of IS came to a halt in Latin America. On first instance, the fact that the region's economies became more (and not less, as initially planned) dependent on imports, implying that economic growth in these nations was strongly attached to the balance of payments. This was particularly grave, especially considering the frequent foreign exchange crises. Secondly, the dependence on a few primary commodity and raw material exports was reinforced. Thirdly, the artificially supported exchange rates negatively affected exports, especially the new or "non-traditional" ones. Coupled with this, the growth of the manufacturing exports was seriously affected by the commercial restrictions imposed in the 1980s by the big majority of Latin American countries.

Both the debt crisis of the 1980s, as well as different problems linked to the import substitution strategy were factors that decisively contributed to the decision of turning again to trade as a driver of economic growth. At the end of that decade, a process of liberalization started first in Bolivia, Chile, and Mexico, and later on in Colombia, Peru and Brazil. Most countries opted for a reduction of their minimum and average tariff rates, the abolition of restrictive import lists, and the elimination of non-tariff barriers to trade. Many of them also launched a liberalization of their foreign exchange markets (GRECO 2002, p. 5).

Table 3.1 – included in the work of Hofman (2001) – depicts some interesting trends concerning the evolution of the volume of exports before, during, and right after the implementation of the IS model in Latin America. As can be observed, the region's performance was similar to other countries analyzed. As noted by Hofman, during the 1913–1950 period the region fared much better in comparison to other countries and regions in the sample. But after the Second World War, a turning point can be identified in this trend: between 1950 and 1973, the export performance was poor. It was, for instance, much lower than the averages of Korea and Taiwan, the United States, and the European countries as a whole.

This fall in the trend coincided with the moment when Latin America erected high tariffs and trade barriers. The situation reverted again between 1973 and 1994: especially in 1980–1994, countries like Argentina, Colombia and Venezuela registered higher rates of growth than in the period 1973–1980. Finally, at the

Table 3.1 Variations in volume of merchandise exports, 1913–2000 (Hofman (2001), Maddison (1995), *Monitoring the World Economy*, 1820–1992, Paris, Organisation for Economic Cooperation and Development (OECD), Development Centre, and International Monetary fund (IMF), *International Financial Statistics*, various issues; Maddison (2001), "The World Economy – A Millennial Perspective", Organisation for Economic Cooperation and Development (OECD), Development Centre, Paris, and ECLAC (Economic Commission for Latin America and the Caribbean) (2001), *Economic Survey of Latin America and the Caribbean*, Santiago de Chile)

	1870–1913	1913–1950	1950–1973	1973–1994	1994–2000
Argentina	5.2	1.6	3.1	5.8	9.0
Brazil	1.8	1.7	4.7	8.9	3.9
Chile	3.4	1.4	2.4	8.8	8.8
Colombia	2.0	3.9	3.8	5.7	5.8
Mexico	5.9	−0.5	4.3	9.7	16.6
Venezuela	4.1	5.4	4.1	−1.9	3.8
Arithmetic average	**3.7**	**2.3**	**3.7**	**6.2**	**8.0**
Korea	0.0	−1.3	20.3	12.6	18.0
Taiwan province of China	4.8	2.6	16.3	10.8	6.6
Arithmetic average	**2.4**	**0.7**	**18.3**	**11.7**	**12.3**
Portugal	2.1	2.0	5.7	8.5	7.9
Spain	3.5	−1.6	9.4	8.2	3.0
Arithmetic average	**2.8**	**0.2**	**7.5**	**8.4**	**5.5**
France	2.8	1.1	8.2	4.4	7.5
Germany	4.1	−2.8	12.4	4.0	7.1
Japan	8.5	2.0	15.4	6.2	3.8
Netherlands	2.3	1.5	10.3	4.3	7.1
UK	2.8	0.0	3.9	3.9	6.8
USA	4.9	2.2	6.4	5.1	7.1
Arithmetic average	**4.2**	**0.7**	**9.4**	**4.7**	**6.6**

end of the twentieth century, an important rise in the volume of exports was registered, especially in Mexico, Argentina, Chile, and Colombia.

3.1.2 Colombia: From an Inward to an Outward-Looking Economic Strategy

It is sometimes believed that the import substitution model was introduced in Colombia during the early postwar years, but long before, there were protectionist initiatives in the country that encouraged the development of alternative productive activities. In that line of argumentation, Garay (2004) stresses the existence of a previous "implicit model of import substitution", that did not respond to any specific theoretical approach still, but did consist of different policies and measures aimed at protecting infant Colombian industries. For instance, between 1904 and 1909, a number of protective measures were taken by the national government. Legislation was enacted to increase tariff protection for final goods, while duties for imported raw materials were reduced. The underlying motivation was to boost manufacturing activities through these tariffs and different subsidies. But these efforts were not very fruitful, taking into account different limitations such as the lack of technology absorption and technical knowledge, as well as the limited dimension of the internal market. Misas (2001) points out how the infant industry ideology developed by Friedrich List, one of the forefathers of the German Historical School, was highly respected in the country at that time.

Berry and Thoumi (1977) identify four different phases of the industrialization process in Colombia within the framework of the IS model: the first one, between 1900 and 1930, corresponds to a time where the country embarked on efforts to introduce a modern manufacturing sector. In the second phase (1930–1945), growth took place in a very complicated international juncture, the Great Depression and the Second World War being two important times. Next (from 1945 and until the late 1960s), the IS model was fully implemented, introducing different protective mechanisms like import controls. Another important feature of this period was the shift towards more complex and capital-intensive sectors. Finally, between the late 1960s and the end of the 1980s a sort of "mixed model" was implemented in the country, where the IS model was combined with different policies that were very successful for boosting a group of minor, "non-traditional" exports in the country. In what follows, the shift from an IS to an EP model in Colombia will be explained in a chronological sequence, based on the line of time proposed by Berry and Thoumi.

At first, the first manufacturing efforts were launched in a significant scale in the country within the period 1900–1930. This phase was characterized by the victory of protectionism over free trade, the expansion of the public infrastructure (railroad system), the remarkable rise of coffee exports, and important capital inflows. During these years, a period of rapid economic growth was spurred by the rise of coffee exports. The revenues obtained from that product, which accounted for a staggering 80% of total foreign sales, were crucial for the national economic development: they allowed to finance the imports of machinery and equipment and boosted the development of productive capacities in the country (Garay 2004).

FDI in Colombia was also of relevance for financing imports. The Colombian economic history calls this phase the "first boom of the non-agricultural economy" (*Primer Auge de la Economía No Agrícola).* In addition to the industrial development that was initiated, the construction of the road and transport systems encouraged the appearance of new industries too (Garay 2004). Hanratty and Meditz (1988) explain how Colombia's industrial sector (including manufacturing, assembly, and construction) was mostly developed after the First World War, using resources accumulated by the coffee and tobacco industries in the nineteenth century.

In the second phase (between the years 1930–1945), industrial activities were highly protected. Both the Great Depression and the Second World War exerted a negative influence upon the economic performance not only of Colombia, but of all Latin American countries. As stated by Garay (2004), the Colombian manufacturing industry began to take off in the 1930s, based primarily on the production of consumer goods. A number of protectionist measures were adopted to prevent competition against the domestic industries. Different sectors experienced positive rates of growth, e.g. the foods, beverages, tobacco, textiles and clothing industries. The lion's share of the manufacturing growth (70–75%) came from the non-durable consumer goods and textile industries (Berry and Thoumi 1977, p. 93). A defined group of intermediate products (rubber, paper, petroleum derivatives and coal) and the metal-metallurgical industries increased its share too (Berry and Thoumi 1977, p. 91).

In the third phase of the industrialization process (1945 – late 1960s) the IS model was fully implemented through different mechanisms such as import controls and import licenses, and a clear advance into more complex and capital-intensive sectors took place (intermediate and capital goods). Different monetary, exchange rate, fiscal and even foreign policies were strongly influenced by the ECLA (United Nations Economic Commission for Latin America and the Caribbean). Within that period, tariff rates were substantially increased, controls in the foreign exchange market were introduced, and the monetary policy was also directed towards the promotion of the industrial sector, through subsidized credits (the so-called *créditos de fomento*). The latter was possible because the coffee growers – who in the 1950s generated approximately 90% of the foreign currency entering the country – made an alliance with the industrialists, that were eager to use this foreign exchange for financing the import of badly needed machinery and technology (Misas 2001). Holmes, Amin Gutiérrez de Piñeres, Curtin (2009) argue that Colombia followed a mixed economic policy: on one side, the national government promoted import substitution to support domestic capitalists. In a parallel manner, export promotion was introduced specifically for the coffee sector, which has been a crucial product in inserting Colombia in global markets. The authors highlight that this pattern of "mixed policy" was a very particular approach, compared to the other Latin American countries. The authors also highlight that "because coffee was such a dominant export crop throughout much of the twentieth century, the Colombian economy has often been tied directly to the market for coffee" (Holmes, Amin Gutiérrez de Piñeres, Curtin 2009).

Misas (2001, p. 114) also agrees that a mixed policy approach was implemented in Colombia in the period of transition between the IS and EP models. Three elements were especially important during this phase: the increase of tariff rates, the coffee revenues, and the offer of subsidized credits. The latter mechanism offered interest rates that were substantially lower to the ones offered in the market, with the objective of promoting capital accumulation.

The exchange rate administration, coupled with subsidized credits, were two cornerstones of the IS model in Colombia within this phase. The creation of big conglomerates with a very limited degree of technology absorption, the very low levels of diversification, and an entrepreneurial class linked to the agrarian-commercial elite, were also some of the most important developments. The industrial sector was almost exclusively dedicated to satisfy domestic demand, and was very poorly integrated in the global markets (Misas 2001).

Important to observe is that most of the fastest growing industries in this stage of industrialization (e.g. metal products, rubber, and paper) were strongly dependent on imported inputs (Berry and Thoumi 1977, p. 93). The creation of the "Industrial Promotion Institute" (*Instituto de Fomento Industrial*), agency of the Colombian government in charge of supporting the Colombian industrial development, was another policy tool implemented. It certainly played an important role in the creation of different industries in the country.

It is also interesting to mention that the import-substituting industrialization was also a reaction to two different problems in the country: the frequent balance-of-payment crises, originated in fluctuations in the terms of trade, as well as the inflation-devaluation cycle. (Berry and Thoumi 1977, p. 93). Particularly between 1957 and 1968, when a period of slow growth of the industrial activities occurred, the contribution of most consumer industries and intermediate goods declined.

At the beginning of the fourth phase, between the late 1960s and the late 1970s, the IS model was combined with an increasing export focus. The economic model in Colombia shifted to a more balanced and even pro-export pattern (Berry and Thoumi 1977). Here, a very important increase in the participation of minor exports (the ones different to coffee and petroleum), took place: these exports increased at an important rate of approximately 25% per year. This trend remained positive until 1975, when the world recession and domestic anti-inflationary policies took their toll.

Hanratty and Meditz (1988) elaborate on several issues dealing with the process of Colombian industrialization. They mention how the industrial sector "grew slowly but steadily up to the 1970s, then declined until the mid-1980s". Under the IS model, which dominated in Latin America during the Great Depression, the new manufacturing efforts were oriented towards meeting the domestic demand or formerly imported goods, placing a special emphasis on the production of consumer – rather than capital – goods. The authors also highlight that Colombia, different to other Latin American nations, was not as negatively affected from the protectionist effects of the IS model as other nations in region. The reason for that was that the country postponed intensive industrialization until the 1950s, and "was a relatively open society politically and economically" (Hanratty and Meditz 1988).

As discussed by Ocampo and Villar (1992), 1967 is considered a decisive turning point in the history of the Colombian commercial regime. Measures adopted were aimed at changing a process of liberalization of the economy that was previously launched in the middle of the 1960s. As a result of a grave currency crisis that took place in 1966, the government decided to reestablish a generalized control of imports, coupled with a rigid control of the foreign exchange market. These measures were accompanied by the introduction of a system of "mini-devaluations", and the creation of a stable system of incentives to the export of "non-traditional" products (Ocampo and Villar 1992, p. 167). On the imports side, at the beginning of the 1970s the average tariff rates were still very high, and the big majority of imports were anchored to a previous license regime. The very rigid control was only relaxed for capital and intermediate goods not produced in the country (Ocampo and Villar 1992, p. 167). Berry and Thoumi (1977, p. 100) argue that the policy measures adopted at the end of the 1960s seem to have been caused by the increased awareness of Colombian policymakers of "the high-cost substitution into more and more complex activities" and the "recurring balance-of-payments crises".

Edwards and Steiner (2000, p. 14) mention two features that are supposed to differentiate Colombia from other Latin American countries: the first one is that there has been a product (coffee) not linked to import substitution, produced by the most influential business group. The second one is that export promotion has been the cornerstone of policy since 1967, despite the official process of opening up the economy officially starting only in the 1990s. Nevertheless, it should be mentioned that these initial timid efforts to open up the economy were launched more as a response to the grave balance of payments crisis that had been caused by the protectionist policies.

Consequently, policymakers introduced some export promotion strategies, which were followed by the development of some industries – mainly, consumer goods (Hanratty and Meditz 1988). The introduction of export subsidies, the creation of *PROEXPO* (export promotion agency), and the introduction of a "crawling peg" exchange rate system, were some of the most relevant initiatives taken to boost Colombian industrial exports. The latter instrument proved especially effective, since the Colombian currency was constantly devalued against the most important currencies traded. Despite the important rise of industrial output and the impressive increase in the share of manufactures within the total value of exports – from 8% in 1967 to 28% in 1975 – , this positive growth trend came to a halt at the end of the 1970s, revealing again the dependence of the Colombian economy on one single commodity: coffee (Hanratty and Meditz 1988). It should be clarified that these reforms were still accompanied by a set of instruments typical of an IS model, such as import controls and licenses. Imports of domestically produced goods were still not allowed.

A myriad of other problems affected the Colombian economy at the end of the 1970s: deindustrialization, the fall of manufactured exports as a percentage of total exports, the dependence on internal demand, the lack of diversification and the low level of investment were factors that decisively contributed to the country's economic decline. Other factors that played a negative role were the so-called "Dutch disease" that the country passed through, due to the boom of coffee exports and the consequent appreciation of the Colombian peso, affecting the competitiveness of manufactured goods. The dismal economic situation was worsened by the debt crisis, especially since 1982, when the capital flows to Latin America were dramatically reduced.

An inflection point within this last stage can be identified by the middle of the 1980s, when the industrial sector showed signs of real growth again. Domestic policies that placed special emphasis on diversification and growth through exports especially contributed in a positive manner (Hanratty and Meditz 1988). Nevertheless, it is important to mention that the growth of industrial output was again mostly explained by the production of consumer and intermediate goods. Industrial goods, as usual, had to be mostly imported to the country.

Edwards & Steiner (2000, p. 18) emphasize that during the 1980s, Colombia and Chile were the best performers among the Latin American economies: different to Argentina and Venezuela – where average GDP growth was negative – and to Peru and Uruguay – where it was barely positive- it reached 3.4% in Colombia. Furthermore, the country experienced positive rates of growth of its per capita GDP, did not need to restructure its foreign debt, and inflation rates were never beyond control. But on the other hand, at the end of the 1980s the Colombian economy suffered from different problems and distortions: a very high degree of protection, an extremely rigid labor legislation, a highly distorted financial sector, and an extensive system of exchange controls (Edwards and Steiner 2000). The authors believe that "from a regional standpoint, in 1985 Colombia was probably the least open of all Latin American economies" (Edwards and Steiner 2000, p. 18). The record deficit levels in the current account and the rapid decrease of the foreign exchange reserves, were also problematic factors (Ocampo and Villar 1992).

By the middle of the 1980s, due to pressures from the World Bank, the national government launched a set of measures geared towards the liberalization of imports. Quantitative restrictions were lifted, the list of "prohibited imports" was significantly reduced, and a wide number of intermediate and capital goods were declared as goods that could be freely imported. In addition, the average tariff was reduced.

The transition to an export promotion model in Colombia took place in a moment when the intra-Latin American trade was gradually improving, a factor that had a positive effect on the minor, "non-traditional" exports. In 1989, the non-coffee exports rose by 170% compared to 1983. This positive development was not the only factor that facilitated the change in the economic approach. Ocampo and Villar (1992) make reference to different factors that altogether explain this shift from an IS to an EP model. First,an intense ideological debate began to be conducted at government level, concerning the role of the state in the economy, the dependency on the domestic market, and the necessity of promoting an "outward-oriented" model. In addition to this, the pressures exerted by the multilateral credit agencies, the poor levels of investment and productivity rates, and the previous changes of economic models in different Latin American countries, played a very important role too. A flexibilization of the labor market and an increased level of competition in the domestic market – as a result of the elimination of oligopolies – , were other positive effects expected from the process (Misas 2001).

This is the background that gave birth to a gradual liberalization program, intended to make trade an engine of economic growth and to successfully insert the country into the global markets. As stated by Rajapatirana (1998, p. 518), the *apertura* (liberalization) policy was seen "as the vehicle for modernization, which would increase efficiency and output growth, as well as raise export growth, employment, and reduce costs to consumers".

A first measure consisted of the progressive elimination of quantitative barriers to trade, which was followed later by a decrease of the average tariff and a nominal devaluation. The new Colombian government that took office in 1990 decided to deepen the opening process, eliminating practically all kinds of import licenses. Tariff rates were substantially reduced, the foreign exchange market was liberalized, and the FDI legislation was reformed offering the same rights to national and foreign investors. Moreover, different institutional measures were taken: the Ministry of Foreign Trade, Industry and Tourism was created, as well as *Proexport* (Colombian national business support organization) and *Bancoldex* (Colombian national export credit agency, which offers lines of credit to Colombian exporters) (Garay 2004).

3.2 The Colombian Commercial and Trade Policy Reforms Since 1990

In February 1990, the Colombian government officially announced its decision to reform the country's economic development model. The so-called "Program for the Modernization and Industrialization" of the industrial apparatus was launched (Ocampo and Villar 1992). Some of the most important measures derived from these policies were related to a gradual liberalization of imports, a substantial reduction of tariffs, the elimination of import licenses and, generally speaking, a host of actions intended to increase the exposure of the national industries to foreign competition. Simultaneously, the institutional framework and tools dealing with the promotion of exports were "upgraded": among others, the *Consejo Superior de Comercio* (High Council of Trade), directed by the Colombian President, was constituted.

As previously mentioned, the Ministry of Trade, Industry and Tourism was established, as well as a national foreign trade bank (*Bancoldex*), the latter with the purpose of improving the credit access to exporting companies. A new international exchange law was also enacted, introducing a free market approach to the exchange rate's fixation. In addition, a remarkably bigger level of independence was granted to the Central Bank with the new constitution of 1991, transforming it into a more autonomous institution, in charge of the monetary and exchange management.

Since the onset of Colombia's process of liberalization, a dynamic trade policy was enacted. Both at the bilateral and multilateral level, great efforts were devoted towards developing a "strategic" network of foreign relations. The underlying motivation was that these free trade agreements, as well as other forms of integration, would render important effects in terms of productivity levels. This policy has also been oriented towards the consolidation of exports as the country's "engine" of economic growth. Through these actions, the ultimate objectives of promoting economic growth and improving the population's welfare conditions, should be pursued. The Colombian Commercial Policy, contained in the so-called "Strategic Exporting Plan", and jointly conceived by the public and private sectors, aims to establish the "competitive foundations" that would allow the country to increase its productivity levels (*Ministerio de Comercio, Industria y Turismo,* 1999).

Five "strategic objectives" have been specified within Colombia's commercial policy: augmenting and diversifying Colombia's exportable offer of goods and services, improving the capacity of foreign sales by attracting international investments, increasing productivity levels and accomplishing a competitive level of exporting activities, "regionalizing" the exporting activities (by promoting "competitive regional advantages" and the consolidation of clusters), and promoting managerial skills and a "managerial culture" (*Ministerio de Comercio, Industria y Turismo*, 1999). The latter strategy is associated with different initiatives, such as supporting the economic development of bordering zones, the widening and following of foreign commercial relations, negotiating Free Trade Agreements (FTAs), and coordinating Colombia's position in international organizations.

As stated by Goldberg and Pavcnik (2005, p. 86),

> Colombia's trade policy underwent significant changes during the past three decades. Although Colombia considerably liberalized its trading environment during the late 1970s, the government increased protection during the early 1980s in an attempt to combat the impact of the exchange rate appreciation and intensified foreign competition. The level of protection varied widely across industries. Manufacturing industries enjoyed especially high levels of protection with an average tariff of 50%. Imports from the two most protected sectors, textiles and apparel, and wood and wood product manufacturing, faced tariffs of over 90% and 60%, respectively. This suggests that Colombia protected relatively unskilled, labor-intensive sectors, which conforms to a finding by Harrison and Hanson (1999) for Mexico. From 1985 to 1994, Colombia gradually liberalized its trading regime by reducing the tariff levels and virtually eliminating the nontariff barriers to trade. Tariff levels declined throughout the period, but the most radical reforms took place in 1985 and 1990–1991.

The concentration of exports in a certain number of sectors – and markets- is certainly a matter of concern for Colombian policy-makers, in the same way it is for many other developing nations. Taking that into account, and hoping to attain

Table 3.2 Colombian bilateral and multilateral commercial agreements (Own elaboration, based on information from the Organization of American States (OAS): Foreign Trade Information System, and the Colombian Ministry of Trade, Industry and Tourism)

Counterpart	Scheme of integration	Year of signature
European union	FTA[a]	2010
Canada	FTA[a]	2008
European Free Trade Association- EFTA	FTA[a]	2008
United States	FTA[a]	2006
"Northern triangle": El Salvador, Honduras, and Guatemala	FTA[a]	2006
Andean Community-Mercosur	FTA	2004
Group of three: Colombia, Mexico, and Venezuela	FTA	1994
Caribbean community and common market (CARICOM)	PPA	1994
Chile	PPA	1993
Panama	PPA	1993
Honduras	PPA	1984
El Salvador	PPA	1984
Costa Rica	PPA	1984
Nicaragua	PPA	1984
Guatemala	PPA	1984
Andean Community	CU	1969

FTA Free Trade Agreement, *PPA* Partial Preferential Agreements, *CU* Customs Union
[a]Negotiations concluded, ratification pending

bigger markets either through the conclusion of commercial agreements or unilateral schemes of preferences offered by developed countries, Colombia has embarked on an active outward-oriented trade policy (in terms of the negotiation and signature of commercial agreements) since the 1990s. As depicted in Table 3.2, seven FTAs have been negotiated since 1994. Besides that, the country is a member of the Andean Community of Nations, and benefits from different unilateral schemes of preferences, such as the US's "Andean Trade Promotion and Drug Eradication Act" or the European Union's "GSP Plus".

Colombian policy makers state that some of the objectives of conducting these negotiations are linked to the accomplishment of goals such as improving the "economic efficiency" through a freer trade environment, expanding the access conditions for Colombian exports, and avoiding a possible "crowding- out" phenomenon of the national products in the world's marketplace (*Consejo Superior de Comercio Exterior, República de Colombia,* 2004).

By the same token, the WTO's 2006 "Trade Policy Review of Colombia" highlights how Colombia has "stepped up its negotiating agenda with different countries". Opening up new markets for Colombian products, and ensuring a preferential and long-term access (which is not provided by unilateral schemes of preferences, that have to be frequently renewed), are the utmost objectives associated with the trade negotiations. Furthermore, the WTO underscores how these negotiations "are in line with the policy recommended by the Joint Committee on Foreign Trade in 2005" (WTO 2006).

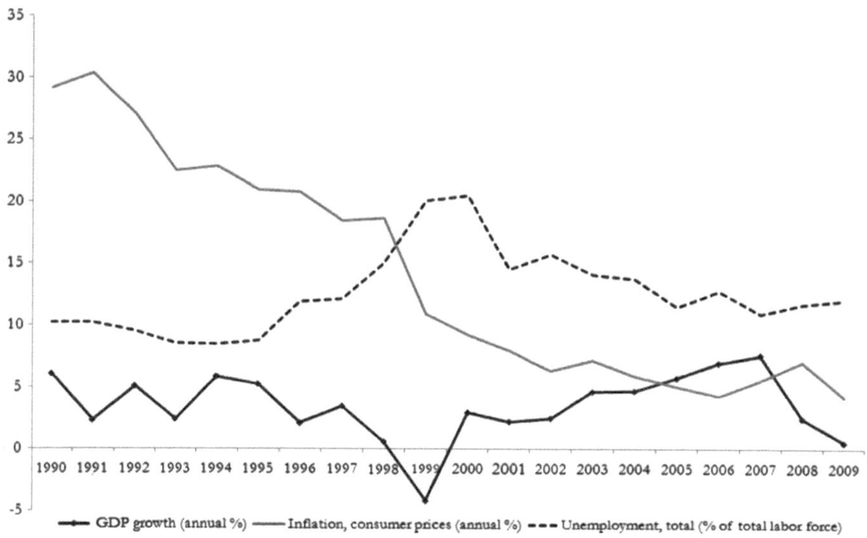

Fig. 3.1 GDP growth, inflation, and unemployment rates in Colombia (1990–2009) (Own elaboration, based on data from World Development Indicators Database and the International Labor Organization, 2009)

Whereas the objectives of opening up to new markets and consolidating stable trade relations are well intentioned, it is nevertheless paradoxical to find out how the composition of Colombian exports remains highly concentrated, and heavily dependent upon a few raw materials. Similar to other Latin American countries, the country has benefited from the increased prices of basic commodities -such as oil, coal, and nickel- during recent years. A slight increase in the participation of the "non traditional" exports was registered in the years 2001 and 2007. But on the contrary, the average rate of growth in the period 1994–2008 is lower than the one registered in 1994.

Figure 3.1 depicts some interesting trends in the period of time analyzed. After the first few years of the opening up of the economy, a severe economic recession took place in 1998, dramatically affecting relevant macroeconomic indicators. In the period 2002–2007, positive rates of economic growth (going up to a level of 8% in 2007), as well as a remarkable trend of declining inflation and unemployment rates, document a positive economic performance in the country. The global economic downturn took its toll on the economy: GDP grew at just 2.4% in 2008 and 0.5% in 2009, and unemployment slightly increased to 12% at the end of the period analyzed.

Figure 3.2 shows a pattern of rather stable growth of the total exports value since 1994, process only interrupted in 1998 (when the economic recession hit the country) in the period 2001–2002, and in the year 2009 (the latter, as a result of the global economic downturn). Remarkable increases have been reported since 2004. Between 2004 and 2008, total foreign sales more than doubled in value, going

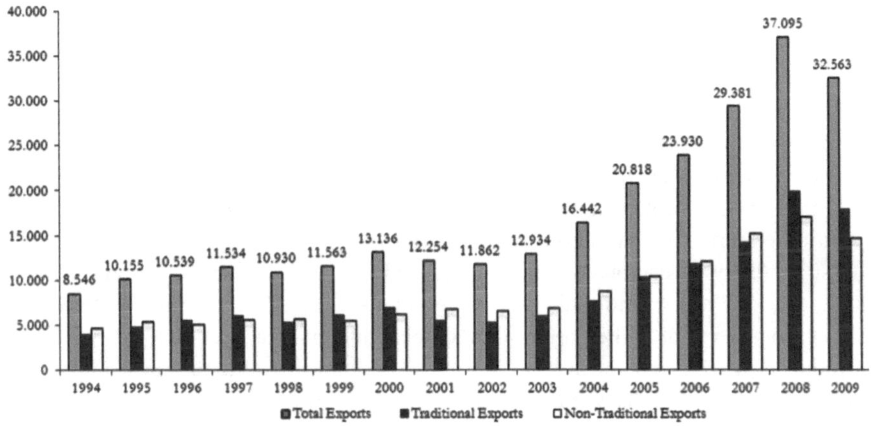

Fig. 3.2 Colombian exports, million USD, 1994–2009 (Own elaboration, based on data from the Colombian Central Bank, 2009)

up from USD $16 to USD $37 billion. This is a positive fact that could be related to an increased degree of openness in the economy. Nevertheless, it should again be highlighted that the greater international demand for commodities had an important influence upon this positive trade performance, especially during the last few years. In 2009, a decreased international demand for Colombian products – associated to the global economic downturn-was reflected in a fall of total exports to USD $32 billion.

3.3 Role and Significance of the "Traditional" and "Non-traditional" Exports for the Colombian Economy

Establishing a clear-cut distinction between "traditional" and "non-traditional" exports is not an easy task, taking into account the variety of definitions that can be found in academic literature. It is, therefore, relevant to start this section by looking at different perspectives that have been considered for approaching this typology.

Starting with the argument of Dijkstra (2001, p. 2), he stresses that it is not possible to establish a universal definition for several reasons. In the first instance, it is generally supposed that "non-traditional" exports started later than "traditional" ones, but "there is no agreement on the moment in history that differentiates traditional from non-traditional". Furthermore, the same export good can be "traditional" in one country and "non-traditional" in another. Consequently, he proposes that "a definition of non-traditional agricultural exports has to be country-specific".

Agosin (2007) discusses that growth that may be enhanced based on the introduction of "new goods" or through investment in "non-traditional goods". Here, an association between the notions of "non-traditional" and "novelty" could be inferred. Amin Gutiérrez de Piñeres and Ferrantino (1997a) utilize the so-called "traditionality index", which is aimed at deriving an empirical measure of traditionality (this methodology is implemented in the next section, for establishing the degree of traditionality of Colombian exports).

One principle that has also been implemented is related to an export share criteria, aimed at introducing some kind of differentiation between these two types of exports. In that sense, several attempts have been undertaken in trade literature to try to establish a distinction. Balassa, 1977, cited in Ng and Yeats, 2002, defined "non-traditional" primary products as those accounting for less than 2% of total exports. The latter authors also underscore that the World Bank introduced in 1997 a definition of "traditional exports", as the ten most important three-digit commodity group in a country's exports in a base year. Non-traditional exports "are, by implication, everything else" (Ng and Yeats 2002, p. 6). In a more recent study, the United Nations 2009 International Trade Statistics Yearbook refers to the "top 10" export commodities at the four-digit level of the Harmonized System.

When it comes to Colombia, the definition of "non-traditional exports" has significantly changed during the last decades. Within the period 1950–1970, all those export commodities different to coffee and petroleum were grouped under that category – at that time, the latter were called "minor exports". From 1970 on, gold and bananas joined the group of the "traditional exports" (GRECO 2002). Since 1997, the National Administrative Department of Statistics (DANE) considers just four export commodities as "traditional" exports: petroleum and derivatives, coffee, coal, and ferronickel. All the remaining agricultural, mining and industrial goods are defined as "non-traditional" exports.

It is important to clarify that the Colombian central bank groups exports within the following categories:

- "Traditional": comprising of coffee, petroleum and its derivatives, coal and nickel;
- "Non-traditional": cut flowers, emeralds, minerals such as gold, and a big variety of agro-industrial and industrial products;
- Services: transport, travel, communication and information services, insurance and financial services, managerial and construction services, and others.

For purposes of clarification, Tables 3.3 and 3.4 list the composition of Colombian exports, as well as their share within the total amount of foreign sales, based on the ISIC Rev.3. In the first instance, it should be observed that the country's reliance upon primary products has significantly increased: In 1995, 47% of exports were composed of "traditional" goods. In 2009, this share increased to 55%. Oil and its derivatives, as well as coal, have now turned to be the principal "traditional" exports of the country, while coffee has progressively decreased its contribution.

Table 3.3 Colombian "traditional" exports, share of total exports, 1995–2009 (Own elaboration, based on information provided by the Colombian Ministry of Trade, Industry and Tourism, 2010)

Division (ISIC Rev. 3)	Product/ Activity	1995 (%)	2000 (%)	2005 (%)	2009 (%)
01 Agriculture, hunting and forestry	Coffee	18	8	7	5
11 Extraction of crude petroleum and natural gas; service activities incidental to oil and gas extraction excluding surveying.	Oil	19	31	19	24
23 Manufacture of coke, refined petroleum products and nuclear fuel.	Oil derivatives	3	6	7	7
10 Mining of coal and lignite; extraction of peat	Coal	6	7	12	16
13 – Mining of metal ores	Nickel	2	2	4	2
Traditional exports (total)		**47**	**53**	**49**	**55**

Figure 3.3 provides another look at these patterns, depicting the participation both of "traditional" and "non-traditional" exports within the total amount of exports. Notice that services exports have *not* been included in the analysis.

As illustrated in Fig. 3.3, between 1991 and 2000 important oscillations in these shares can be appreciated: by the middle of the 1990s, 53% of the foreign sales originated in the so-called "non-traditional" exports, while "traditional" ones had a share of 47%, process interrupted between 1999 and 2000. In 2001, a "tipping point" can be observed: "non-traditional" exports surpass again the "traditional" ones, pattern that can be observed until 2007. However, in the last 3 years, the participation of the "non-traditional" exports decreased from 53% in 2007, to 47% in 2008 and 45% in 2009.

Some important aspects should be noted when analyzing these trends. The first one is that the data shown in Figs. 3.2 and 3.3 demonstrate that the objective of diversifying the composition of Colombian exports has not been fully accomplished, especially when it comes to fostering the "non-traditional" ones. The latter have importantly increased from 47% in 2000, to 55% in 2009. Last year's trend can be explained by the increased contribution of the exports of raw materials such as oil, coal, and nickel. Oil, for instance, significantly increased from a share of 18% in 2007 to a participation of 24% of the total foreign sales for 2009.

Furthermore, it should be clarified that within the so-called "non-traditional" exports, besides industrial products, some raw materials still play a very important role. Within Colombia's balance of payments, primary products such as bananas, emeralds, cut flowers, "other farming products" and the so-called "other mining products" are of great relevance. In 2008, these five sectors accounted for 13% of the total amount of foreign sales. But excluding some types of basic technologies involved in the agro-industrial and mining sectors, these goods are clearly *not* industrial exports. And as mentioned, their participation is very significant. Hence, the term"non-traditional" exports does not necessarily make reference to industrial exports.

Table 3.4 Colombian "non-traditional" exports, share of total exports, 1995–2008 (Own elaboration, based on data provided by the Colombian Ministry of Trade, Industry, and Tourism, 2010)

Division (ISIC Rev. 3)	Product/Activity	1995 (%)	2000 (%)	2005 (%)	2009 (%)
14 – Other mining and quarrying	Emeralds	4	1	0.3	0.3
01 – Agriculture, hunting and related service activities	Bananas, cut flowers	9	8	7	6
13 – Mining of metal ores	Other mining products	2	1	5	6
05 – Fishing, operation of fish hatcheries and fish farms; service activities incidental to fishing.					
011 – Growing of crops; market gardening; horticulture	Other farming products.	3	3	3	3
15 – Manufacture of food products and beverages	Agro-industrial products	6	5	5	5
17 – Manufacture of textiles. 18 – Manufacture of wearing apparel; dressing and dyeing of fur. 19 – Tanning and dressing of leather; manufacture of luggage, handbags, saddlery, harness and footwear. 22 – Publishing, printing and reproduction of recorded media. 25 – Manufacture of rubber and plastics products. 24 – Manufacture of chemicals and chemical products.	Light manufactures.	16	13	14	11
27 – Manufacture of basic metals. 28- Manufacture of fabricated metal products, except machinery and equipment.	Manufacture of basic iron and steel. Manufacture of basic precious and non-ferrous metals.	9	13	11	10
29 – Manufacture of machinery and equipment n.e.c. 30 – Manufacture of office, accounting and computing machinery. 31 – Manufacture of electrical machinery and apparatus n.e.c. 32 – Manufacture of radio, television and communication equipment and apparatus. 33 – Manufacture of medical, precision and optical instruments, watches and clocks.	Manufacture of general purpose machinery. Manufacture of special purpose machinery. Manufacture of domestic appliances n.e.c.	3	3	3	4
34 – Manufacture of motor vehicles, trailers and semi-trailers. 35 – Manufacture of other transport equipment.	Automotive industry.	1	2	3	1
Total		53	47	51	47

Note: *NEC* Not elsewhere classified

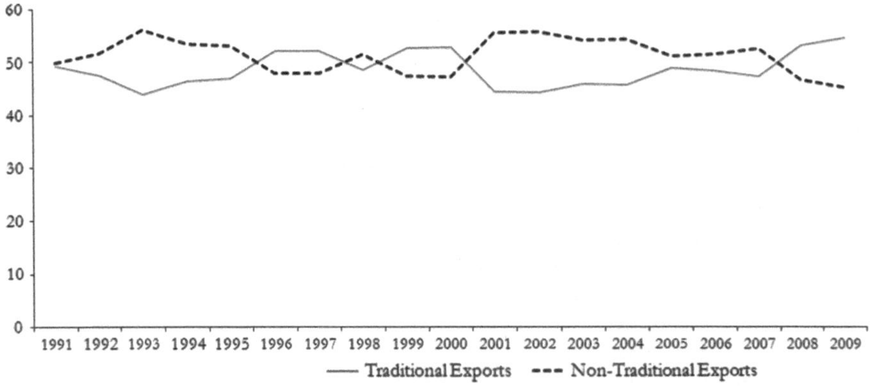

Fig. 3.3 Share of "traditional" and "non traditional" exports, 1994–2009 (Own elaboration, based on data provided by the Colombian Ministry of Trade, Industry and Tourism, 2010)

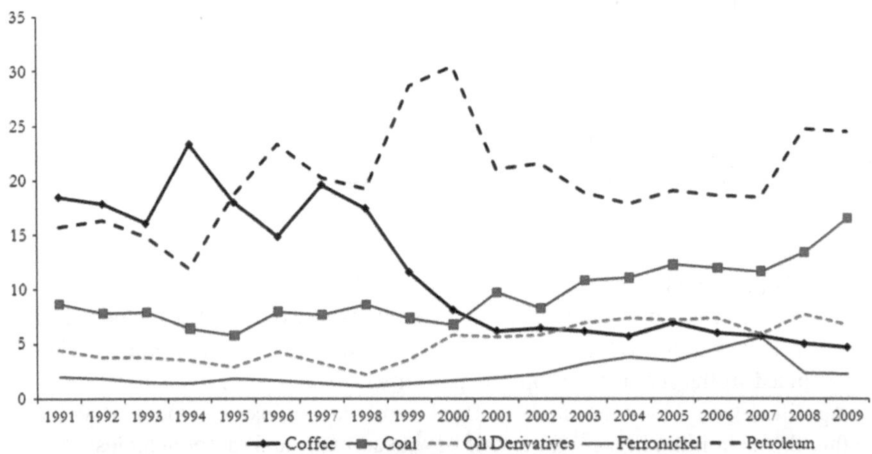

Fig. 3.4 The five "traditional" Colombian export products (share of total exports), 1991–2009 (Own elaboration, based on data provided by the Colombian Central Bank)

Again, it can be observed that the "non-traditional" exports average rate of growth at the end of the current decade has actually been inferior to the level registered by the middle of the 1990s (in terms of its participation within the total amount of exports).

Another interesting trend of the Colombian foreign trade can be observed in Fig. 3.4: coffee, the most important export product at the beginning of the 1990s, is displaced by petroleum (crude oil) since 1995. On the other hand, coal and nickel become gradually more relevant within Colombia's offer of "traditional exports".

Should the aforementioned "export share" criteria of the World Bank's and the United Nations' be literally taken into account, the definition of Colombian

Table 3.5 Colombian "traditional" exports according to the export share criteria: "top 10" export commodities at the four-digit level, 2008 (Own elaboration, based on data from the United Nations International Merchandise Trade Statistics)

HS code	Industry	Exports in value (USD thousands)	Exports as a share of total exports	Exports as a share of world exports	Growth of exports in value (%p.a.)
2709	Crude petroleum oils	9,306,210	24.73	0.64	33
2701	Coal; briquettes, ovoids & similar solid fuels manufactured from coal	4,593,574	12.21	4.82	27
2710	Petroleum oils, not crude	2,736,320	7.27	0.37	22
0901	Coffee, tea, mate and spices	1,923,023	5.11	5.9	19
0603	Cut flowers and flower buds for bouquets, fresh or dried	1,094,472	2.91	15.21	12
7108	Gold unwrought or in semi-manuf forms	891,303	2.37	0.9	12
0201	Meat of bovine animals, fresh or chilled	742,593	1.97	3.91	130
0803	Bananas, including plantains, fresh or dried	654,357	1.74	7.87	11
8703	Motor cars and other motor vehicles principally designed for the transport	255,725	0.68	0.04	1

"traditional" exports would be quite different to the one currently adopted by the Colombian economic authorities. Some products like petroleum and its derivatives, coal and briquettes, coffee, and ferroalloys (ferronickel) would still be included in that group. But, in addition to these export goods, an additional number of products should be included in the list of the "top 10" performers. Table 3.5 depicts how this new composition would look: as can be noticed, some new industries would be included within this definition, like gold, meat of bovine animals, and motor vehicles.

Based on the same "export share" criteria, the "non-traditional" exports would be comprised of all the other export goods which are not included in the "top 10" list. Table 3.6 depicts their composition.

3.4 Export Diversification in Colombia: An Empirical Analysis

3.4.1 The Cumulative Export Experience Function and the Industry-Specific Traditionality Index

When analyzing diversification and structural change in exports, a simple association of *traditionality* with primary products and *non-traditionality* with manufactures, fails to represent the experience of developing nations (Amin

Table 3.6 Colombian "non-traditional" exports, export share criteria, 2008 (Own elaboration, based on data from the United Nations International Merchandise Trade Statistics)

Industry	Exports in value (USD thousands)	Exports as a share of total exports	Exports as a share of world exports	Growth of exports in value (%p.a.)
Paper & paperboard, articles of pulp, paper and board	628,767	1.67	0.36	19
Boilers, machinery; nuclear reactors, etc.	624,033	1.66	0.03	22
Articles of apparel, accessories, not knit or crochet	603,204	1.6	0.34	3
Articles of apparel, accessories, knit or crochet	588,840	1.57	0.33	16
Vehicles other than railway, tramway	567,196	1.51	0.05	7
Electrical, electronic equipment	560,985	1.49	0.03	28
Essential oils, perfumes, cosmetics, toileteries	438,416	1.17	0.51	36
Animal,vegetable fats and oils, cleavage products	399,600	1.06	0.45	29
Sugars and sugar confectionery	397,880	1.06	1.26	1
Raw hides and skins (other than furskins) and leather	378,117	1	1.32	38
Pharmaceutical products	365,228	0.97	0.09	13
Articles of iron or steel	336,618	0.89	0.11	17
Miscellaneous edible preparations	334,523	0.89	0.77	22
Copper and articles thereof	295,808	0.79	0.2	52
Miscellaneous chemical products	257,110	0.68	0.17	2
Ceramic products	237,971	0.63	0.6	20
Knitted or crocheted fabric	237,538	0.63	1	39
Printed books, newspapers, pictures etc.	232,966	0.62	0.49	11
Salt, sulphur, earth, stone, plaster, lime and cement	222,882	0.59	0.46	19
Footwear, gaiters and the like, parts thereof	220,681	0.59	0.24	50
Furniture, lighting, signs, prefabricated buildings	220,508	0.59	0.13	27

(continued)

Table 3.6 (continued)

Industry	Exports in value (USD thousands)	Exports as a share of total exports	Exports as a share of world exports	Growth of exports in value (%p.a.)
Aluminium and articles thereof	209,188	0.56	0.13	13
Tanning, dyeing extracts, tannins, derivs, pigments etc.	203,745	0.54	0.3	44
Fish, crustaceans, molluscs, aquatic invertebrates nes	202,079	0.54	0.28	11
Rubber and articles thereof	196,093	0.52	0.13	21
Organic chemicals	173,419	0.46	0.05	24
Cotton	163,070	0.43	0.31	31
Glass and glassware	150,126	0.4	0.23	11
Tools, implements, cutlery, etc. of base metal	148,242	0.39	0.28	44
Aircraft, spacecraft, and parts thereof	142,649	0.38	0.07	72
Other made textile articles, sets, worn clothing etc.	139,898	0.37	0.32	21
Soaps, lubricants, waxes, candles, modelling pastes	139,176	0.37	0.3	25
Cereal, flour, starch, milk preparations and products	132,765	0.35	0.29	23
Inorganic chemicals, precious metal compound, isotopes	128,122	0.34	0.11	27
Ores, slag and ash	112,499	0.3	0.08	35
Dairy products, eggs, honey, edible animal product nes	112,058	0.3	0.16	19
Products of animal origin, nes	108,931	0.29	1.49	117
Edible vegetables and certain roots and tubers	97,849	0.26	0.2	48
Miscellaneous articles of base metal	94,334	0.25	0.17	41
Articles of leather, animal gut, harness, travel goods	91,029	0.24	0.18	12
Manmade staple fibres	85,131	0.23	0.27	33
Miscellaneous manufactured articles	82,218	0.22	0.32	20

(continued)

Table 3.6 (continued)

Industry	Exports in value (USD thousands)	Exports as a share of total exports	Exports as a share of world exports	Growth of exports in value (%p.a.)
Optical, photo, technical, medical, etc. apparatus	80,019	0.21	0.02	23
Manmade filaments	79,322	0.21	0.19	26
Cocoa and cocoa preparations	76,942	0.2	0.24	15
Stone, plaster, cement, asbestos, mica, etc. articles	70,688	0.19	0.17	20
Wood and articles of wood, wood charcoal	69,396	0.18	0.06	21
Fertilizers	67,341	0.18	0.09	47
Special woven or tufted fabric, lace, tapestry etc.	67,157	0.18	0.48	32
Beverages, spirits and vinegar	57,227	0.15	0.06	10
Impregnated, coated or laminated textile fabric	49,607	0.13	0.24	22
Albuminoids, modified starches, glues, enzymes	42,550	0.11	0.2	10
Vegetable, fruit, nut, etc. food preparations	41,403	0.11	0.08	6
Wadding, felt, nonwovens, yarns, twine, cordage, etc.	41,399	0.11	0.22	3
Meat, fish and seafood food preparations nes	37,937	0.1	0.1	9
Tobacco and manufactured tobacco substitutes	37,344	0.1	0.11	−19
Toys, games, sports requisites	30,113	0.08	0.03	5
Live animals	26,418	0.07	0.16	−37
Milling products, malt, starches, inulin, wheat gluten	25,726	0.07	0.17	4
Residues, wastes of food industry, animal fodder	24,830	0.07	0.05	49
Nickel and articles thereof	15,260	0.04	0.05	27
Oil seed, oleagic fruits, grain, seed, fruit, etc., nes	14,116	0.04	0.02	16
Ships, boats and other floating structures	13,431	0.04	0.01	23

(continued)

Table 3.6 (continued)

Industry	Exports in value (USD thousands)	Exports as a share of total exports	Exports as a share of world exports	Growth of exports in value (%p.a.)
Headgear and parts thereof	10,422	0.03	0.18	24
Cereals	6,707	0.02	0.01	52
Carpets and other textile floor coverings	6,235	0.02	0.04	9
Lead and articles thereof	6,224	0.02	0.09	7
Commodities not elsewhere specified	5,597	0.01	0	39
Arms and ammunition, parts and accessories thereof	3,188	0.01	0.04	101
Furskins and artificial fur, manufactures thereof	2,940	0.01	0.04	22
Wool, animal hair, horsehair yarn and fabric thereof	2,085	0.01	0.02	−4
Lac, gums, resins, vegetable saps and extracts nes	1,773	0	0.04	75
Vegetable plaiting materials, vegetable products nes	1,706	0	0.26	21
Clocks and watches and parts thereof	1,577	0	0	20
Photographic or cinematographic goods	1,369	0	0.01	−2
Works of art, collectors pieces and antiques	1,227	0	0.01	6
Explosives, pyrotechnics, matches, pyrophorics, etc.	1,087	0	0.03	19
Other base metals, cermets, articles thereof	528	0	0	27
Pulp of wood, fibrous cellulosic material, waste etc.	485	0	0	−10
Musical instruments, parts and accessories	435	0	0.01	43
Zinc and articles thereof	424	0	0	16
Railway, tramway locomotives, rolling stock, equipment	309	0	0	28
Cork and articles of cork	309	0	0.02	−13

(continued)

Table 3.6 (continued)

Industry	Exports in value (USD thousands)	Exports as a share of total exports	Exports as a share of world exports	Growth of exports in value (%p.a.)
Bird skin, feathers, artificial flowers, human hair	298	0	0.01	21
Umbrellas, walking-sticks, seat-sticks, whips, etc.	249	0	0.01	30
Vegetable textile fibres nes, paper yarn, woven fabric	230	0	0.01	45
Manufactures of plaiting material, basketwork, etc.	224	0	0.01	−9
Tin and articles thereof	48	0	0	−6

Gutiérrez de Piñeres and Ferrantino 1997a, p. 377). The same argument holds for Colombia, as will be analyzed in the current section. In the light of that evidence, and trying to derive empirical measures of the *traditionality* of some export industries, the authors propose the calculation of a cumulative export experience function for each commodity. It is defined as

$$c_{it} = \frac{\sum_{i}^{t} {=}_{t0} e_{it}}{\sum_{i}^{t1} {=}_{t0} e_{it}} \tag{3.1}$$

where c_{it} denotes the cumulative export experience function of industry i in year t, t_0 and t_1 represent the initial and final periods of the sample, and e_{it} denotes the exports by industry i in year t. The variable c_{it} has properties similar to that of a cumulative distribution function: it takes on values at or near 0 at the beginning of the sample period and rises to 1 in the final year (Amin Gutiérrez de Piñeres and Ferrantino 1997a, p. 379).

A cumulative export production function was calculated for the full set of 65 Colombian industries for the period 1991–2008, based on data from the United Nations Commodity Trade Statistics Database – *COMTRADE*, at the two-digit level. Exports were calculated in constant (1984) US Dollars. As previously mentioned, this indicator is considered as a common measure of diversification and structural changes in exports for a given industry (ESCAP 2004).

When plotted, the cumulative export experience function of an industry whose export experience has been concentrated in the initial period of the sample is expected to have a plot shifted to the left. As can be observed in Fig. 3.5, for the case of Colombian coffee and articles of apparel and clothing are the industries that

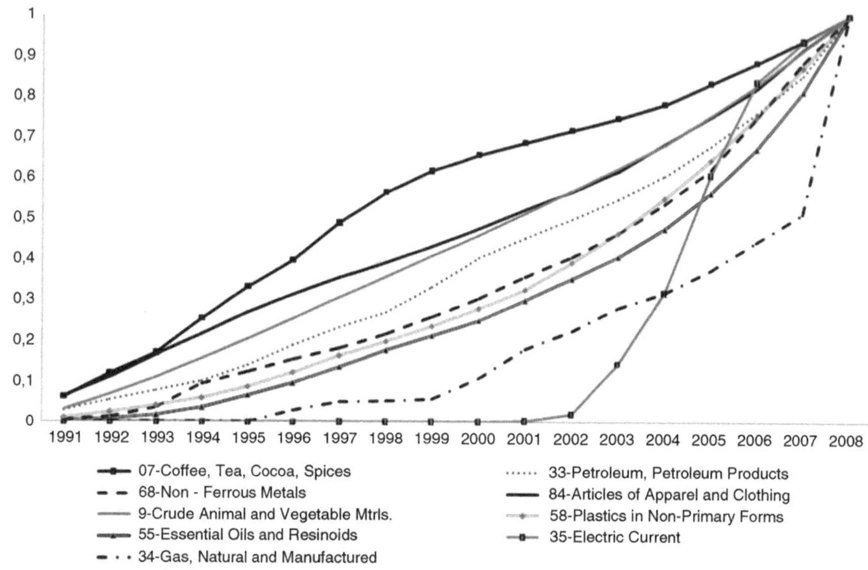

Fig. 3.5 Cumulative export experience function for specific Colombian industries, 1991–2008 (Own calculations, based on data from the United Nations Statistics Division)

are shifted more to the left, showing that a large share of its exports took place early in the sample period. The crude animals and vegetable materials industry has an almost linear shape, indicating that real exports were almost constant in the period of time analyzed. These industries, as well as petroleum and petroleum products, would fit into the category of "traditional exports".

On the other hand, the so-called "non-traditional exports" are comprised of those industries whose export experience has been concentrated on the last period of the sample, implying a right-shifted cumulative export experience function. This is the case of the non-ferrous metals, plastics in non-primary form, essential oils and resinoids, natural gas, and electric current industries, for which the export experience is more recent. Especially remarkable is the case of the latter two industries, which only initiated their export experience in the second half of the 1990s.

Figure 3.6 depicts the cumulative export experience functions for some of the most important "non-traditional" exports in Colombia – some of the largest contributors to the total amount of exports. Despite the fact that all these industries are considered as "non-traditional exports", it should be noted how some of them – e.g. non-metallic mineral manufactures, vegetables and fruits, apparel and clothing, chemical materials and products – are more "traditional" than the ones shifted to the right – general industrial machinery and equipment, paper and paperboard.

The comparison of cumulative export experience functions across different industries may shed light on the diversification of the export industries (ESCAP 2004). The industries for which the plots are shifted further to the

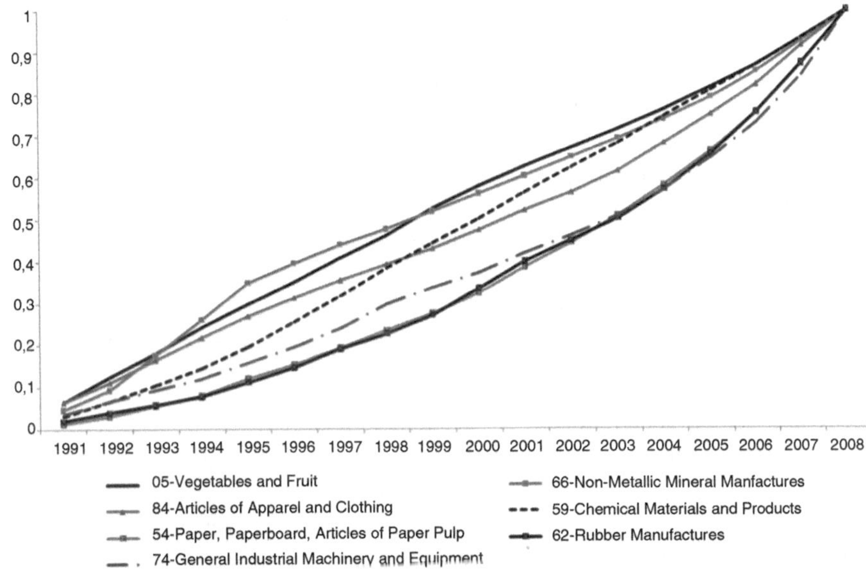

Fig. 3.6 Cumulative export experience function for specific Colombian "non-traditional" industries, 1991–2008 (Own calculations, based on data from the United Nations Statistics Division)

right should not only be considered to be more "non-traditional exports" but they should also be expected to be more vertically diversified (ESCAP 2004).

The industry-specific traditionality index offers another possibility of ranking the exports of a country according to the "traditionality attribute". This is accomplished by calculating the mean of the cumulative export experience index for each industry, and it is defined as

$$T_i = \frac{\sum_{t}^{t1} =_{t0} c_{it}}{t_1 - t_0 + 1} \tag{3.2}$$

where T_i denotes the traditionality index for industry I, and c_{it} is the cumulative export experience function. As stated by Amin Gutiérrez de Piñeres and Ferrantino (1997a, p. 380), more traditional industries have a higher score for T_i. Furthermore, the variance of the traditionality index can also be estimated, in order to test the robustness of the indicator (ESCAP 2004). It is defined as

$$VT_i = \frac{\sum_{t}^{t1} =_{t0} (c_{it} - \overline{c_i})^2}{t_1 - t_0 + 1} \tag{3.3}$$

A first analysis based both on the cumulative export experience function and the traditionality index (see Table 3.5) for a certain industry allows identifying the extent of diversification of a country's export mix. In the case of the coffee industry, for instance, it is possible to observe that the distribution is shifted to the left, which is coupled with a high score of the traditionality index in the period of time analyzed (0.57). The same holds true for the petroleum and derivatives industry, which shows an almost linear cumulative export distribution and a high value for the traditionality index. This implies that little or no diversification and no remarkable structural changes have taken place for the particular case of these industries. Nevertheless, it should be highlighted that the shape of the distribution of the coffee industry has significantly shifted to the left, indicating that Colombia has progressively decreased its dependency on its traditional main export product.

As previously mentioned, this trend is also confirmed by the impressive decrease in the share of coffee within the total value of Colombian exports: from a participation of 18% in 1995, it went down to 5% in 2008. Conversely, the dependency of the country on the petroleum and derivatives industries has experienced a dramatic increase: from a share of 22% of the total value of exports in 1995, it peaked at 33% in 2008.

At this point, it is important to recall the distinction between vertical and horizontal diversification, introduced in Chap. 1. The first category is related to the move between different categories of goods – e.g. the shift from primary commodities to manufactures-, through value-added mechanisms. The second category implies expanding the export basket, by "diversifying into goods within the same broad category of goods" (Agosin 2006, p. 7). The latter would be the case of shifting, for example, from coffee for the mass market to gourmet coffee (Agosin 2006). Additionally, export diversification may be accomplished either by adjusting shares of commodities in the existing export mix, or by adding new commodities to it (Ali et al. 1991). Horizontal diversification implies the modification of the primary export mix, contributing to neutralize the volatility of global commodity prices. On the other hand, vertical diversification implies value-adding activities (ESCAP 2004).

For the cases of coal and non-ferrous metals, with more right-shifted distributions and lower values for the traditionality index, this reflects that some sort of vertical diversification has taken place in these industries. Figure 3.7 depicts the cumulative export experience distributions for the Colombian "traditional exports".

When it comes to the so-called "non-traditional" exports, it is possible to identify some interesting trends, considering the cumulative export experience function and the traditionality index together. As depicted in Fig. 3.8, some industries – like meat and meat preparations, natural gas, electric current, iron and steel, non-ferrous metals, rubber manufactures, and general industrial machinery and equipment – have distributions shifted to the right. These same industries have low values of the traditionality index, indicating that greater export experience has been acquired during the last years of the sample (see Table 3.7).

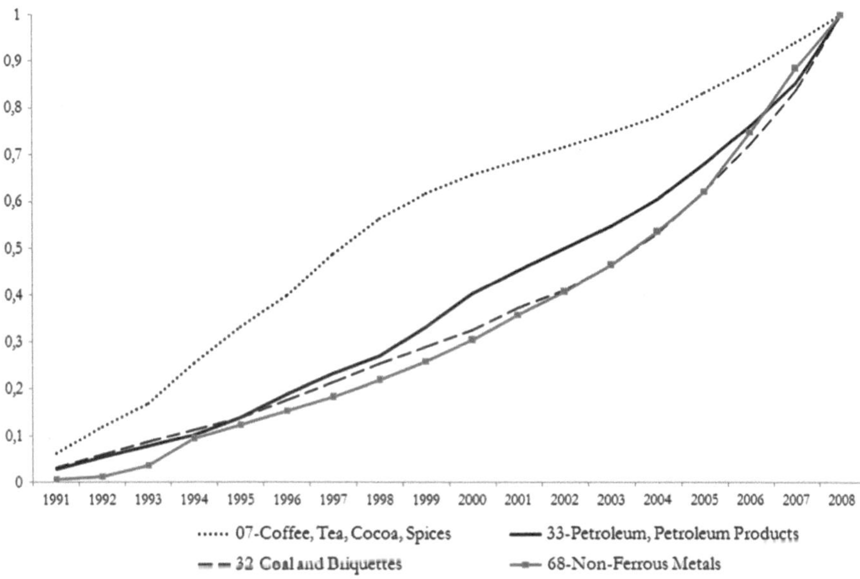

Fig. 3.7 Cumulative export experience function for Colombian "traditional" exports, 1991–2008 (Own calculations, based on data from the United Nations Statistics Division)

Conversely, in the cases of the metal-working machinery and non-metallic mineral manufactures industries, the plots are quite flat and the traditionality index is high, implying that no significant structural changes took place in the period of time analyzed. As shown in Table 3.7, from the 65 industries included in the Standard International Trade Classification (SITC) Revision 3, 37 show a traditionality index equal or lower to 0.41 (average value). Coupled with that, it can be noticed in Fig. 3.8 that the plots of different industries are shifted to the right, which indicates more exporting experience during the last years of the sample.

Based on the plots of the cumulative export experience functions, the traditionality index, and its variance, it is possible to identify some interesting trends in Colombia within the period of time analyzed:

- The coffee and petroleum industries, two of the most important "traditional" exports, do not show to have experienced remarkable structural changes. Neither horizontal nor vertical diversification are identifiable. Their traditionality indexes are high. Conversely, the coal and non-ferrous metals, with more right-shifted distributions and lower values for the traditionality index, suggest that some sort of vertical diversification has taken place in these industries.
- As far as the so-called "non-traditional" exports are concerned, the balance looks rather mixed. On one hand, it is possible to observe that some industries show distributions shifted to the right and low traditionality indexes, suggesting a process of diversification. However, it could not be affirmed that this process has been broad-based or generalized, since for other "non-traditional" exports, the

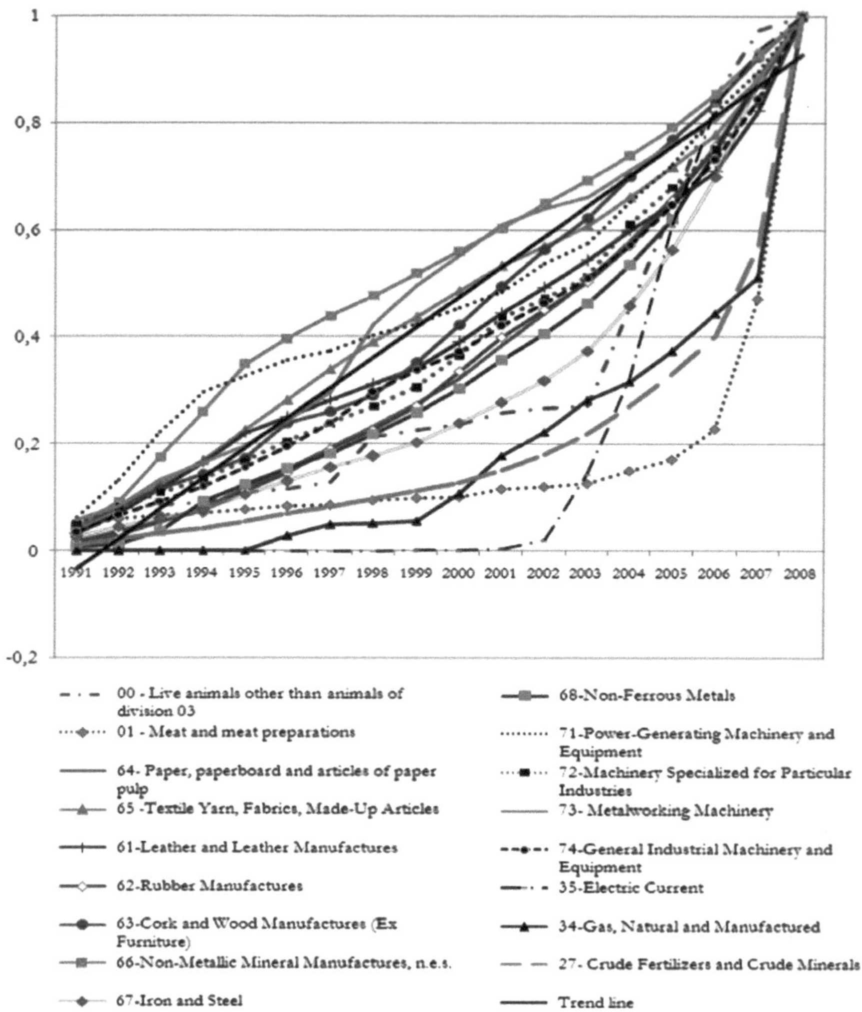

Fig. 3.8 Cumulative export experience function for Colombian "non-traditional" exports, 1991–2008 (Own calculations, based on data from the United Nations Statistics Division)

plot is either linear or even quite shifted to the left, suggesting that little or no diversification has taken place in these sectors. This suggests that a process of vertical diversification has taken place, but limited to some specific export goods.

- The curves of four sectors are particularly pronounced, namely the ones corresponding to meat and meat preparations, crude fertilizers and crude minerals, natural gas, and electric current industries, implying that these are export goods that are more recent and therefore, more "non-traditional". This is further confirmed by the fact that the traditionality index for these industries is

Table 3.7 Industry-specific traditionality index and its variance, Colombia, 1991–2008 (Own elaboration)

Rank	SITC code	Industry	Traditionality index	Variance of traditionality index	Cumulative real exports 2008, US $ (millions)
1	01	Meat and meat preparations	0.17633	0.05159	880
2	34	Gas, natural and manufactured	0.20139	0.06765	203
3	27	Crude fertilizers, other than those of division 56, and crude minerals (excluding coal, petroleum and precious stones)	0.21013	0.06100	198
4	35	Electric current	0.21510	0.13161	365
5	28	Metalliferous ores and metal scrap	0.23125	0.07757	1,266
6	97	Gold, non-monetary (excluding gold ores and concentrates)	0.25708	0.09096	3,436
7	42	Fixed vegetable fats and oils, crude, refined or fractionated	0.25901	0.08134	902
8	24	Cork and wood	0.30367	0.07377	113
9	78	Road vehicles (including air-cushion vehicles)	0.30789	0.09835	3,817
10	76	Telecommunications and sound-recording and reproducing apparatus and equipment	0.30958	0.09702	179
11	55	Essential oils and resinoids and perfume materials; toilet, polishing and cleansing preparations	0.31022	0.08686	1,863
12	75	Office machines and automatic data-processing machines	0.31242	0.10571	80
13	82	Furniture, and parts thereof; bedding, mattresses, mattress supports, cushions.	0.31307	0.08722	736
14	09	Miscellaneous edible products	0.32045	0.09569	683
15	67	Iron and steel	0.32233	0.08511	6,637
16	79	Other transport equipment	0.32761	0.07345	425
17	02	Dairy products and birds' eggs	0.32960	0.10795	455
18	00	Live animals other than animals of division 03	0.33653	0.09938	636
19	58	Plastics in non-primary forms	0.34559	0.09403	1,580
20	08	Feeding stuff for animals (not including unmilled cereals)	0.34761	0.09117	94
21	43	Animal or vegetable fats and oils, processed; waxes of animal or vegetable origin; inedible mixtures or preparations of animal or vegetable fats or oils, n.e.s	0.35034	0.11577	63
22	11	Beverages	0.35036	0.08921	287

(continued)

Table 3.7 (continued)

Rank	SITC code	Industry	Traditionality index	Variance of traditionality index	Cumulative real exports 2008, US $ (millions)
23	68	Non-ferrous metals	0.35594	0.09013	852
24	77	Electrical machinery, apparatus and appliances, n.e.s., and electrical parts thereof	0.35711	0.08194	2,566
25	32	Coal	0.36899	0.07851	18,928
26	81	Prefabricated buildings; sanitary, plumbing, heating and lighting fixtures and fittings, n.e.s.	0.36942	0.08775	469
27	62	Rubber manufactures, n.e.s.	0.37114	0.09098	889
28	64	Paper, paperboard and articles of paper pulp, of paper or of paperboard	0.37118	0.09132	2,943
29	96	Coin (other than gold coin), not being legal tender	0.39377	0.22940	0.56
30	74	General industrial machinery and equipment, n.e.s., and machine parts	0.39433	0.07836	974
31	54	Medicinal and pharmaceutical products	0.40042	0.10871	2,380
32	33	Petroleum, petroleum products and related materials	0.40149	0.08606	49,963
33	72	Machinery specialized for particular industries	0.40223	0.07894	511
34	69	Manufactures of metals, n.e.s.	0.40521	0.08209	2,150
35	57	Plastics in primary forms	0.40937	0.08202	4,240
36	04	Cereals and cereal preparations	0.40993	0.08466	705
37	61	Leather, leather manufactures, n.e.s., and dressed furskins	0.41362	0.07204	1,356
38	56	Fertilizers (other than those of group 272)	0.42243	0.07687	181
39	88	Photographic apparatus, equipment and supplies and optical goods, n.e.s.; watches and clocks	0.42282	0.06601	74
40	87	Professional, scientific and controlling instruments.	0.42741	0.08736	289
41	53	Dyeing, tanning and colouring materials	0.44408	0.15189	1,503
42	63	Cork and wood manufactures (excluding furniture)	0.44711	0.09307	236
43	25	Pulp and waste paper	0.45119	0.13132	6
44	21	Hides, skins and furskins, raw	0.45466	0.11187	142
45	29	Crude animal and vegetable materials, n.e.s.	0.45791	0.08858	8,723
46	51	Organic chemicals	0.46135	0.08554	1,021

(continued)

Table 3.7 (continued)

Rank	SITC code	Industry	Traditionality index	Variance of traditionality index	Cumulative real exports 2008, US $ (millions)
47	65	Textile yarn, fabrics, made-up articles, n.e.s., and related products	0.46210	0.07863	4,143
48	06	Sugars, sugar preparations and honey	0.46805	0.09970	4,333
49	89	Miscellaneous manufactured articles, n.e.s.	0.46860	0.08061	4,522
50	52	Inorganic chemicals	0.46975	0.09498	702
51	59	Chemical materials and products, n.e.s.	0.48147	0.09861	2,891
52	84	Articles of apparel and clothing accessories	0.48160	0.07628	8,919
53	73	Metalworking machinery	0.48456	0.08703	33
54	71	Power-generating machinery and equipment	0.48612	0.06571	329
55	23	Crude rubber (including synthetic and reclaimed)	0.51234	0.06484	11
56	12	Tobacco and tobacco manufactures	0.52727	0.08154	566
57	66	Non-metallic mineral manufactures, n.e.s.	0.53177	0.07830	5,539
58	05	Vegetables and fruit	0.53470	0.08213	7,711
59	41	Animal oils and fats	0.53765	0.10563	3
60	85	Footwear	0.55086	0.05120	1,006
61	07	Coffee, tea, cocoa, spices, and manufactures thereof	0.56932	0.08379	22,000
62	03	Fish (not marine mammals), crustaceans, molluscs and aquatic invertebrates, and preparations thereof	0.57006	0.08695	2,656
63	22	Oil-seeds and oleaginous fruits	0.59239	0.04632	24
64	83	Travel goods, handbags and similar containers	0.62580	0.06688	741
65	26	Textile fibres and their wastes (not manufactured into yarn or fabric)	0.74140	0.04486	383

the lowest. The variance of the traditionality index is low for the first three industries, indicating that the export diversification in these cases has been achieved with rather stable export earnings. Conversely, in the case of electric current, the variance of the traditionality index is one of the highest from the entire sample. This shows that the export earnings for that particular industry were very unstable along the period of time analyzed.

- Besides that, the aforementioned three industries are the ones where the plots are most shifted to the right, indicating that real exports have grown more rapidly in those sectors.
- The ranking of the different industries according to their traditionality index included in Table 3.5 shows that the distinction between "traditional" and "non-traditional" exports in Colombia should not be associated with agricultural exports. Some of the industries that have shown to be more "traditional" along the period of time analyzed are, indeed, manufactures (e.g. textiles, footwear, non-metallic mineral manufactures, and apparel and clothing, among others). On the other hand, some of the newest Colombian "non-traditional" exports belong to the mining sector (e.g. natural gas, metal ores).

3.4.2 The Herfindahl-Hirschman Index of Export Concentration

Different indexes are used to estimate concentration ratios of exports, like the Ogive index, the entropy index, and the Herfindahl-Hirschmann index (HHI). As stated by Ali et al. (1991), it has been argued that all three of the indices provide similar scores of export concentration and therefore, may be used interchangeably. For the purpose of the current study, the HHI index will be analyzed, which is a measure of the degree of market concentration (UNCTAD 2006, p. 191). It is normalized to obtain values ranking from 0 to 1 (maximum concentration), and it takes the form

$$HHI_j = \sum_i \left(\frac{x_{ij}}{x_j}\right)^2 \tag{3.4}$$

where x_{ij} is the value of exports of good i by country j and x_j represents the value of total exports of country j. If a single export product produces all the revenues, the value of H will be one. Still, if one country's revenues are equally distributed over a large number of products, the value will be close to 0 (Lederman and Maloney 2003). This indicator is detailed enough to capture, however imperfectly, both vertical and horizontal diversification (Agosin 2006, p. 7).

The HHI index for developed nations was of 0.056 in 1995, 0.07 in 2000, 0.067 in 2005, and 0.06 in 2008. The index for developing Asian economies was of 0.098 in 1995, 0.13 in 2000, and 0.12 in 2005 and 2008 (UNCTAD 2010). As can be observed in Table 3.8, the latter values were – in almost all cases – much lower than the scores obtained by the South American countries. For comparison purposes, some interesting observations can be made concerning the performance of Colombia and generally speaking, the whole South American region.

Firstly, it should be noted that the experiences of the countries in the region are quite different. On one hand, there are some economies where the HHI has

Table 3.8 Herfindahl–hirschman export concentration index, selected South American countries, 1980–2008 (Agosin (2006), UNCTAD handbook of statistics 2010)

	1980	1986	1995	2000	2005	2008
Argentina	0.15	0.17	0.13	0.14	0.14	0.15
Brazil	0.15	0.12	0.09	0.09	0.09	0.11
Bolivia	0.39	0.52	0.22	0.20	0.36	0.46
Chile	0.41	0.37	0.31	0.29	0.32	0.37
Colombia	0.58	0.58	0.24	0.30	0.21	0.25
Ecuador	0.55	0.45	0.38	0.45	0.54	0.56
Peru	0.26	0.25	0.24	0.23	0.24	0.25
Paraguay	0.28	0.40	0.34	0.34	0.37	0.40
Uruguay	0.24	0.20	0.16	0.17	0.21	0.20
Venezuela	0.67	0.57	0.52	0.62	0.86	0.93

dramatically fallen between 1980 and 2008. The cases of Brazil (approaching a level of 0.09 in 2000 and 2005, which is very near to the one of the developed nations), Colombia, and Chile are particularly interesting, where an important fall of the index took place. This is clearly an indication of a process of exports diversification and structural change of the exports in these nations.

In contrast, another group of nations (Venezuela, Bolivia, and Paraguay) has actually experienced an increase in their scores, indicating that their export revenues were more concentrated at the end of the period than they were at the beginning. Especially striking is the case of Venezuela, explained by the overdependence on a single export commodity, petroleum. Finally, Argentina, Ecuador, Peru, and Uruguay show more stable trends for the index within the period of time analyzed.

Despite the process of export diversification in some of the South American countries, it is also possible to identify how during recent years (2000–2005), the HHI index has actually increased for all the countries but Uruguay. This trend may be associated with the increased demand for raw materials, as well as the rise of their prices in the world market.

3.4.3 *The Export Diversification Index*

It is an index that ranges from 0 to 1, capturing the extent of the differences between the structure of trade of the country or country group and the world average (UNCTAD 2006, p. 204). If the score is close to 1, it indicates a larger difference from the world average. The export diversification index is calculated by measuring the absolute deviation of the country share from the world structure, and it takes the form

$$S_j = \frac{\sum_i \left| h_{ij} - h_i \right|}{2} \tag{3.5}$$

Table 3.9 Export diversification index, South American countries, 1995–2008 (UNCTAD, handbook of statistics, 2009)

	1995	2000	2005	2008
Argentina	0.57	0.55	0.56	0.57
Bolivia	0.73	0.77	0.76	0.66
Brazil	0.52	0.51	0.47	0.47
Chile	0.78	0.75	0.76	0.74
Colombia	0.65	0.64	0.59	0.57
Ecuador	0.79	0.74	0.75	0.73
Paraguay	0.70	0.76	0.78	0.76
Peru	0.79	0.79	0.79	0.77
Uruguay	0.64	0.62	0.67	0.66
Venezuela	0.76	0.79	0.84	0.82

where h_{ij} = share of product i in total exports or imports of the country j, and h_i is the share of product i in total world exports.

As in the case of the HHI, the values of the export diversification index for developed nations are low: 0.12 in 1995, 0.13 in 2000, 0.16 in 2005 and 0.17 in 2008. Table 3.9 shows the performance of the South American countries, indicating a very similar trend to the one of the HHI. In the first instance, countries like Brazil, Chile, and Colombia have significantly improved their scores between 1995 and 2008. Other economies, such as Argentina, Peru and Uruguay have not experienced significant changes. Finally, Paraguay, Uruguay, and Venezuela, have actually experienced an increase in the score of the index, suggesting a larger difference between their trade structure and the world average.

The scores for Colombia, similar to the case of the HHI, show a progressive decrease. Especially significant is the reduction registered between 2000 and 2005.

3.4.4 The Intensive and Extensive Margins of Export Growth in Colombia After 1990

When it comes to the growth of exports, two other indicators have been proposed in the academic literature: the intensive and extensive margin of exports. The former refers to a situation where the increase is based on the expansion of existing products to old markets. The latter can be related either to the increase of existing and new products to new geographic markets, and/or the expansion of new products to old markets (Brenton and Newfarmer 2009). As indicated by Besesedes and Prusa (2007), there is an important debate concerning the relative impact of each margin. While some authors have concluded that the extensive margin is the primary channel for export growth – like Hummels and Klenow, 2005–, others argue that the intensive margin plays the dominant role (Eaton et al. 2008; Helpman et al. 2008; Brenton and Newfarmer 2009).

Based on the methodology proposed by Evenett and Venables (2002), an analysis of Colombian exports at the two-digit level of trade (SITC Rev.3) for the period 1991–2008 was conducted. Two sub-periods were identified: 1991–1994 (which corresponds to the beginning of the export promotion model in Colombia) and 2005–2008. This decomposition was conducted, as proposed by Evenett and Venables (2002), based on the following assumptions:

X_{ij}^{k} (1991/1994) is the mean value of nation *i*'s (Colombia's) exports of good *k* to the world in 1991–1994.

X_{ij}^{k} (2005/2008) is the mean value of nation *i*'s (Colombia's) exports of good *k* to the world in 2005–2008.

$\Delta X_{ij}^{k} = X_{ij}^{k}$ (2005/2008) $- X_{ij}^{k}$ (1991/1994), the change in the value of Colombia's exports of good *k* to the world;

$$X_i^k(1991/1994) = \sum_j X_{ij}^k(1991-1994), \quad \text{the value of } \textit{Colombia's} \text{total exports of good } k \text{ in } 1991-1994 \tag{3.6}$$

$$X_i^k(2005/2008) = \sum_j X_{ij}^k(2005-2008), \quad \text{thevalue of } \textit{Colombia's} \text{total exports of good } k \text{ in } 2005-2008 \tag{3.7}$$

$$X_i^k = X_i^k(2005-2008) - X_i^k(1991-1994), \quad \text{the change in the value of } \textit{Colombia's} \text{exports of good } k \tag{3.8}$$

$$\Delta X_i^k = \sum\nolimits_k \Delta X_i^k, \text{ the change in } \textit{Colombia's} \text{ total exports} \tag{3.9}$$

Following the empirical strategy of Evenett and Venables (2002), a decomposition of Colombia's exports by product line was conducted, with the purpose of identifying to which extent the export behavior was based on the introduction of new products, the "death" of previously exported products, or volume changes on existing products. For accomplishing that objective, two indicators created by the latter authors were also used, in order to identify whether Colombia traded good *k* in 1991–1994 and 2005–2008. A threshold level of trade of $50.000 pa., denoted as $\$\bar{x}$, was introduced.

Taking that into consideration, the following two indicators were used (Evenett and Venables 2002):

$$I\left(X_i^k(1991-1994)\right) = 1 \; \textit{if} \; X_i^k\ (1991-1994) \geq \bar{x}, \quad 0 \; \textit{otherwise}. \tag{3.10}$$

$$I\left(X_i^k(2005-2008)\right)=1 \qquad \begin{array}{l} \textit{if } X_i^k(2005-2008) \geq \bar{x}, \\ 0 \textit{ otherwise}. \end{array} \tag{3.11}$$

Based on the latter two indicators, each pair i (Colombia) k has been classified into one of the next four sets:

$$D_i \equiv \left\{k \middle| I\left(X_i^k(1991-1994)\right)=1 \cap I\left(X_i^k(2005-2008)\right)=0\right\}, \tag{3.12}$$

the set of product lines k that Colombia exported in 1991–1994, but no longer exported in 2005–2008;

$$N_i \equiv \left\{k \middle| I\left(X_i^k(1991-1994)\right)=0 \cap I\left(X_i^k(2005-2008)\right)=1\right\}, \tag{3.13}$$

the set of product lines k that Colombia did not export in 1991–1994, but did export in 2005–2008;

$$C_i \equiv \left\{k \middle| I\left(X_i^k(1991-1994)\right)=1 \cap I\left(X_i^k(2005-2008)\right)=1\right\}, \tag{3.14}$$

the set of product lines k that Colombia exported in 1991–1994 and continued to export in 2005–2008;

$$O_i \equiv \left\{k \middle| I\left(X_i^k(1991-1994)\right)=1 \cap I\left(X_i^k(2005-2008)\right)=1\right\}, \tag{3.15}$$

the set of product lines k that Colombia did not export in either 1991–1994 or 2005–2008.

Evenett and Venables (2002, p. 6) propose that set D_i is composed of all those product lines by country i that "died", set N_i contains all the "newly exported goods", and set C_i contains those goods that were exported at the beginning of the period and continued to be exported at the end of the period. Finally, set O_i is composed of the goods that were not exported in any of these periods, or that were exported beneath the threshold $\$\bar{x}$ in both periods.

For obtaining the total change in exports associated to each of the sets, the following calculation was performed:

$$\sum_{k \in D_i} \Delta X_i^k, \sum_{k \in N_i} \Delta X_i^k, \sum_{k \in C_i} \Delta X_i^k, \sum_{k \in O_i} \Delta X_i^k \tag{3.16}$$

Based on data from the United Nations Commodity Trade Statistics Database (UN COMTRADE), an analysis of Colombian exports to the world was conducted at the two-digit level of the SITC Rev.3. Following the approach of Evenett and Venables (2002), the decompositions undertaken considered the changes in real exports from their annual averages in the period 1991–1994 to their annual averages in 2005–2008.

From the 66 product lines that were exported in the period 2005–2008, 61 had also been exported in the period 1991–1994. This means that 99.09% of Colombia's real export growth during the period was based on already existing product lines. Four new product lines appeared at the end of the period, accounting for 0.91% of the country's real export growth: gas (natural and manufactured), electric current, animal oils and fats, and special transactions and commodities not classified according to kind. Only one product line was exported beneath the threshold, namely, coin (other than gold coin), not being legal tender.

The results obtained are in line with previous empirical studies, showing that the most important source of export growth in developing countries comes from increases in existing bilateral trade flows (the intensive margin), rather than increases in new products or in old products to new geographic markets (the extensive margin) (Brenton et al. 2009). Evenett and Venables (2002, p. 7) report for instance, for the case of Argentina, that from its overall real export growth during the period, 98% was in continuing product lines, 2% in new product lines while product lines that died, amounted to 0.00% of the total export growth. Similar results were obtained for countries like Brazil, China, India, and Mexico. Besedes and Prusa (2007) state that their findings support the argument of the majority of growth of trade being based on the intensive margin, rather than the extensive margin of trade. Likewise, Amurgo-Pacheco and Pierola (2008), cited in Brenton et al. (2009), report that in all of the developing regions, the dominant source of export growth was associated with the intensive margin.

3.4.5 *Diversification of Markets and Trade Performance of Colombian Export Sectors*

Conventionally, the trade performance of countries has been measured by indicators like the level of openness, or the growth of exports over a given period (International Trade Centre 2007). Recent studies dealing with the linkage between trade and growth state that openness by itself is not sufficient for accomplishing increased levels of growth. It has been proposed that additional factors, like the type of product, the positioning on quality ladders, or the level of market and economic diversification, play a prominent role at the moment of boosting growth (International Trade Centre 2007).

In what follows, an analysis of the trade performance of the full set of export sectors (14) contained within the SITC Rev.3 is conducted for Colombia. These trade performance indicators have been produced by the International Trade Centre (ITC), based on the UN COMTRADE database. In addition to the value of exports, the share in national exports, and the share in the world market, one indicator is analyzed at the sectoral level: the market diversification index (number of equivalent markets). The analysis is undertaken for the period 2004–2008, years for which the trade performance indexes have been produced by the ITC. The share in national exports refers to the participation of each sector within the total amount of a country's exports. The share in world markets makes reference, for each sector, to the ratio of a country's total exports to total world exports. Finally, the diversification of markets index (equivalent number) is used for capturing the extent of market diversification (ITC 2007, p. 9).

It is defined as

$$NE_i^t = \frac{1}{\sum_{j=1}^{p} \left(\frac{X_{ijcl}^t}{X_{i.cl}^t}\right)^2} \tag{3.17}$$

where X_{ijcl}^t is country i exports of all products that belong to the cluster cl to country j in year t, $X_{i.cl}^t$ is country i total exports of all products that make part of cluster cl, and $X_{ijcl}/X_{i.cl}$ is the share of market j in country i total exports of products belonging to the cluster cl (ITC 2007, p. 9).

In the previous section, it was stressed that one of the dimensions of export diversification is related to the expansion of existing and new products to new geographic markets (extensive margin). The underlying idea behind the diversification of markets is that it may reduce a country's dependence on a small number of export markets and consequently the vulnerability to shocks within destination countries (ITC 2007, p. 9). The primary objective of this section is, therefore, to complement the findings of the decomposition of Colombian exports by product line with the diversification of markets index.

The market diversification equivalent number identifies, for each country, the number of partner economies weighed according to their importance. The increase in rank is a function of the increase in the level of diversification of markets. The bigger the index value, the greater the diversification of markets and consequently, the better the ranking (ITC 2007, p. 9).

From the 14 Colombian export sectors analyzed, which accounted for more than 95% of Colombian exports between 2004 and 2008, the following findings can be reported:

- Only two sectors registered an increase in the diversification of markets index between 2004 and 2008, namely, fresh food (see Table A.2) and transport equipment (Table A.12). This means that in the period of time analyzed, only these two sectors managed to diversify their exports by breaking into new markets.
- On the other hand, eight sectors registered a decrease in their scores of the same index: processed food (Table A.3), wood products (Table A.4), textiles (Table A.5), leather products (Table A.7), basic manufactures (Table A.8), non-electronic machinery (Table A.9), electronic components (Table A.11), and miscellaneous manufacturing (Table A.14). Especially pronounced has been the fall for wood products, textiles, leather products, electronic components, and miscellaneous manufacturing export sectors.
- Four sectors did not experience a change in the rank, comparing the years 2004 and 2008: chemicals (Table A.6), IT and consumer electronics (Table A.10), clothing (Table A.13), and minerals (Table A.15).

- The share in national exports has substantially increased for one single export sector, namely, minerals: from a participation of 38% in 2004, it increased to 48% in 2008. Leather and leather products and electronic components sectors registered small increases in their participation. Fresh food, chemicals, basic manufactures, processed food, clothing and transport equipment show a fall in their shares. The remaining five sectors (miscellaneous manufacturing, wood products, textiles, non-electronic machinery, and IT and consumer electronics) did not experience a change in their participations, comparing the years 2004 and 2008.
- Concerning the share in world markets, some sectors experienced an increase in their participations. Especially relevant were the improvements for leather products, textiles, fresh food, wood products, and minerals sectors. The electronic components, miscellaneous manufacturing, chemicals, transport equipment, and non-electronic machinery sectors also registered small increases in their shares. Nonetheless, four sectors (basic manufactures, processed food, IT and consumer electronics, and clothing) registered a fall in their participations.

The analysis of markets diversification can be complemented by the evaluation of the share of Colombia's main export partners within the total value of Colombian exports. As depicted in Fig. 3.9, the main export destinations have remained practically unchanged within the period of time analyzed. At the beginning of the liberalization process in 1991, 83.2% of the country's foreign sales went to just five markets, namely: the NAFTA countries (with a share of 37.1%), the European

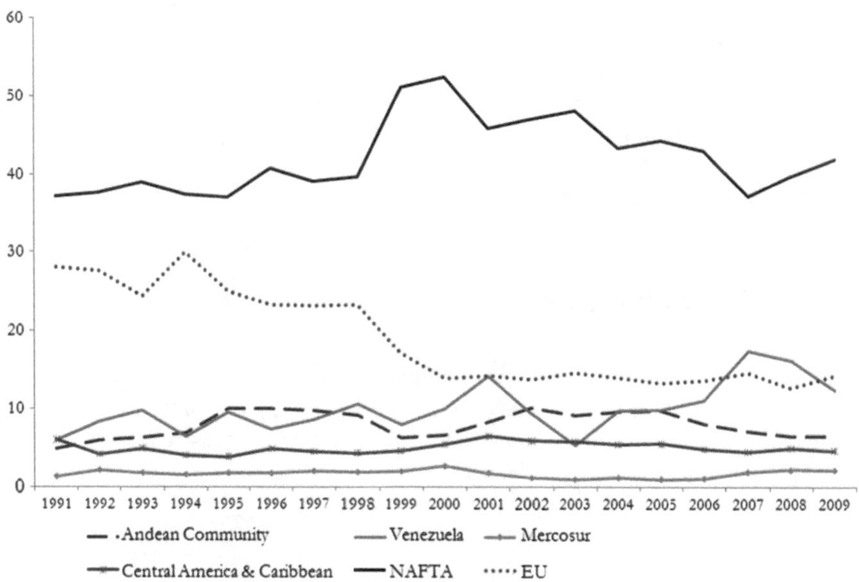

Fig. 3.9 Colombia's main export markets, 1991–2009 (Own elaboration, based on data from the Colombian Ministry of Trade, Industry and Tourism)

Union (28.1%), the Central American and Caribbean countries (6%), Venezuela (5.9%), the Andean Community (4.8%), and Mercosur (1.3%). In 2009, the participation of these markets slightly decreased to a level of 82%. But the composition shows a very similar trend at the end of the period, the same six destinations being the principal export destinations for Colombia.

Some changes can, nevertheless, be reported concerning the "ranking" of these destinations: At the end of the period, both NAFTA and the EU continue to be the first and second destination, but as shown in Fig. 3.9, it can be observed that the participation of the EU has significantly decreased (from 28.1% in 1991 to 14.3% in 2009). The loss of importance of the EU has been compensated by an increasing importance of the NAFTA: from a share of 37.1% in 1991, it peaked to a level of 52.5% in 2000, and registered a participation of 42% in 2009. The explanation for the increasing trend in the share of trade with NAFTA is strongly associated to the very significant value of sales of petroleum to the United States – this single product accounted for 49% of the Colombian exports to that country in 2009. Still, just 5% of the Colombian exports to the EU consisted of petroleum in that same year.

Bilateral trade with Venezuela peaked in 2007, representing a share of 17.4% and temporarily surpassing the EU. But in the last 2 years, an important decrease in the amount of exports took place, a trend explained by the tense situation in political bilateral relations. Trade with the Andean Community has slightly increased to a participation of 6.5% in 2009. Trade with Mercosur and the Central American and Caribbean countries has practically remained the same.

Nonetheless, some interesting changes can be reported for other export markets that, altogether, represented a participation of 7.5% in 1991 and, by 2009, increased to a share of 11.7%. As depicted in Fig. 3.10, the EFTA countries have been playing an increasingly important role for Colombia's exports since 2006. China has also significantly increased its participation (from 0.2% to 2.9%), as well as the "other Asian countries" (from 0.2% to 1.7%). However, trade with Japan (traditionally one of Colombia's most important markets for coffee in the world) experienced a dramatic fall in the period of time analyzed.

3.4.6 Intra-Industry Trade and the Grubel-Lloyd Index

Another interesting perspective of Colombia's trade pattern can be derived from applying the Grubel & Lloyd index of trade overlap (1975), one of the most utilized indicators for measuring intra-industry trade levels. For an industry i, with exports X_i and imports M_i, the index is defined as

$$IIT_i = \frac{(X_i + M_i) - |X_i - M_i|}{(X_i + M_i)} \tag{3.18}$$

Fig. 3.10 Colombian "minor" export markets, 1991–2009 (Own elaboration, based on data from the Colombian Ministry of Trade, Industry and Tourism)

or,

$$IIT_i = 1 - \left(\frac{|X_i - M_i|}{(X_i + M_i)}\right) \tag{3.19}$$

As explained by Krugman and Obstfeld (2006), the index can take values between zero -indicating inter-industry trade, where a country either exports or imports a good, not both- to one -indicating complete intra-industry trade, if a country's exports and imports within an industry are equal.

When Colombia's industrial exports are analyzed from the Grubel & Lloyd Index's perspective, it is found that most of the intra-industry trade is conducted either in "resource-based" industries- such as tobacco, miscellaneous edible preparations, or edible animal products- or "low technology" industries – like plastics, glass and glassware or footwear. On the other hand, the industries at the bottom of the table – reporting values closer to zero- are the ones where almost no intra-industry trade takes place: e.g. In boilers, machinery, and nuclear reactors; Colombia is basically just an importer. In others like sugars and sugar confectionary, the country is mostly an exporter (see Table 3.10).

Lall (1998) proposes an interesting technological typology for manufactures, comprised of "resource- based technologies", "low technologies", "medium technologies", and "high technologies".

Resource-based technologies are comprised of manufactures such as processed foods and tobacco, simple wood products, refined petroleum products,

Table 3.10 Grubel–lloyd index for selected Colombian industries, 1995–2008 (Own calculations, based on data provided by the United Nations Commodity Trade Statistics Database, UNCOMTRADE)

HS code	Industry	1995	2000	2005	2008
3808	Insecticides, fungicides, herbicides packaged for retail sale	0.57	0.66	0.80	0.97
7010	Carboy, bottle & other container of glass	0.39	0.71	0.81	0.91
7306	Tubes, pipes and hollow profiles of iron or steel, nes	0.09	0.46	0.43	0.91
2106	Food preparations, nes	0.66	0.36	0.87	0.90
8418	Refrigerator, freezer, etc.	0.66	0.64	0.75	0.83
6403	Footwear, upper of leather	0.49	0.88	0.94	0.82
4820	Registers, acct, note, order books etc.;other stationary articles of paper	0.58	0.39	0.67	0.82
9406	Prefabricated buildings	0.90	0.38	0.67	0.79
7604	Aluminum bars, rods and profiles	0.66	0.56	0.61	0.75
2402	Cigars, cheroots, cigarillos & cigarettes	0.04	0.64	0.76	0.74
7312	Iron & steel strandd wire, ropes, cables, etc., not electrically insulated	0.99	1.00	0.98	0.73
7013	Glassware usd for table, kitchen, toilet office, etc.	0.88	0.88	0.53	0.72
9403	Other furniture and parts thereof	0.50	0.61	0.41	0.72
4802	Uncoated paper for writing, printing etc.	1.00	0.83	0.87	0.72
2710	Petroleum oils, not crude	0.89	0.38	0.42	0.72
2904	Hydrocarbon derivatives, sulfonated, nitrated	0.70	0.63	0.53	0.64
3004	Medicament mixtures	0.81	0.82	0.76	0.63
3304	Beauty, make-up & skin-care preparations	0.72	0.98	0.66	0.63
3812	Prepared rubber accelerators; compound plasticizers, & other compound stabilizers	0.83	0.89	0.79	0.63
4901	Printed books, brochures, leaflets & similar printed matter	0.79	0.62	0.53	0.59
8544	Insulated wire/cable	0.13	0.99	0.54	0.58
4011	New pneumatic tires, of rubber	0.45	0.61	0.56	0.53
6204	Women's suits, jackets, dresses skirts etc.&shorts	0.25	0.24	0.15	0.40
4016	Articles of vulcanised rubber o/t hard rubber,	0.17	0.27	0.31	0.29
8703	Cars (incl. station wagon)	0.12	0.60	0.67	0.27
2716	Electrical energy	0.00	0.00	0.04	0.24
6203	Men's suits, jackets, trousers etc. & shorts	0.24	0.10	0.07	0.24
3904	Polymers of vinyl chloride/other halogenated olefins, in primary forms	0.44	0.29	0.30	0.21
1704	Sugar confectionery (incl white choc), not containing cocoa	0.65	0.16	0.15	0.18
8704	Trucks, motor vehicles for the transport of goods	0.20	0.68	0.46	0.17
3902	Polymers of propylene or of other olefins, in primary forms	0.50	0.70	0.21	0.15
7202	Ferro-alloys	0.11	0.08	0.06	0.13
2709	Crude petroleum oils	0.00	0.02	0.06	0.05
0901	Coffee	0.00	0.00	0.03	0.02
0603	Cut flowers and flower buds for bouquets, fresh or dried	0.00	0.00	0.01	0.01
2704	Coke & semicoke of..coal, lignite, peat; retort carbon	0.00	0.00	0.00	0.00
2701	Coal; briquettes, ovoids & similar solid fuels manufactured from coal	0.00	0.00	0.00	0.00

dyes, leather -not leather products-, rubber and cellulose products, and organic chemicals. The group of low technology manufactures is integrated by labor-intensive manufactures such as textiles, garments, footwear, toys, simple metal and plastic products, furniture, and glassware. Within the group of medium technologies, "complex but not fast-moving technologies (though some entail considerable engineering and design effort)" are found: automotive products, chemicals, industrial machinery, and simple consumer electronics. Finally, high technology is comprised of fine chemicals, pharmaceuticals, complex electrical and electronic machinery, aircraft, and precision instruments. He further observes that there is an intense geographical concentration of manufactured exports where Asia takes the lead and is followed in a very distant second place by Latin American countries.

For the particular case of Colombia, as will later be explained, it is interesting to observe how the biggest share of intra-industry trade is represented either by "resource-based" or "low" technology categories. Turning now to the analysis of Colombia's industrial trade, and applying the typology proposed by Lall (1998), the country's industrial exports could be grouped as follows:

- "Resource-based technologies": comprised mainly of agro-industrial products and processed food.
- "Low technology manufactures" (light industry): textiles and apparel, footwear, metal and plastic products, among others.
- "Medium technologies": where the remaining sectors depicted in the following figures, would be included: automotive industry, chemicals, industrial machinery.

Figure 3.11 illustrates the evolution of Colombia's industrial trade. Light industry (manufactures), basic industry (metallurgy, basic chemicals and paper) and agro-industry are the sectors accounting for most of the foreign sales. On the other hand, the machinery and equipment sector occupies the first place when it comes to industrial imports. These figures could somehow illustrate Colombia's pattern of specialization in low-skilled labor or resource- based industries. Import products mostly belong to capital or knowledge- intensive industries.

The trends depicted on the last figure provides further evidence of the fact that Colombian industrial exports have not substantially increased in the period of time analyzed. With the exception of 2001 and 2002, levels are practically the same (or even inferior) to the share registered in 1994 (33% of total exports).

In the meantime, it is important to briefly recall how intra-industry trade (IIT) is defined as a two-way trade in products falling under the same industry classification. As has been previously reviewed in the first section, specialization allows unleashing the potentials associated with economies of scale, and it increases consumption possibilities. It is expected that the pattern of trade taking place between developed nations – with similar factor endowments, technologies and tastes- will mostly have an intra-industrial character, taking into account their similarities in terms of in capital-labor ratios. Conversely, inter-industry trade

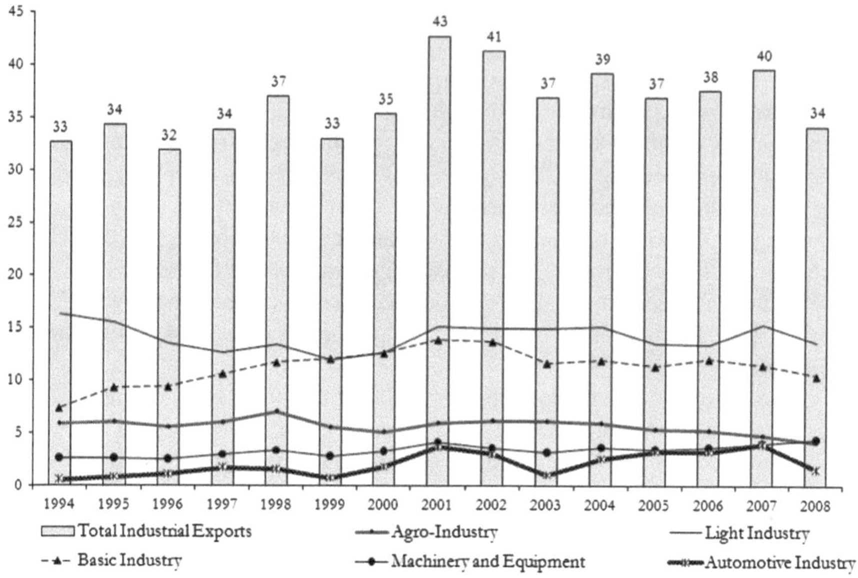

Fig. 3.11 Colombian industrial exports, share of total exports, 1994–2008 (Own elaboration, based on data provided by the Colombian Ministry of Trade, Industry and Tourism, 2009)

will dominate between countries with big differences in these same ratios, reflecting comparative advantage.

When analyzing Colombia's pattern of industrial trade with some selected regional groups of integration, the above mentioned proposition clearly holds: in the case of developed counterparts, such as the NAFTA or the European Union, inter-industry trade distinctly predominates. In NAFTA's case, as documented in Fig. 3.12, just 14% of Colombian exports were comprised of industrial products in 2008 – the figure has, indeed, decreased since 2004. Labor-intensive light industry is, by far, the most relevant export. Conversely, more than 80% of Colombian imports from NAFTA have usually been composed of capital-intensive industrial goods, such as machinery and equipment.

3.4.7 Trade Specialization: The Revealed Comparative Advantage (RCA) Index

Furthermore, the RCA index also provides important information concerning Colombia's pattern of trade. As pointed out by Laursen (1998), since Balassa's introduction of this measure in 1965, it has been broadly used as a measure of international trade specialization, both by international organizations and academic researchers. It can be calculated by using the equation,

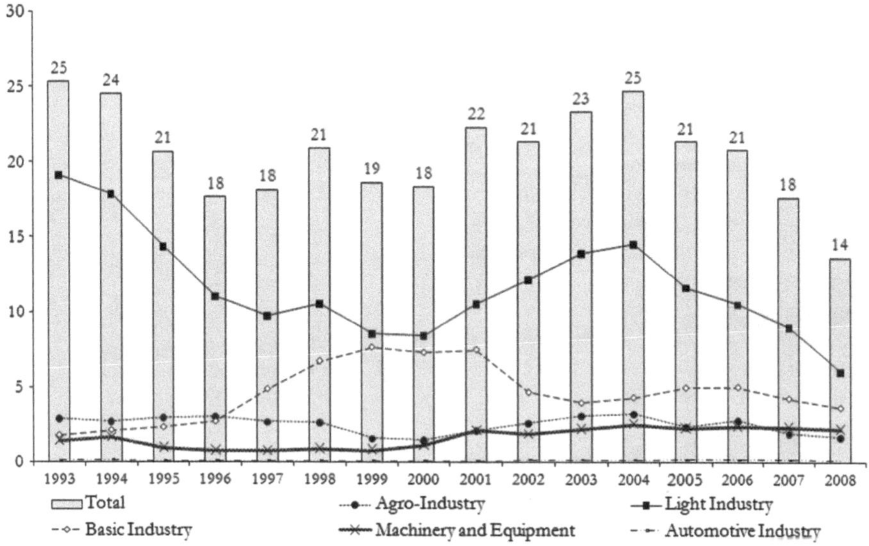

Fig. 3.12 Colombian industrial exports to the NAFTA: share of the total amount of exports (%), 1993–2007 (Own calculations, based on data provided by the Colombian Ministry of Trade, Industry and Tourism, 2010)

$$RCA_{ij} = \left(X_{ij} / \sum_i X_{ij}\right) / \left(\sum_j X_{ij} / \sum_i \sum_j X_{ij}\right) \quad (3.20)$$

If the RCA value > 1, it implies that the country possesses a comparative advantage in that industry. If the RCA value < 1, the country has a comparative disadvantage.

Table 3.11 lists a number of Colombian industries that, according to the RCA index, show a comparative advantage. As can be observed, many of them are related to the minerals, food, and light manufactures sectors.

These two indexes provide evidence on Colombia's pattern of specialization. The analysis can be complemented by following the behavior of the country's bilateral industrial trade with some selected markets.

Starting with the NAFTA, as previously mentioned, Colombia is currently waiting for the eventual ratification of a free trade agreement with the United States. Colombian policymakers have placed great expectations on this treaty, mentioning the objective of increasing the exports of manufactures to that market.

In the meantime, just 14% of Colombian exports to the NAFTA are composed of industrial products, as shown in Fig. 3.12. Primary products overwhelmingly account for the difference (86%). The so-called "traditional exports" – only five products- represented 68% of the sales to that market in 2007. Conversely, more than 80% of Colombian imports from NAFTA have usually been composed of capital-intensive industrial goods, such as machinery and equipment.

Table 3.11 Revealed comparative advantage for some selected Colombian industries, 2002 and 2006 (International Trade Center, Trade competitiveness map, 2009)

Industry	2002	2006
Live trees, plants, bulbs, roots, cut flowers etc.	37,7	33,3
Coffee, tea, mate and spices	35,7	32,4
Sugars and sugar confectionery	11,2	9,4
Edible fruit, nuts, peel of citrus fruit, melons	7,7	5,3
Miscellaneous edible preparations	3,5	3,5
Mineral fuels, oils, distillation products, etc.	3,8	2,6
Ceramic products	2,0	2,5
Printed books, newspapers, pictures etc.	2,5	2,4
Salt, sulphur, earth, stone, plaster, lime and cement	3,0	2,3
Raw hides and skins (other than furskins) and leather	2,1	2,1
Pearls, precious stones, metals, coins, etc.	1,0	2,0
Iron and steel	1,4	1,9
Essential oils, perfumes, cosmetics, toileteries	1,3	1,9
Articles of apparel, accessories, not knit or crochet	1,7	1,7
Articles of apparel, accessories, knit or crochet	1,1	1,7
Knitted or crocheted fabric	1,1	1,6
Glass and glassware	1,4	1,5
Animal, vegetable fats and oils, cleavage products, etc.	1,1	1,5
Paper & paperboard, articles of pulp, paper and board	1,3	1,4
Cereal, flour, starch, milk preparations and products	1,3	1,4
Plastics and articles thereof	1,2	1,3
Miscellaneous manufactured articles	1,1	1,2
Cocoa and cocoa preparations	1,1	1,2
Special woven or tufted fabric, lace, tapestry etc.	1,0	1,2
Fish, crustaceans, molluscs, aquatic invertebrates	1,7	1,1
Milling products, malt, starches, inulin, wheat gluten	1,4	1,1
Soaps, lubricants, waxes, candles, modelling pastes	1,3	1,1
Albuminoids, modified starches, glues, enzymes	1,1	1,1
Miscellaneous chemical products	1,8	1,0
Wadding, felt, nonwovens, yarns, twine, cordage, etc.	1,6	1,0
Other made textile articles, sets, worn clothing etc.	1,3	1,0

Bilateral trade with the European Union is characterized even more by an inter-industry pattern. Between 1993 and 2008, Colombian industrial sales oscillated between 12% and 15% of the total exports. The latter can be observed in Fig. 3.13. In the year 2008, 85% of the exports were comprised of primary products (especially coffee, oil and coal). Different to the NAFTA's case, agro-industrial exports are the most important sales.

The European Union has recently launched the negotiations of a bilateral commercial agreement with Colombia, within the framework of the Andean Community of Nations. Nevertheless, it should be said that the challenge here is even bigger, taking into account the very scarce use of the current *GSP-Plus* by national industries, as well as the degree of concentration on primary products. Value-added products do not represent a significant share of the sales to that market.

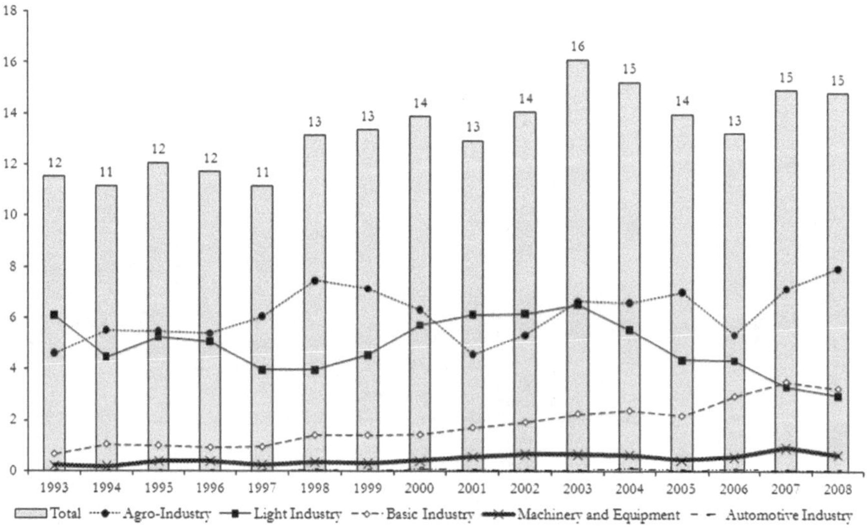

Fig. 3.13 Colombian industrial exports to the EU, share of the total amount of exports (%), 1993–2008 (Own elaboration, based on data from the Colombian Ministry of Trade, Industry and Tourism, 2010)

Conversely, the so called "natural markets" are by far Colombia's most important commercial counterparts, when intra-industry trade is considered. Countries such as Venezuela, Ecuador, Perú, and the Central American ones, are of critical importance for a wide variety of industrial sectors.

Industrial exports to the Andean Community of Nations have traditionally oscillated between 85% and 91% of total exports in the period 1993–2008 (see Fig. 3.14). Imports show a very similar tendency, fluctuating between 75% and 90%. It is also important to mention that manufactures play a very important role in the bilateral trade. Industries such as textiles and apparel, cosmetics and toiletry, machinery and equipment, paper and basic chemicals, greatly benefit from that market. However, Colombian main imports are comprised of basic chemical products and a number of manufactures.

Trade with Mercosur, especially with Brazil and Argentina, is gradually getting to be more important for Colombia. Nevertheless, a concerning development is associated to the visible decrease of Colombian industrial exports to that market, as depicted in Fig. 3.15. It is rather striking to observe that by the middle of the 1990s, 18% of exports to Mercosur were comprised of primary products, while 82% were industrial goods. On the contrary, in 2008 these percentages were of 46% and 54% respectively. The latter can be explained by the increasing participation of raw materials, such as oil, coal, and nickel.

Finally, the Central American Common Market is also an important counterpart, both in terms of industrial exports and imports. As shown in Fig. 3.16, 53% of Colombian sales to that market were comprised of industrial products in 2008. Sectors such as apparel, plastics, cosmetics, and toiletries are especially benefited.

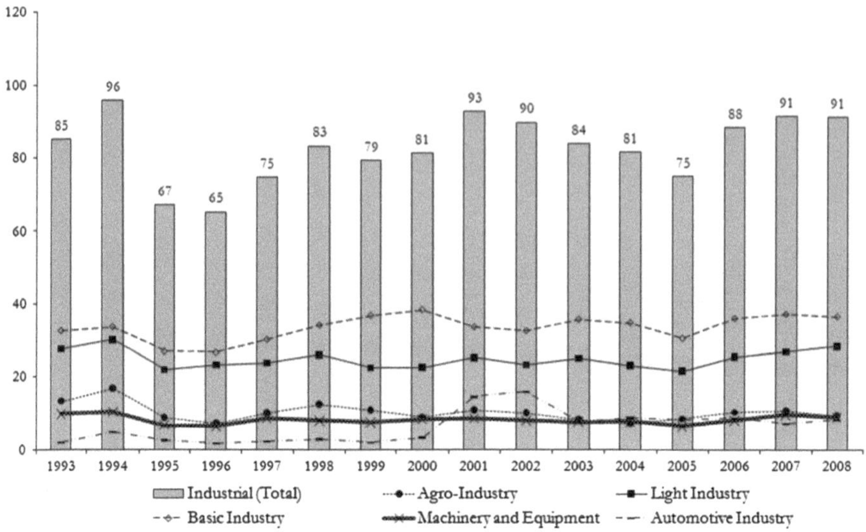

Fig. 3.14 Colombian industrial exports to the Andean community of nations, share of the total amount of exports (%), 1993–2008 (Own elaboration, based on data provided by the Colombian Ministry of Trade, Industry and Tourism, 2010)

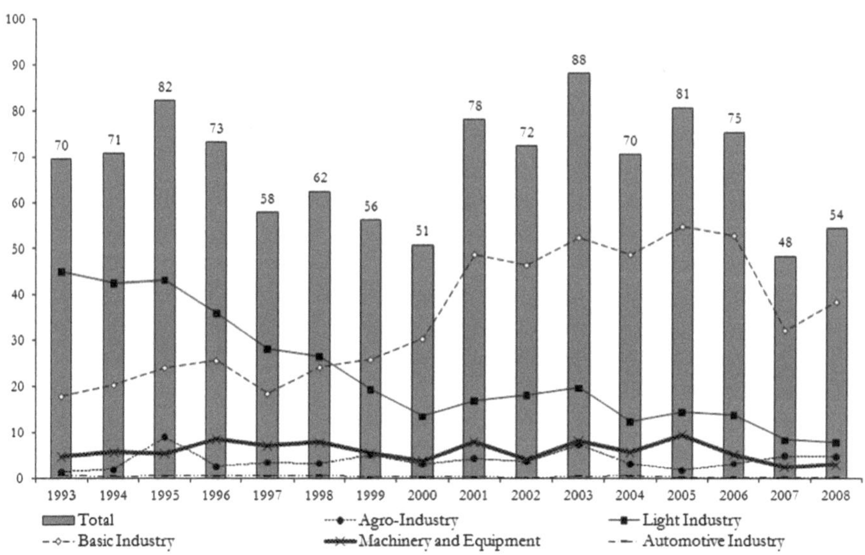

Fig. 3.15 Colombian industrial exports to the Mercosur, share of the total amount of exports (%), 1993–2008 (Own elaboration, based on data provided by the Colombian Ministry of Trade, Industry and Tourism, 2010)

On the side of the imports, 71% of the Colombian purchases are comprised of industrial products. Plastics, basic chemicals, and machinery are some of the products that the country buys from Central American countries.

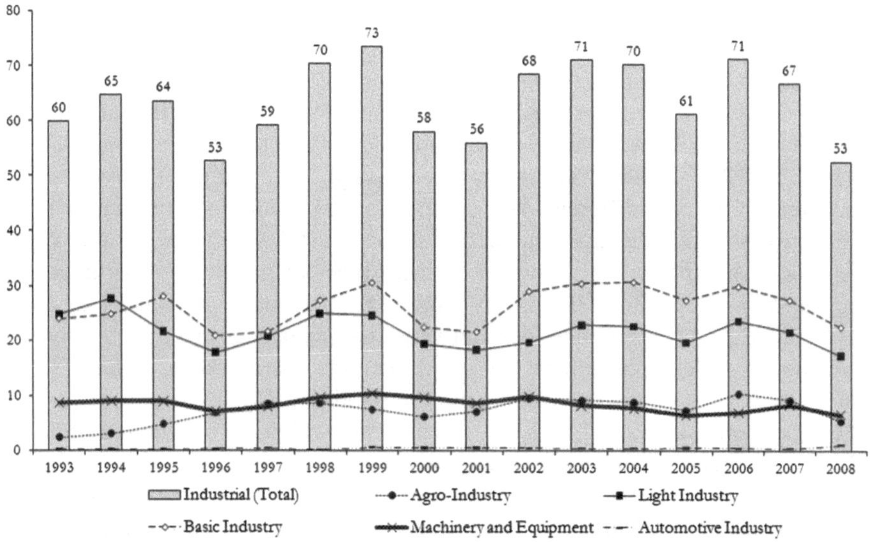

Fig. 3.16 Colombian industrial exports to Central America and the Caribbean, share of the total amount of exports (%), 1993–2008 (Own elaboration, based on data from the Colombian Ministry of Trade, Industry and Tourism, 2010)

3.5 Concluding Remarks

In a similar manner to other Latin American nations, Colombia resorted to import substitution partially as a response to the international context of the postwar period. But the particularity of the Colombian experience with the IS model has been addressed in the literature, taking into account that the country followed a mixed economic policy approach that was quite different to the one of other Latin American nations. On one hand, the national government promoted import substitution to support domestic capitalists. In a parallel manner, export promotion was introduced specifically for the coffee sector, which has been a crucial product for the insertion of Colombia to global markets. This pattern of mixed policy is considered by different authors as a very particular approach, compared to that of the other Latin American countries.

Between 1990, a time considered to be the starting point of the export promotion model in Colombia, and 2008, some positive patterns can be reported: a stable growth of the total exports value since 1994, (process briefly interrupted in 1998 when the economic recession hit the country, and in the period 2001–2002), and very remarkable increases since 2004. Between 2004 and 2008, total foreign sales more than doubled in value, going up from USD $ 16 to USD $37 billion. This is a positive fact that may be related to an increased degree of openness of the economy. Nevertheless, it should be highlighted that the greater demand of primary commodities had an important influence on this positive trade performance.

The country's reliance upon primary products has actually increased within the period of time analyzed. Petroleum and its derivatives, as well as coal, have now turned out to be the principal "traditional" exports of the country, while coffee has progressively decreased its contribution. While in 1995, these "traditional" exports accounted for 47% of Colombian foreign sales, that participation increased to 54.64% in 2009. On the other hand, the so-called "non-traditional" exports (all the other export goods different to the aforementioned "traditional" ones) have been losing ground within the total amount of exports. In 1997, 47.90% of the total value of Colombian exports was generated by these types of goods. That participation decreased to 45.36% in 2009, and is projected to become even smaller in 2010 (37.27%). The analysis of these descriptive statistics indicates that the objective of diversifying the composition of Colombian exports has not been accomplished, especially when it comes to fostering the "non-traditional" ones.

Furthermore, it should be clarified that in the definition of "non-traditional" exports adopted by the Colombian economic authorities, besides industrial products, some raw materials still play a crucial role. Products such as bananas, emeralds, cut flowers, "other farming products" and the so-called "other mining products" are of great relevance: in 2008, these five sectors accounted for 13% of the total amount of foreign sales. But apart from some types of basic technologies involved in the agro-industrial and mining sectors, these goods are not industrial exports. Hence, the term "non-traditional" exports is not necessarily associated with industrial exports in Colombia.

When analyzing diversification and structural change in exports, a simple association of *traditionality* with primary products and *non-traditionality* with manufactures, fails to represent the experience of developing nations (Amin Gutiérrez de Piñeres and Ferrantino 1997a, p. 377). The same argument holds for Colombia. While there is not a consensus about where to draw the line between the concepts of "traditional" and "non-traditional" exports, the literature refers to some recent proposals such as the "export share" criteria of the World Bank. A classification of Colombian exports according to that measure would be quite different to the one currently adopted by the Colombian economic authorities. Other export goods currently considered as "non-traditional" (like cut flowers, bananas, gold, meat of bovine animals, and motor vehicles), would join the list of "traditional" exports.

The analysis of the cumulative export experience functions, the traditionality index, and its variance, allow observing some interesting trends in terms of the composition of exports in Colombia between 1991 and 2008. The coffee and petroleum industries, two of the most important "traditional" exports, do not show to have experienced remarkable structural changes. On the contrary, the coal and non-ferrous metals, with more right-shifted distributions and lower values for the traditionality index, suggest that some sort of vertical diversification has taken place in these industries. As far as the so-called "non-traditional exports" are concerned, the balance looks rather mixed. On one hand, it is possible to observe that some industries show distributions shifted to the right and low traditionality indexes, suggesting a process of diversification. But it could not be affirmed that this process has been broad-based or generalized, since for other "non-traditional" exports, the plot is either linear or even quite shifted to the left, suggesting that little or no diversification has taken place in these sectors. This suggests that a process of vertical diversification has taken place, but limited to some specific export goods.

The curves of four sectors look particularly pronounced, namely the ones corresponding to the meat and meat preparations, crude fertilizers and crude minerals, natural gas, and electric current industries, implying that these are export goods that are more recent and therefore, more "non-traditional". The variance of the traditionality index is low for the first three industries, indicating that the export diversification in these cases has been achieved with rather stable export earnings. The ranking of the different industries according to their traditionality index shows that the distinction between "traditional" and "non-traditional" exports in Colombia should not be associated with agricultural exports. Some of the industries that have shown to be more "traditional" along the period of time analyzed are, indeed, manufactures (e.g. textiles, footwear, non-metallic mineral manufactures, and apparel and clothing, among others). On the other hand, some of the newest Colombian "non-traditional" exports belong to the mining sector (e.g. natural gas, metal ores).

The rather mixed performance of Colombia in terms of diversification may also be complemented by the analysis of the behavior of the Herfindahl – Hirschman Index (HHI) of export concentration. Between 1980 and 2000, Colombia (together with Brazil and Chile) was one of the best performers in Latin America: a dramatic fall in that indicator suggests that the country managed to more equally distribute its revenues over a larger number of products. This is also shown by the score in terms of the export diversification index, which demonstrates that Colombia significantly narrowed its difference from the world average between 1995 and 2008. On the other hand, however, the HHI's score for 2008, compared to the one of 2005, indicates a larger degree of market concentration than the one of 2005. This trend may be associated with the increased demand for raw materials, as well as the rise of their prices in the world market.

The decomposition of Colombia's exports by product line, following the methodology proposed by Evenett and Venables (2002), indicates that from the 66 product lines that were exported in the period 2005–2008, 61 had also been exported in the period 1991–1994. This means that 99.09% of Colombia's real export growth during the period was based on already existing product lines (the intensive margin of exports). Only four new product lines appeared at the end of the period, accounting for 0.91% of the country's real export growth. The results obtained are in line with previous empirical studies, showing that the most important source of export growth in developing countries comes from increases in existing bilateral trade flows (the intensive margin), rather than increases in new products or in old products to new geographic markets (the extensive margin). In Colombia, as in other developing nations, the relative expansion of exports has taken place in export commodities that are neither industrial in nature nor have a high value-added component.

Furthermore, the market diversification index and the analysis of the trade performance of Colombia's export sectors suggest that only two sectors (out of the full set of 14 sectors contained within the SITC Rev.3) registered an increase in the diversification of markets between 2004 and 2008 and therefore, managed to diversify their exports by breaking into new markets. Conversely, eight sectors registered a decrease in their scores of the same index, showing a larger degree of concentration of markets. The share in national exports has substantially increased for one single export sector, namely, minerals: from a participation of 38% in 2004, it increased to 48% in 2008.

The analysis of markets diversification can be complemented by the evaluation of the share of Colombia's main export partners within the total value of Colombian exports. The analysis of descriptive statistics demonstrates that the main export destinations have remained practically unchanged between 1990 and 2009. At the beginning of the liberalization process in 1991, 83.2% of the country's foreign sales went to just six markets. In 2009, the participation of these markets slightly decreased to a level of 82%. But the composition shows a very similar trend at the end of the period, the same six destinations being the principal export destinations for Colombia.

When Colombia's industrial exports were analyzed from the Grubel & Lloyd Index's perspective, it was found that most of the intra-industry trade was conducted either in "resource-based" industries- such as tobacco, miscellaneous edible preparations, or edible animal products- or "low technology" industries – like plastics, glass and glassware or footwear. These figures somehow illustrate Colombia's pattern of specialization in low-skilled labor or resource- based industries, while import products mostly belong to capital or knowledge- intensive industries. The trends analyzed provide further evidence of the fact that Colombian industrial exports did not substantially increase in the period of time analyzed. With the exception of 2001 and 2002, levels are practically the same (or even inferior) to the share registered in 1994 (33% of total exports).

At the moment of analyzing Colombia's pattern of industrial trade with some selected regional groups of integration, inter-industry trade distinctly predominates with developed counterparts, such as the NAFTA or the European Union. However, most of Colombia's intra-industrial trade takes place with other developing nations with similar factor endowments, technologies and tastes, taking into account their similarities in terms of in capital-labor ratios.

Furthermore, the RCA index also provides important information concerning Colombia's pattern of trade. As mentioned by Moreno and Posada (2006), Colombia's specialization continues to be heavily dependent upon comparative advantage, centered on the production of goods abundant in natural resources and low-skilled labor. The latter, taking into account the scarcity in terms of qualified human capital, as well as the technological gap, which in turn seriously undermine the productivity of Colombian industrial exports.

Chapter 4
Commercial Relations Between Colombia and the European Union: An Empirical Approximation in the Light of the Gravity Model

The current chapter examines the impact of the European Generalized System of Preferences on Colombian exports over the period 1990–2008. Based on the gravity model of international trade, an augmented gravity equation is tested, capturing economic, geographic, cultural, and institutional factors that are believed to exert an influence upon Colombian trade. The findings indicate that Colombian exports have positively benefited from the unilateral scheme of preferences offered by the European Union, and that this trade mechanism had a large and positive effect on Colombian exports within the period of time analyzed. But, as will be addressed in a next section, this is not synonymous to a more diversified export basket with the EU.

The contribution of this empirical work to the field of knowledge is intended to be twofold: on first instance, to increase the very limited amount of empirical studies addressing the commercial relations between Colombia and the European Union. Second, to apply two estimators that have not been – to the author's knowledge- previously used in other empirical studies analyzing the bilateral trade relations between Colombia and the EU, namely the Hausman and Taylor (1981) estimator and the Amemiya MaCurdy (1986) estimator.

4.1 Evolution of the Bilateral Commercial Relations

4.1.1 Significance of the European Union for Colombia's Foreign Trade

Before analyzing the commercial relations between the EU and Colombia, it is first important to understand how the linkages between that regional block and Latin America have evolved and more specifically, to get acquainted with the role that

J.F. Mejía, *Export Diversification and Economic Growth*, Contributions to Economics, DOI 10.1007/978-3-7908-2742-2_4,

Colombia plays for the EU's political, economic and commercial interests in the region.

The EU is Latin America's second most important trading partner, and the first trading partner of *Mercosur* and Chile. The EU's Commission highlights how the volume of trade with that region has more than doubled since the beginning of the current decade. Furthermore, trade in goods with Latin America amounted to €71 billion for imports and €63.4 billion for exports in 2009, representing 6% of EU's total trade (European Commission 2010b). With regard to trade in services, imports of €19 billion and exports of €28 billion respectively were registered in that same year (European Commission 2010b). It is also relevant to mention that the trade balance for the EU has been lately negative in goods, but positive in services: since 2002, a deficit in trade in goods with the 17 countries composing Latin America has been reported. Concerning the trade composition in the year 2009, 68% of the EU's imports from Latin America were composed of primary goods – agricultural products, fuels and mining products–, and 27% of manufactures – mainly machinery and transport equipment, and chemicals– (European Commission 2010a). EU's exports to that region were mainly of machinery and transport equipment (46%), chemicals (19%), and manufactured goods (11.6%) (European Commission 2010a). The EU also plays a paramount role in Latin America in terms of FDI: in 2009, EU's direct investment in Latin America went to €275.4 billion, confirming its position as the region's main foreign investor.

Figure 4.1 depicts the evolution of the EU's trade in goods with Latin America during the last 10 years.

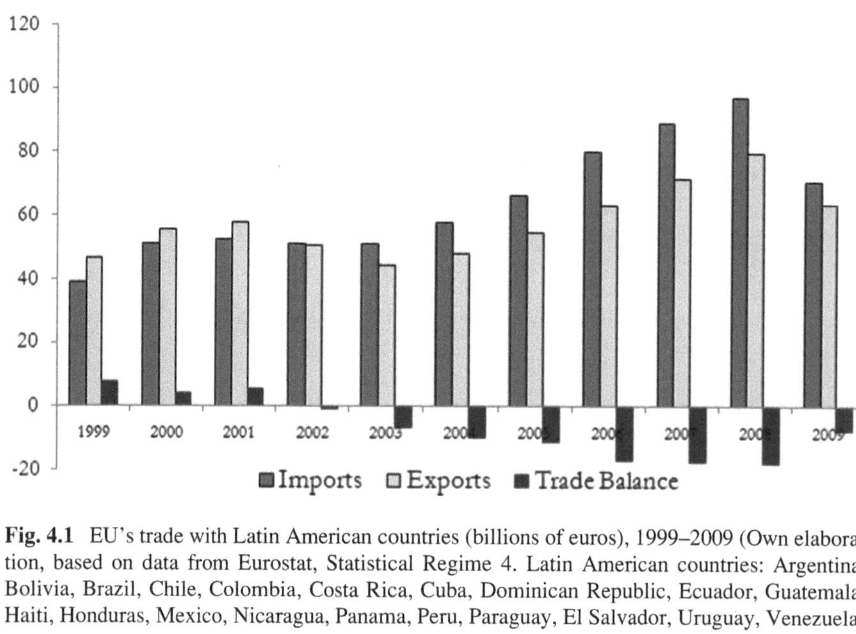

Fig. 4.1 EU's trade with Latin American countries (billions of euros), 1999–2009 (Own elaboration, based on data from Eurostat, Statistical Regime 4. Latin American countries: Argentina, Bolivia, Brazil, Chile, Colombia, Costa Rica, Cuba, Dominican Republic, Ecuador, Guatemala, Haiti, Honduras, Mexico, Nicaragua, Panama, Peru, Paraguay, El Salvador, Uruguay, Venezuela)

Commercial relations between the EU and Latin America have been structured both at the bilateral and multilateral levels. Starting with Mexico and Chile, it should be mentioned that these were the first countries in the region to sign FTAs with the EU, which entered into force at the beginning of the current decade. Recently, Colombia and Peru signed an association agreement that still needs to be ratified by their respective parliaments. At a multilateral level, negotiations with Mercosur have been re-launched afresh, seeking to the signature of a trade agreement. Finally, with the Central American countries (Costa Rica, Guatemala, Honduras, Nicaragua, Panamá and El Salvador), the EU has also recently concluded negotiations on an association agreement, aimed to replace the temporary preferences granted by the EU to these countries under the unilateral *GSP Plus* to a permanent scheme of preferences (European Commission 2010a).

Among 20 Latin American countries, Colombia is nowadays the EU's sixth trade partner, accounting for 0.3% of its total extra-EU 27 trade in 2009. This figure is low, compared to the shares of Brazil (2.1%), Mexico (1.1%), Argentina (0.6%) and even Chile (0.5%). Nevertheless, it should also be noted how Colombia's share doubled between 1999 and 2008, as depicted in Fig. 4.2.

As can be observed in Fig. 4.3, after the United States, the EU has traditionally been the second most important destination for Colombian exports –except for the years 2007 and 2008, when Venezuela's share was larger than the EU's participation. During the last year, 39% of Colombian exports were destined to the US market and 14% to the EU's market. Venezuela, the Andean Community of Nations, the Central American and Caribbean countries, and *Mercosur* were the other most important export destinations in that same year (with shares of 12%, 7%, 5% and 2% respectively).

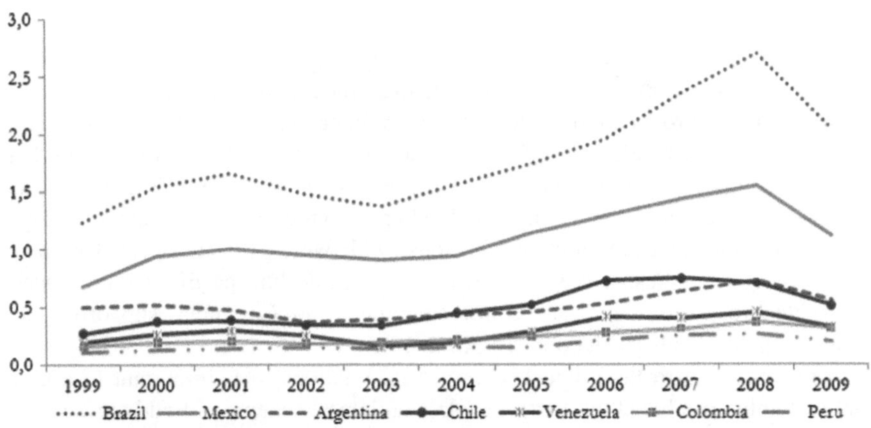

Fig. 4.2 EU's trade with main Latin American partners (share of total extra-EU trade), 1999–2009 (Own elaboration, based on data from Eurostat, Statistical Regime 4)

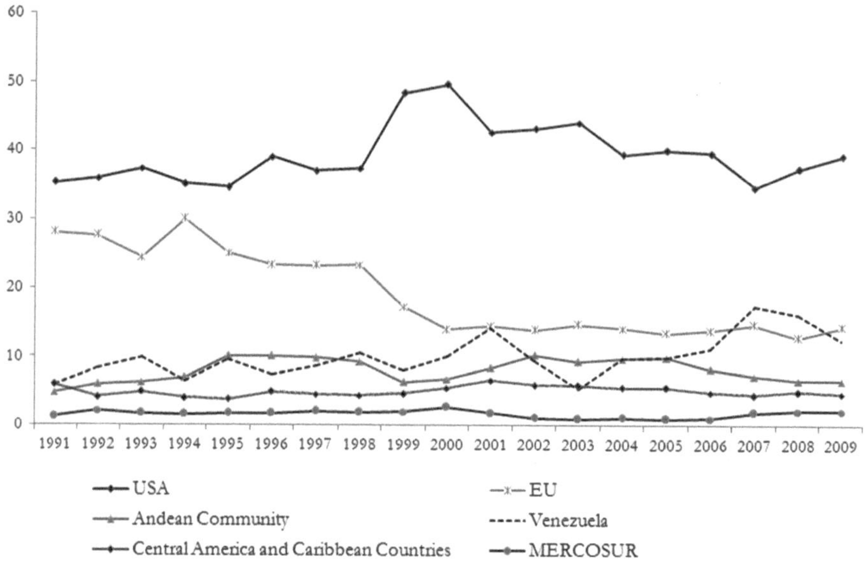

Fig. 4.3 Colombia's main export partners, share of total exports, 1991–2009 (Own illustration, based on data from the Colombian Ministry of Trade, Industry and Tourism)

4.1.2 The Andean GSP, the GSP Plus, and the Multiparty Trade Agreement

For the Colombian foreign policy, relations with Europe are a political priority, taking into account factors such as the European Union's influence in the multilateral scenario, its investment levels in the country, as well as its large domestic market. Being a primary source of international cooperation, of which Colombia is a major beneficiary, is also considered a very important aspect. Besides that, Colombian policymakers underscore that the bilateral relations are based on a historical bond grounded on three pillars: political dialogue, cooperation, and economic and trade relations (Ministerio de Relaciones Exteriores de Colombia 2010). Likewise, the Commission of the European Union recognizes Colombia as an important partner in Latin America, due in part to the role that the country plays within the Andean Community of Nations, with which the European Union is looking for closer ties. It is also relevant to mention that the EU has long been committed to promoting peace and reconciliation in Colombia, supporting its combat against drugs production (EEAS 2010).

With reference to the bilateral commercial relations, it is important to notice that Colombia has benefited from the EU's unilateral scheme of trade preferences since 1991 – aimed to provide preferential access for developing countries to that market. This trade mechanism, initially called the *Andean Generalized System of Preferences*, was offered as a special support to the Andean countries (Bolivia, Colombia, Ecuador, Peru and Venezuela) in their fight against the production and trafficking of illegal drugs. It consisted on the elimination from tariff charges for approximately 90% of the imports to the EU proceeding from the Andean nations – excluding some products such as bananas, citrus, milk and meat– in addition to the items that had zero tariffs by the principle of Most Favored Nation – MFN (Orozco 2002). In 2005, this trade mechanism – which was renamed *GSP Plus*- was upgraded and extended until the year 2015, offering now a preferential access for approximately 7.200 products. In a parallel manner, the negotiations of a bilateral free trade agreement have aimed to replace this temporary mechanism for a permanent, reciprocal agreement covering other topics of mutual interest like services, intellectual property, trade defense, and investment (EEAS 2010).

As aforementioned, the EU, Colombia, and Peru recently concluded the negotiations of a so-called "Multy-Party Trade Agreement", that was signed within the framework of the fourth EU-Latin America and the Caribbean Summit in May 2010, agreement that could enter into force as soon as 2011. Having the same status as other Latin American nations that have previously negotiated FTAs with the European Union (e.g. Mexico and Chile), increasing the level of certainty for Colombian exporters, and attracting larger amounts of FDI to the country, are some of the most important benefits expected by Colombian policymakers from this bilateral agreement.

One interesting observation frequently made when it comes to the EU's *GSP Plus* is related to the low degree of utilization both by Colombian and Andean exporters. For the particular case of Colombia, it is striking to notice how the country has been exporting just 17% of the products covered during the last years. This is clearly a paradoxical aspect since, as mentioned above, the trade preferences are offered to approximately 7.200 products (Koetsenruijter 2006). Undoubtedly, one of the main reasons that explain this situation is the concentration of Colombian exports to the EU in a few mining and agricultural industries. Since the middle of the 1990s, more than 80% of that country's sales to the EU have been composed by just eight products –coffee, coal, ferronickel, oil and its derivatives, bananas, emeralds, and flowers. The participation of these goods increased to a level of 87% in the year 2009. On the contrary, the share of industrial exports to the European Union decreased from 12% in 1995, to 10% in 2009. An evident concentration of Colombian exports, coupled with the low productivity of some industries, have been frequently proposed as factors that could help to explain this trend (see Fig. 4.4).

4.2 Theoretical Framework: The Gravity Model of International Trade

4.2.1 Previous Empirical Studies

As stated by Baldwin and Taglioni (2006), the gravity model is a workhorse tool that has been used in a wide range of empirical fields, being the impact of trade agreements, exchange rate volatility, currency unions, FDI between countries, and the so-called 'border effect', some of its common applications. Three aspects have

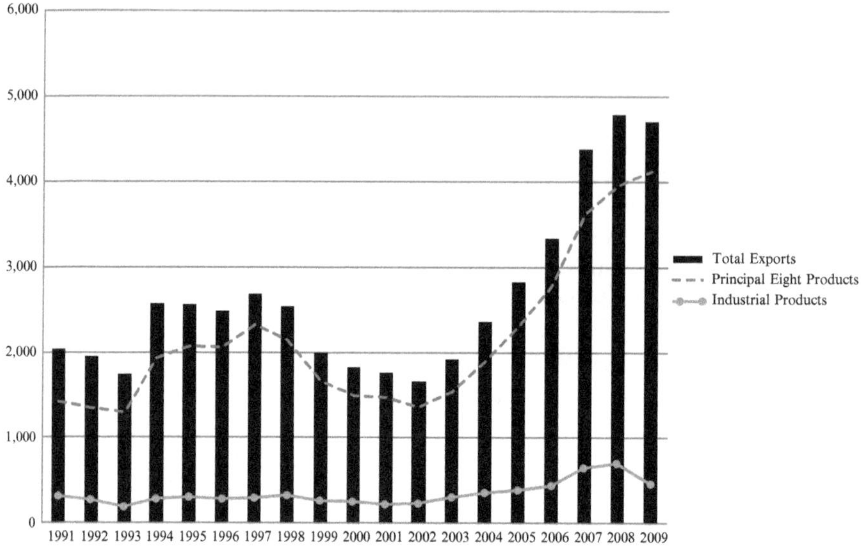

Fig. 4.4 Colombian exports to the European union (FOB), million USD, 1991–2009 (Own illustration, based on data provided by the Colombian Ministry of Trade, Industry and Commerce. Principal eight products: coffee, coal, ferronickel, oil and its derivatives, bananas, emeralds, and flowers)

been crucial for its recognition: its suitability for explaining international trade flows, the accessibility of the data needed for its estimation, and the respectability of a number of seminal papers that have established the gravity model's reputation and proposed a set of standard practices that are used to address different empirical questions. It is a mathematical model derived from an analogy with Newton's gravitational law, used to explain aggregate human behaviors related to spatial interaction such as migration and traffic flows (World Bank 2002).

The gravity model appeared in the 1960s as an empirical specification with some theoretical foundations. As noted by Deardorff (1995), Tinbergen (1962) and Poyhonen (1963a) conducted the first econometric estimations of trade flows using the gravity equation, being the approach mainly intuitive. Later, Linnemann (1966) proposed a theoretical justification based on the Walrasian general equilibrium system. He argued that the gravity model was a reduced form from a four-equation partial equilibrium model of export supply and import demand (Bergstrand 1985). Deardorff (1995, p. 7) also notes how "...Leamer and Stern (1970) followed Savage and Deutsch (1960) in deriving it from a probability model of transactions". Afterward, attempts were made to derive the gravity equation from models that assumed product differentiation, starting with Anderson (1979). He made the so-called "Armington Assumption" – where products were differentiated by country of origin.

Anderson (1979) obtained a simple form of the gravity equation by deriving a Cobb-Douglas expenditure system, where he could consider a framework of many goods and transit cost as a function of distance (Correia 2008). Subsequently, Bergstrand (1985, 1989) derived a gravity equation from a general equilibrium model of international trade, introducing factor endowment differences, two differentiated product-industries and two factors of production. He argued that the gravity model fitted both the Heckscher–Ohlin and the Helpman–Krugman models of trade (Correia 2008). As stated by Cárdenas and García (2004), despite the empirical success, only until the works of Anderson (1979), Bergstrand (1985, 1989, 1990), Krugman (1979b), Helpman and Krugman (1985) and, more recently, Anderson and Van Wincoop (2003), was a theoretical foundation given to the gravity equation.

Deardorff also highlights how Bergstrand (1989, 1990) assumed Dixit-Stiglitz (1977) monopolistic competition, implying product differentiation across firms rather than among countries.

Deardorff further states that:

> Bergstrand's later work therefore serves to bring together the earlier Armington-based approaches to deriving the gravity equation with a second strand of literature in which gravity equations were derived from simple monopolistic competition models. Almost from the start of the New Trade Theory's attention to such models, it was recognized that they provided an immediate and simple justification for the gravity equation. (p. 7).

In addition to the above mentioned theoretical foundations, Rose (2000) argues that other approaches have also been linked to the gravity model, like models with national technological differences, "reciprocal dumping" models of homogenous goods and models with internationally varying factor endowments. Moreover, he remarks that there is not a clear consensus about "which particular theoretical model best describes the empirical findings of the gravity model" (p. 8).

In one of the most influential empirical papers dealing with the gravity equation, Rose (2000), notes that the gravity model of international trade "has a remarkably consistent history of success as an empirical tool" (p. 8). He also cites Leamer and Levinsohn (1995, p. 1384), who describe the gravity model as having provided "some of the clearest and most robust empirical findings in economics." It relates bilateral trade flows to GDP, distance, and other factors that affect trade barriers (Anderson and van Wincoop 2003), modelling the flow of international trade between a pair of countries as "proportional to their economic mass and inversely proportional to the distance between them" (Rose 2000, p. 7). Anderson (1979, p. 106) states that the gravity equation is "probably the most successful empirical trade device of the last 25 years". Influential empirical studies dealing with the gravity equation include the works of Anderson and van Wincoop (2003), Feenstra et al. (2001), Evenett and Keller (2002), Eaton and Kortum (2002), Rose (2000, 2004), Soloaga and Winters (2001), and Subramanian and Wei (2007), among others.

Membership in a specific free trade agreement has been traditionally represented introducing dummy variables in the testable gravity equation. The same approach holds when considering other factors that could exert an influence on trade, like geographical or cultural factors (Lederman and Özden 2007).

4.2.2 Foundations and Assumptions of the Model

As argued by Baldwin and Taglioni (2006, p. 4), the gravity model is inspired on the field of physics and more specifically on the law of gravity, where the force of gravity between two objects "is proportional to the product of the masses of the two objects divided by the square of the distance between them" (p. 4). The equation takes the form

$$F = G\frac{M_1 M_2}{(dist_{12})^2} \tag{4.1}$$

Where F denotes the magnitude of the gravitational force between the two masses, G is the gravitational constant, M_1 and M_2 are the masses, and $dist_{12}$ is the distance between them.

When applied to international trade, the force of gravity is replaced with the value of bilateral trade, and the masses, with the trade partners' GDPs. In its simplest version, the gravity equation takes the functional form

$$T_{ij} = A\frac{Y_i Y_j}{D_{ij}} \tag{4.2}$$

where T_{ij} denotes the value of exports from country i to country j, Y_i is country's i national income, Y_j is country's j national income, D_{ij} is the distance between the trade partners, and A is a constant of proportionality.

Anderson (1979) introduced a theoretical underpinning for the gravity model based on constant elasticity of substitution (CES) preferences and goods differentiated by origin. Subsequent extensions, like the ones of Bergstrand (1989, 1990) and Deardorff (1998), maintained the CES preference structure and included monopolistic competition or a Heckscher–Ohlin structure, with the purpose of explaining specialization.

With the purpose of presenting the theoretical foundations of the gravity model, the derivation proposed by Anderson and van Wincoop (2003) is now briefly introduced. As stated by the latter authors, the first assumption of the gravity model is related to the differentiation of all goods by place of origin, being each region specialized in the production of only one good, and being the supply of each good fixed. Identical, homothetic preferences, approximated by a CES utility function, are also assumed. Denoting c_{ij} the consumption by region j consumers of goods from region i, consumers in region j maximize

$$\left(\sum_i \beta_i^{(1-\sigma)/\sigma} c_{ij}^{(\sigma-1)/\sigma}\right)^{\sigma/(\sigma-1)} \tag{4.3}$$

under the budget constraint

$$\sum_i p_{ij} c_{ij} = y_j \tag{4.4}$$

Being σ the elasticity of substitution between all goods, β_i a positive distribution parameter, y_j the nominal income of region j residents, and p_{ij} the price of region i goods for region j consumers.

The exporter's supply price, net of trade costs, is denoted by p_i and t_{ij} is the trade cost factor between i and j

$$p_{ij} = p_i t_{ij} \tag{4.5}$$

Anderson and van Wincoop define the nominal demand for region i goods by region j consumers, satisfying utility maximization, under the budget constraint, as

$$x_{ij} = \left(\frac{\beta_i p_i t_{ij}}{P_j}\right)^{(1-\sigma)} y_j, \tag{4.6}$$

P_j is the consumer price index of j, given by

$$P_j = \left[\sum_i (\beta_i p_i t_{ij})^{1-\sigma}\right]^{1/(1-\sigma)}. \tag{4.7}$$

In a general equilibrium scenario, market clearance implies

$$y_i = \sum_j x_{ij} \tag{4.8}$$

$$= \sum_j (\beta_i t_{ij} p_i / P_j)^{1-\sigma} y_j$$

$$= (\beta_i p_i)^{1-\sigma} \sum_j (t_{ij}/P_j)^{1-\sigma} y_j, \forall i.$$

The world nominal income is represented as $y^W \equiv \sum_j y_j$. Income shares are defined as $\theta_j \equiv \frac{y_j}{y^W}$.

Then

$$x_{ij} = \frac{y_i y_j}{y^W} \left(\frac{t_{ij}}{\prod_i P_j}\right)^{1-\sigma} \tag{4.9}$$

and

$$\prod_i \equiv \left(\sum_j \left(\frac{t_{ij}}{P_j}\right)^{1-\sigma} \theta_j\right)^{1/(1-\sigma)}. \tag{4.10}$$

Now, Anderson and van Wincoop substitute the equilibrium scaled prices into (4.7), obtaining

$$P_j = \left(\sum_i \left(t_{ij}/\prod_i\right)^{1-\sigma}\theta_i\right)^{1/1-\sigma} \tag{4.11}$$

The authors later explain how (4.10) and (4.11) "can be solved for all $\prod_i$'s and P_i's in terms of income shares $\{\theta_i\}$, bilateral trade barriers $\{t_{ij}\}$ and σ" (Anderson and van Wincoop 2003, p. 176).

Trade barriers are assumed to be symmetric, $t_{ij} = t_{ji}$. Based on the latter assumption, the solution proposed to (4.10) and (4.11) is $\prod_i = P_i$, and

$$P_j^{1-\sigma} = \sum_i P_i^{\theta-1}\theta_i t_{ij}^{1-\sigma}\forall_j. \tag{4.12}$$

The gravity equation is defined as

$$x_{ij} = \frac{y_i y_j}{y^W}\left(\frac{t_{ij}}{P_i P_j}\right)^{1-\sigma}. \tag{4.13}$$

Rose (2004) states that usually, when the gravity equation has been tested, the estimated effects of distance and output have shown to be economically and statistically significant, and reasonably consistent across studies. Besides that, the gravity model has been able to explain most of the variation in international trade. In Rose own words, "the model seems reliable and fits the data well" (p. 4).

4.3 Empirical Methodology and Data

The main research question explored in the current empirical analysis is the possible influence that the EU's unilateral generalized system of preferences has exerted upon Colombian of exports, between 1990 –year when the Colombian economy started a process of opening up and an ambitious strategy of internationalization, after decades of implementation of an imports substitution model—and 2008. Following the approach of Rose (2004), the estimation of the effect of the European Union's GSP is based on the standard gravity model of bilateral trade which, as already mentioned, explains trade as a function of distance and income. The basic gravity equation is augmented, trying to include all the relevant variables that could exert an influence upon trade. A variable representing the real exchange rate has also been included, with the aim of controlling for changes in the value of the currency. The latter is based on the approach suggested by Belke and Spies (2008).

Different empirical studies have included a number of additional variables – besides the traditional ones that account for the gravity effects, namely output and distance— to account for cultural, geographical or time-specific characteristics of the trade partners (Correia 2008). For the purpose of the current investigation, a set of dummy variables has been introduced: the existence of a border between the trade partners (*Border*), the possibility of one of the countries being a landlocked nation (*Landl*), and the fact of one of the partners being an island (*Island*) have all been defined as binary variables. Sharing a common language (*Lang*) is also included, variable that reflects some sort of cultural proximity. Finally, the remaining control variables have been introduced, seeking to capture the effects of some institutional relations. These dummy variables are $GSPEU_{it}$ (which is unity if the Colombian exports to its trade partner are covered by the European Union's GSP), and RTA_{ijt} (which is unity if both commercial partners make part of the same regional trade agreement).

The empirical version of the model can be specified as

$$X_{ijt} = \beta_0 (Y_{it})^{\beta 1} (Y_{jt})^{\beta 2} (D_{ij})^{\beta 3} \exp(\beta 4 \Gamma_{ijt}) \exp(\varepsilon_{ijt}) \tag{4.14}$$

Where X_{ijt} denotes trade between partners i and j in the year t, Y_{it} is the output of country i at time t, Y_{jt} is the output of country j at time t, D_{ij} is the distance between country i and country j, Γ_{ijt} is a vector of additional explanatory variables (capturing geographical, cultural, and institutional characteristics of the trade partners), and ε_{ijt} is the error term, normally distributed, with mean zero (Cárdenas and García 2004). In a logarithmic form, the equation takes the form

$$\ln X_{ijt} = \ln \beta 0 + \beta 1 \ln Y_{it} + \beta 2 \ln Y_{jt} + \beta 3 \ln D_{ij} + \beta 4 \Gamma_{ijt} + \varepsilon_{ijt} \tag{4.15}$$

The testable log-linearized gravity equation is defined as

$$\begin{aligned} \ln EXP_{ijt} = {} & \beta 0 + \beta 1 \ln GDP_{it} + \beta 2 \ln GDP_{jt} + \beta 3 \ln D_{ij} + \beta 4 \ln re_{ijt} \\ & + \beta 5 Border_{ij} + \beta 6 Landl_{ij} + \beta 7 Island_{ij} + \beta 8 Lang_{ij} \\ & + \beta 9 GSPEU_{it} + \beta 10 RTA_{ijt} + \varepsilon_{ijt} \end{aligned} \tag{4.16}$$

where i and j denote countries, and t denotes time. (EXP_{ijt}) is the value of Colombian exports to country j at time t, GDP_{it} is Colombia's GDP, GDP_{jt} is the partner country's GDP, accounting respectively for export supply and demand conditions. D_{ij} is the great-circle distance between Colombia and the capital city of its trade partner, which is a proxy for the transportation costs. As mentioned before, re_{ijt} seeks to capture the influence of the bilateral real exchange rate upon trade between both partners. The set of binary dummy variables capturing geographical factors is composed by $Border_{ij}$, which is unity if the countries share a land border, $Landl_{ij}$, which is unity if one of the countries is a landlocked territory, and $Island_{ij}$, which is unity if one of the trade partners is an island. $Lang_{ij}$ takes the value of one if both countries share the same language. Finally, two binary dummy variables represent institutional factors exerting an influence upon Colombia's exports: $GSPEU_{it}$, which takes the value of one if the exports have been covered by the European Union's GSP, and RTA_{ijt}, *which* is unity if both countries make part of any regional trade agreement, or if Colombia receives any other preferences from the trade partner.

The equation was estimated based on 855 observations within the period 1990–2008, covering the panel of data the exports of Colombia to 45 countries. More than 80% of Colombia's exports are destined to these countries. The dataset was constructed based on information provided by the International Monetary Fund (International Financial Statistics), the World Bank (World Development Indicators Database), the United Nations National Accounts Main Aggregates Database, the Commission of the European Union, the Organization of American States (OAS), and the CIA World Factbook website.

The expected coefficients are:

$$\beta 1>0, \beta 2>0, \beta 3<0, \beta 4>0, \beta 5>0, \beta 6<0, \beta 7<0, \beta 8>0, \beta 9>0, \beta 10>0 \quad (4.17)$$

Considering that $\ln GDP_{it}$ and $\ln GDP_{jt}$ account for export supply and demand conditions respectively, these variables are expected to exert a positive influence on the Colombian exports. Distance, a proxy for trading costs, is expected to negatively affect exports since countries that are farther apart trade less (Rose 2004). Batra (2004), cited in Correia (2008), argues that distance can also be a proxy for the time elapsed during shipment, synchronization costs, transaction costs or cultural distance. The bilateral real exchange rate, captured in $\ln re_{ijt}$, is intended to measure the purchasing power of the respective foreign currencies in Colombia's market. If it increases, it would imply an increased purchasing capacity for the importing partners.

As previously stated, $Border_{ij}$, $Landl_{ij}$, and $Island_{ij}$ are variables that have been included to capture geographical factors that affect trade. The first one is expected to positively impact Colombian exports, taking into account that trade partners sharing a land border are expected to trade more. This has also been founded for countries sharing the same language, or making part of a common regional trade association (Rose 2004). On the contrary, being a landlocked territory or an island is supposed to imply larger trade costs, which would in turn negatively affect trade between partners. Finally, unilateral schemes of preferences and trade associations are intended to enhance trade, by means of decreasing import tariffs. Consequently, the variables $GSPEU_{it}$and RTA_{ijt} are expected to positively influence Colombian exports.

In what concerns the estimation methods, a pooled OLS (POLS) estimation was first conducted. As in Rose (2000), the underlying motivation for including this method was to show some benchmark estimates of the gravity equation. Nevertheless, as highlighted by Johnston and DiNardo (1997), POLS ignores the panel structure of the data, treating the observations as being serially uncorrelated for a given individual, with homoscedastic errors across individuals and time periods. The latter is supported by the F-test following the fixed effects (FE) regression, which demonstrated significant individual effects. Baltagi (2008) also explains that

OLS estimates ignoring the country dummies suffer from an omission variables problem, resulting in biased and inconsistent estimators.

Next, the fixed effects method is introduced, decision based on the results derived from the Breusch and Pagan Lagrange multiplier (LM) test for random effects, and the Hausman test statistic. The first one indicated specific individual-level effects. In the second one, different point estimates were generated by the random effects (RE) estimator. Consequently, the Hausman test's null hypothesis—that the RE estimator is consistent—was soundly rejected. The Hausman test rejected the hypothesis of no correlation between the individual effects and the explanatory variables, which also justifies the use of instrumental variable (IV) methods (Baltagi 2008).

Baum (2006, p. 232) also argues that if the Hausman test indicates that the RE individual level effects cannot be considered orthogonal to the individual-level error, an instrumental variables (IV) estimator may be used to generate consistent estimates of the coefficients on the time-invariant variables. Taking that into account, the Hausman–Taylor (HT) estimator was applied within the current empirical analysis. Furthermore, Baltagi (2008) also proposes this method when some of the explanatory variables are related to the individual level effects, that is, when endogeneity occurs through the unobserved individual effects.

Introducing the FE estimation also goes in line with the empirical work of Glick and Rose (2002), where this estimator was selected based on the Hausman test. Nevertheless, while this method offers unbiased estimators for the time-varying variables (Belke and Spies 2008), it cannot estimate the effect of time-invariant variables, which are wiped out (Baltagi 2008). Therefore, the variables capturing geographical and cultural factors that affect trade (*ldist, border, landl, island, commlang*) would not be possible to estimate under the latter methodology. Considering that aspect, as well as the aforementioned result of the Hausman test, two IV methods were introduced into the analysis. First, the Hausman and Taylor (HT) estimator was considered, in which some of the covariates are correlated with the unobserved individual-level random effect (Stata Press 2009). Furthermore, a Hausman test on the difference between HT and the within estimator, according to the suggestions of Baltagi (2008), showed the set of instruments chose to be legitimate. This methodology has been previously utilized in empirical works, like the ones of Belke and Spies (2008), Carrère (2006), and Egger (2002). Taking all these arguments into account, the alternative offered by the HT method has been chosen. Finally, the Amemiya MaCurdy (AM) estimator was also used, another IV estimator which also assumes that some of the explanatory variables are correlated with the individual-level effects. The latter uses extra instruments to gain efficiency at the cost of additional assumptions on the data-generating process (Stata Press p. 166). The results were close to the HT estimates, as in the example provided by Baltagi (2008).

As aforementioned, although the fixed effects estimation (FE) provides unbiased estimates of the coefficients, the time-invariant explanatory variables cannot be estimated under this methodology. Belke and Spies (2008, p. 377), citing Plümper and Troeger (2007), also underscore the fact that despite of the coefficients being provided for variables that hardly change over time, the FE absorbs most of their explanatory power and estimates of these variables become inefficient.

Considering that both the HT method and the AM method permit an estimation of time-invariant and almost time-invariant variables, and based on the above mentioned justification for selecting these IV estimators, the analysis of the results is based on the latter two estimators. For comparability purposes, the results obtained under POLS and FE, are also shown.

4.4 Results

While columns 1 and 2 in Table 4.1 depict benchmark POLS and FE estimators, the HT and AM estimators are shown in columns 3 and 4. Robust standard errors are reported for the first two methodologies, while standard errors are reported for the other two estimators.

Table 4.1 Estimation results (Author's own calculations)

	(1) POLS	(2) FE	(3) HT	(4) AM
	0.84[a]	1.64[a]	1.64[a]	1.64[a]
lgdpcol	(0.25)	(0.63)	(0.35)	(0.35)
	1.36[a]	0.50	0.50[b]	0.50[b]
lgdppart	(0.06)	(0.54)	(0.36)	(0.36)
	−2.97[a]		−4.55[a]	−4.55[a]
ldist	(0.24)		(0.67)	(0.67)
	0.10[c]	0.62[c]	0.62[a]	0.62[a]
lgexr	(0.05)	(0.38)	(0.07)	(0.07)
	−1.00		−2.32	−2.37
border	(0.25)		(1.37)	(1.38)
	−0.13		−1.03	−1.05
landl	(0.35)		(1.13)	(1.14)
	0.38		−3.30[a]	−3.33[a]
island	(0.33)		(1.31)	(1.32)
	1.03[a]		−3.77	−3.81
commlang	(0.31)		(1.70)	(1.71)
	1.44[a]	0.51	0.51[b]	0.51[b]
gspeu	(0.19)	(0.49)	(0.34)	(0.34)
	0.16	−0.05	−0.05	−0.05
rta	(0.19)	(0.59)	(0.50)	(0.50)
Observations	855	855	855	855
R-squared	0.62	0.73	0.62	0.62

Robust standard errors reported for the POLS and FE methods

[a]Significant at 1%

[b]Significant at 10%

[c]Significant at 5%

On first instance, it should be noted that the so-called "standard features of the gravity model" –GDP and distance variables, as Rose (2000) calls them– show the expected signs and coefficients. Both Colombia's GDP and the trade partner's GDP exert a positive and significant influence on Colombian exports. When the Colombian GDP increases by 1%, Colombian exports increase by 1.64%. A 1% increase of the trade partner's GDP, raises Colombian exports by 0.50%. The latter finding is in line with other empirical studies where both the exporter and importer countries' GDP turned out to be positive and significant, such as the ones of Rose (2000), Cafiero (2005), and Martínez-Zarzoso et al. (2003), among others. As predicted by the model, when the GDPs of the trading partners increase, the magnitude of trade between them is also expected to get larger. The fact that the exporting country's coefficient is larger than the one of the importing country, underscores the importance of the productive capacity of a country for boosting its exports, as suggested by Martínez-Zarzoso et al. (2003).

Within the gravity model, the flow of international trade between a pair of countries is supposed to be inversely proportional to the distance between them (Rose 2000). In the current empirical study, the elasticity of trade with respect to distance reflects that holding all other factors constant, a 1% increase in the distance implies a decrease of 4.55% in trade. This finding is also in line with previous empirical studies, reporting a negative and significant coefficient for this variable. As previously mentioned, the variable *distance* has been included as a proxy for different factors that exert an effect on exports, like the trading costs between the country pair or the shipment times.

What appears rather striking is the fact that the estimated distance elasticity is higher than the one reported in other studies, aspect that could be explained based on different arguments. Brun et al. (2005, p. 1), for instance, point out that it is commonly believed that the current wave of globalization, much like the first, should have led to the "death of distance." The latter authors propose that globalization should imply "a dispersion of economic activity, reflecting a decline in transaction costs, especially transport costs". Nevertheless, they highlight how different studies based on the gravity model do not come to that conclusion: when the model has been estimated for several years, the absolute value of the coefficient increases over time (Brun et al. 2005, p 1.).

Another relevant affirmation made by them is that previous studies dividing the sample between high-income and low-income countries have founded that the elasticity of bilateral trade with respect to distance falls for bilateral trade between high-income countries, but there is not such a trend for low-income countries. Hence, it has been proposed that the latter group of countries has been marginalized from the current wave of globalization, as a result of their infrastructure offer. The effect of distance on trade would then be much larger for a developing country, such as Colombia.

As will be explained in a next section of the dissertation, the very poor status of the Colombian infrastructure is undoubtedly a factor that has been frequently underscored in different investigations: in the 2009–2010 World Economic Forum's Global Competitiveness Report, the critical need of improvement of the

Colombian infrastructure is underscored, and is considered as an element that seriously hinders Colombia's competitive potential in the world marketplace. In the same study, the inadequate supply of infrastructure is mentioned as one of the most problematic factors at the moment of conducting business in Colombia. This infrastructure limitation, coupled with the associated high transport costs inflicted to Colombian exporters, could be an explanation for the higher value of the coefficient reported within the current study.

Previous empirical studies support the latter argument. Martínez-Zarzoso and Suárez-Burguet (2005, p. 369) conduct a study of Latin American imports from the EU, coming to the conclusion that "improving the infrastructure of Latin American countries as well as improving their ports" efficiency will contribute to reducing transport costs and therefore to increasing the volume of trade. This is then a serious limitation affecting not only the Colombian, but also the regional export capacity.

The bilateral real exchange rate variable seeks to capture the value of Colombia's goods against those of the partner country, and has been calculated as the product of the nominal exchange rate (in all the cases, the cost for the foreign country of a Colombian peso) and the ratio of prices between the two countries. A real appreciation for the partner country, in terms of Colombian goods, would be associated with an increased purchasing power for the trade partner. The coefficient has the expected sign and is statistically significant, meaning that a 1% appreciation of the partner's currency raises Colombian exports by 0.6%.

From the four variables capturing geographical and cultural factors that affect trade, only *island* is statistically significant: as expected, if the importing country is an island, this is supposed to imply larger trade costs, affecting negatively trade between partners. The coefficient shows a decrease of 96% in Colombian exports– given by exp (−3.30)-1–, when the trade partner is an island.

As mentioned before, a positive coefficient was expected for the variable *GSPEU*, based on the perception that preferential treatment granted to exporters boosts the exports of the benefited countries, and that countries receiving these preferences face more favorable access to the EU's market. As can be observed in Table 4.1, the coefficient presents the expected positive sign and statistical significance. This would mean that Colombian exports have positively benefited from the unilateral scheme of preferences offered by the European Union, and that this trade mechanism had a large and positive effect on Colombian exports within the period of time analyzed. Exports to European Union member states, holding all other factors fixed, are estimated to be 61% (exp.0.51–1) more than the ones directed to other countries that do not offer this trade mechanism. While the coefficient might seem large, this finding is consistent with others included in previous empirical studies. Lederman and Özden (2007), for instance, report that Andean countries covered by the U.S. Andean Trade Preference Act (unilateral scheme of preferences) export 42% more than countries not benefited by these commercial preferences (See Tables 4.2, 4.3 and 4.4).

This finding is also in line with studies that have reported positive and statistically significant coefficients for institutional variables. DeRosa (2008) concludes that being a beneficiary of a generalized system of preferences has a positive impact on trade for the eligible countries. Aiello and Demaria (2010), when analyzing the evidence from the EU's GSP concerning the possible enhancement of exports from developing countries, find a positive and significant impact of the trade preferences

Table 4.2 List of variables

Variable	Definition	Source
EXP_{ijt}	FOB value of exports to trade partner *j* at time *t* (in current US$)	IMF's Direction of Trade Statistics (CD ROM)
GDP_{it}	Colombian GDP (in current US$)	United Nations National Accounts Main Aggregates Database
GDP_{jt}	Trade partner's GDP (in current US$)	United Nations National Accounts Main Aggregates Database
D_{ij}	Great-circle distance between the trade partners	CIA World Factbook (latitudes and longitudes, capital cities). US Federal Communications Commission Website, Converter
re_{ijt}	Bilateral real exchange rate	IMF's International Financial Statistics Database (nominal exchange rates, producer price indexes)
$Border_{ij}$	Binary dummy variable, unity if the country pair shares a land border	CIA World Factbook
$Landl_{ij}$	Dummy variable, takes the value of one if any of the countries is a landlocked territory	CIA World Factbook
$Island_{ij}$	Dummy variable, unity if one of the countries is an island	CIA World Factbook
$Lang_{ij}$	Dummy variable, takes the value of one if both countries share a common language	CIA World Factbook
$GSPEU_{it}$	Dummy variable, unity if the Colombian exports to the trade partner have been covered by the European GSP	European Union Commission's Website
RTA_{ijt}	Dummy variable, unity if both countries make part of the same regional trade agreement	Organization of American States' Foreign Trade Information System

Table 4.3 Countries

Argentina	Austria	Belgium	Bolivia	Brazil
Bulgaria	Canada	Chile	Costa Rica	Cyprus
Czech Republic	Denmark	Ecuador	El Salvador	Estonia
Finland	France	Germany	Greece	Guatemala
Honduras	Hungary	Iceland	Ireland	Italy
Latvia	Lithuania	Luxembourg	Malta	Mexico
Netherlands	Norway	Panama	Peru	Poland
Portugal	Romania	Slovak Republic	Slovenia	Spain
Sweden	Switzerland	Trinidad and Tobago	United Kingdom	United States
Venezuela				

Table 4.4 Descriptive statistics

Variable	Observations	Mean	Std. Dev.	Min	Max
EXP_{ijt}	855	16.61	4.20	0	23.25
GDP_{it}	855	25.35	.40	24.70	26.22
GDP_{jt}	855	25.18	1.93	21.66	30.28
D_{ij}	855	8.62	.80	6.59	9.33
re_{ijt}	855	5.41	2.37	−2.74	9.10
$Border_{ij}$	855	.11	.31	0	1
$Landl_{ij}$	855	.13	.34	0	1
$Island_{ij}$	855	.13	.34	0	1
$Lang_{ij}$	855	.29	.45	0	1
$GSPEU_{it}$	855	.34	.47	0	1
RTA_{ijt}	855	.19	.39	0	1

on the agricultural exports of preferred countries. Furthermore, the so-called *GSP Drugs*—nowadays called *GSP Plus*—was founded by the latter authors to be effective in some products where Colombia is highly specialized when trading with the European Union, such as oils. Using a gravity model based on disaggregated trade flows from 161 developing countries to 15 EU member countries, Cipollina and Salvatici (2010) find that EU preferences have a positive impact on developing countries agricultural exports, both at the extensive and intensive margins, although with significant differences across sectors. Lederman and Özden (2007), analyzing different U.S.reciprocal and unilateral preferential market access programs, conclude that such programs have economically large and statistically significant effects on the exports of the beneficiary countries. The study is also based on the estimation of a gravity equation, based on data of the exports from 173 countries and 98 product categories to the US. Other studies supporting this positive effect are the ones of Nilsson (2002) and Agostino et al. (2008).

Another important reason for the large impact might be related to the fact that approximately 85% of the Colombian exports to the EU are covered by the GSP Plus. Products that have a very large participation within the basket of goods exported, like coal, fuel oils, coffee, nickel and cut flowers, do not pay any import duties when entering that market. The reminding 17% that does pay duties is comprised of agricultural products, such as bananas.

As well as in the case of the unilateral schemes of preferences, regional agreements are expected to have positive effects on the volume of bilateral trade among member countries. Interestingly, the variable RTA – capturing institutional relations within the framework of different regional trade agreements where Colombia participates, such as the Andean Community of Nations – did not show to be statistically significant. One possible reason for this finding is that of the 855 bilateral export flows analyzed, just 19% were covered by preferential trade schemes different to the EU's GSP. Some important FTAs, such as the ones signed with the so-called "Northern Triangle" (Guatemala, El Salvador, Honduras) or Canada, have not entered into force yet and still need to be ratified.

4.5 Concluding Remarks

Compared to other large Latin American economies such as the Brazilian, Mexican, Argentinean, or Chilean, it could be argued that Colombia's share in the total extra-EU 27 trade is rather low. Nevertheless, between 1999 and 2009 this share doubled, which is a positive trend.

The enhanced commercial relations, the existence of important levels of FDI in the country, and the role that Colombia plays within the Andean Community of Nations, are all factors that have increased the attractiveness of the Colombian economy for the EU. The signature of a bilateral free trade agreement in May 2010 –which, if ratified, would be the third in the region after the ones signed with Mexico and Chile- is a proof of the renewed economic interest that the EU has been lately showing towards Colombia.

When applied to the pattern of Colombian exports for the period 1990–2008, the gravity equation fits the data well. The explanatory variables contribute in a significant manner to explain those factors exerting an influence on Colombian exports. The so-called "standard features of the gravity model" –GDP and distance variables – show the expected signs and coefficients. The results obtained from the empirical estimations conducted under the different econometric methodologies, especially under the Hausman Taylor and Amemiya MaCurdy estimators, allow to conclude that the EU GSP has exerted a positive and significant impact on Colombian exports. Exports to EU, holding all other factors fixed, are estimated to be 61.3% (exp.0.51–1) more than the ones directed to other countries that do not offer this trade mechanism. This finding is in line with previous empirical studies that have also reported positive and statistically significant coefficients for unilateral schemes of preferences.

Although the influence of the unilateral scheme of preferences shows to be positive, the underutilization of the program by Colombian exporters, as well as the evident concentration in a few export goods, can be observed in the bilateral commercial relations. Despite of the preferences being offered to approximately 7.200 products, the country has been exporting just 17% of the products covered during the last years. Furthermore, since the middle of the 1990s, more than 80% of the country's sales to the EU have been composed by just eight products –coffee, coal, ferronickel, oil and its derivatives, bananas, emeralds, and flowers, figure that increased to a staggering 87% in 2009. Increasing the productivity of the Colombian industrial exports, improving the degree of utilization of the *GSP Plus*, and boosting the diversification of the export mix based on a structural transformation of the economy, seem to be some of the most important challenges to be addressed by Colombian policymakers in coming decades.

Chapter 5
Export Competitiveness in Colombia: Strengths and Weaknesses of the Economy's Competitive Foundations

Chiefly, the current chapter aims to evaluate if Colombia is, indeed, strongly grounded in the "competitive fundamentals" that it requires for a successful process of export diversification. As has been suggested by Cramer (1999), while it is commonly believed that significant benefits could be expected from export diversification, this positive outcome should not be taken for granted. Domestic conditions are required, along with the diversification process.

First, the concepts of "competitiveness" and "export competitiveness" are discussed, from the point of view of the academic literature. Section 5.2 considers the institutional framework that has been established in Colombia, aimed to improve productivity and competitive levels of the Colombian economy.

Next, an empirical analysis of the country's "export competitiveness" is conducted. Finally, some conclusions are drawn, dealing with the most important strengths and weakness associated to Colombia's "export competitiveness."

5.1 The Concepts of "Competitiveness" and "Export Competitiveness"

As is widely known, the "competitiveness debate" is a pretty controversial one. Undoubtedly, one of the more disseminated stances is the one defended by Krugman (1994), who warns about the "dangerous obsession" and "pervasive rhetoric" associated to it. The statement highlights the importance of noticing that the "idea that a country's economic fortunes" are linked to its performance on world markets is a hypothesis that – as an empirical matter- "is flatly wrong" (Krugman 1994, p. 30). Nations do not behave the way corporations do. National productivity, rather than competition in the world's marketplace, is the one leading to higher living standards. He also proposes that the problem should be tackled from the perspective of domestic productivity.

J.F. Mejía, *Export Diversification and Economic Growth*, Contributions to Economics,
DOI 10.1007/978-3-7908-2742-2_5,

The controversy originated by the term "competitiveness" is also addressed by Oughton (1997), when analyzing the United Kingdom's industrial and trade policies between 1950 and 1994, as well as its decline of its position in the "league table of European economies." Her analysis seems to support Krugman's argument: rather than a problem of "competitiveness," the real issue to be analyzed is the poor rate of productivity growth. Interestingly, Oughton asserts that the word has become sort of an "umbrella" concept that tries to integrate a number of industrial and trade policies. Again, the vague and elusive character of the definition is proposed.

A four-factor decomposition of "competitiveness" is depicted by Klein (1988), the latter concept being determined by relative prices. In turn, these are determined based on the unit cost (wage rate), productivity, profit margin and exchange rate. According to Klein, holding down unit labor costs either through wage restraint or productivity enhancement is the way for a country to become competitive.

Cheptea et al. (2005) propose that the gains or losses of world market shares by individual countries are often considered as an indicator of their trade competitiveness. They also argue that market share growth depends also on structural factors. The market share growth of an economy will be influenced by its geographical and sectoral specialization too.

Contrary to the above mentioned contributions, Klein does not appear to reject the term: e.g., he recognizes how a deterioration of a country's "international competitiveness" may take place, where "domestic goods are crowded out by foreign goods" (p. 309). Furthermore, and in the same line of argumentation of highly reputed institutions such as the OECD or the World Economic Forum, Klein believes that "competitiveness" is linked to a wide range of social and institutional factors. Hence, the "buildup of a country's export position," education, work ethic and technology, are some of the underlying forces to be considered (p. 309).

Haddad et al. (2006, p. 121) further state that the definition of competitiveness in developing nations,

> ...is not to be confused with natural resource abundance, cheap labor or continued devaluation of the currency. Competitiveness based on cheap labor is not a formula for boosting prosperity in the long-run, especially when relative productivity is taken into account versus neighboring countries, some of which also have relatively cheap labor on a productivity-adjusted basis. Nor should competitiveness be confused with export growth rates or foreign exchange generation based on mineral wealth or hydroelectric power. While these will be important generators of government revenues, they will not create large numbers of investment and innovation driven jobs.

When dealing with a survey of the term "competitiveness," a reference to Porter's concept of "competitive advantage" should not be missed. As Dunning (1992) points out, the latter refers to the ability of a country –or more specifically, local firms of a country- to use its location-bound resources in a way that will enable it (them) to be competitive in international markets. The "strength, composition and sustainability of a nation's competitive advantage will be revealed in the value of its national product (more particularly, the part that enters into international transactions), and/or the rate of growth of that product, *relative to that of its leading competitors*" (Dunning 1992).

In this line of argumentation, it is proposed that a principal component of a country's export strategy should be the improvement of "competitiveness" (Von Kirchbach 2003). A center point of Porter's "competitive advantage" notion is the idea that it can be created and maintained. "National Competitiveness" is therefore based on four principal "facets," namely: Resources, an innovation-seeking business environment, a demanding local market and the presence of supporting industries. The government's intervention is expected, in terms of "creating a competitive advantage" in growth sectors.

Michael Porter's determinants of competitiveness and his "competitiveness diamond" have been frequently used as a basis for determining a country's competitiveness and economic growth potential (Haddad et al., 2006). According to Porter's approach, a sound macroeconomic, political, legal, and social context are crucial elements for improving a country's competitiveness. This should also be accompanied by a permanent drive to improve the microeconomic environment, promote the sophistication of local companies, and increase domestic competition (Haddad 2006).

Another strand of the literature makes reference to the concepts of trade competitiveness and export competitiveness. Brenton et al. (2008) argue that policies geared towards promoting trade and trade competitiveness are of paramount importance within growth strategies. The authors propose that, for improving export competitiveness, some specific factors should be taken into account. Ensuring the quality of institutions that promote trade, relying on the market to determine prices, and addressing market failures where possible are of utmost importance. Furthermore, the access to an efficient transportation and telecommunications infrastructure, a well-functioning tax and customs service, the support provided to exporters for meeting quality standards (through metrology, testing, and conformity assessment facilities), stable macroeconomic policies, an efficient financial sector, and an open trade policy are all elements required for promoting export competitiveness.

The improvement of export competitiveness could be accomplished, based on the implementation of three different elements: the incentives regime (guaranteeing that domestic resources are channeled to the most productive sectors and firms), the cost reduction of the so-called "backbone" services (e.g. energy, telecommunications, customs services, transport and logistics, security), and the implementation of pro-active policies supporting trade (export and investment promotion entities, agencies to support innovation and clustering, mechanisms geared towards limiting the costs of adjustment) (Brenton et al. 2008).

Starting with some institutional stakeholders, the Organization of Economic Cooperation and Development – OECD defines the concept as "a measure of a country's advantage or disadvantage in selling its products in international markets." Different factors that exert an influence over a country's macroeconomic performance, like productivity and technological innovation -which depend on human and physical capital-, and the policy environment, should therefore be taken into account (Durand et al. 1992). Similarly, the World Economic Forum-

WEF describes "competitiveness" as "the set of institutions, policies, and factors that determine the level of productivity of a country" (World Economic Forum 2008).

The World Bank (2006, p. 122) defines competitiveness as sustainable increases in productivity resulting in improved incomes for the average citizen. Competitiveness is also associated to the capacity for a country to produce goods and services that are able to "meet the test" of the global market, improving the average income of its citizens. The latter improvement should be accomplished without the need of resorting to protection or subsidies. Competitiveness is believed to be important for developing nations for improving their export performance, reaping benefits from the signature of bilateral free trade agreements (mechanisms that imply the reduction of tariff barriers and the need of boosting productivity), encouraging growth (especially in export-oriented sectors), generating employment opportunities, and reducing poverty (World Bank 2006).

In their study conducted for the World Economic Forum's *Global Competitiveness Report*, Sala-i-Martin et al. (2010b, p. 4) define competitiveness as the set of institutions, policies, and factors that determine the level of productivity of a country. The level of prosperity accomplished by a country is therefore determined by its level of productivity. Consequently, "more competitive economies tend to be able to produce higher levels of income for their citizens" (Sala-i-Martin et al. 2010, p. 4). Taking into account that productivity levels also determines the rates of return within the economy, countries with a higher level of competitiveness tend to grow faster (Sala-i-Martin et al. 2010, p. 4).

For the particular case of Colombia, policy-makers currently defend the argument that an increased degree of openness, represented both in a more diversified structure of foreign commercial relations and a bigger offer of exports, would indeed entail very important benefits for the country. Taking that into account, different actions and initiatives have been undertaken toward strengthening the country's "competitive position." As in a wide variety of countries all around the world, the term "competitiveness" has been embedded within the country's technical and political agenda. This interest is derived from "the increasing levels of competition both in the domestic and international markets, implying the necessity of improving it, supported by national policies" (CONPES 2006).

The definition of "competitiveness" in Colombia goes in line with the one provided by the before mentioned institutional agents, namely the World Economic Forum and the OECD. As mentioned in a number of policy documents, the concept is understood as "the capability of producing goods and services able to successfully compete in global markets, while improving the income and welfare conditions of the population" (CONPES 2006). Policy-makers highlight how the betterment of Colombia's "competitiveness" and productivity must be strongly attached to the commercial strategy of "internationalization." Competitiveness indicators and reports elaborated by the World Economic Forum are carefully analyzed, as well as the evolution of the different "factors" comprising "competitiveness," (e.g. productivity, macroeconomic environment, infrastructure, telecommunications, scientific and technological development, human capital, and the institutional framework, just to name a few).

5.2 The Institutional Framework of Competitiveness in Colombia

In a parallel manner to the initiation of the liberalization process in Colombia, the national government launched in 1990 the so-called "Modernization and Internationalization Program." Some of the most important objectives expressed in that document were related to facing competition, increasing productivity levels, boosting investment in technology and promoting a reallocation of the production (Ocampo and Villar 1992). Reaping the benefits derived from the global marketplace would be accomplished by means of increasing the "competitive performance," both at the national and sectoral level.

Meanwhile, the term "competitiveness" has been progressively more and more been embedded in the Colombian political agenda: the underlying idea that has been frequently discussed at the government level is that increased levels of trade –which in turn, could lead to higher levels of economic growth-, could be achieved by improving "competitiveness." Taking these facts into account, it is now appropriate to analyze the institutional framework that has been established in Colombia, with the objective of strengthening the competitive foundations of the economy.

In 1999, Colombia's "National Productivity and Competitiveness Policy" was launched, gathering different strategies and efforts previously undertaken since the beginning of the 1990s.

By the same token, more recently the so-called *Sistema Nacional de Competitividad* (National Competitiveness System) was introduced in 2006, similarly to a wide range of nations that have established "councils," "institutes," "centers," "committees," and the like. The National Competitiveness System is defined by the Colombian government as the "set of guidelines, rules, activities, resources, programs, and public and private institutions that promote the implementation of a productivity and competitiveness policy" in the country (Alta Consejería Presidencial para la Competitividad y las Regiones 2010).

Since its creation, the National Competitiveness System was established with a dual character: its main objective is to coordinate the activities of all the public and private entities that work to enhance the productivity and competitiveness of the Colombian economy (Ministerio de Comercio, Industria y Turismo 2006). It directly reports to the Colombian President, and is coordinated by the National Competitiveness Commission. The latter institution is composed by the Colombian President, the presidential advisor for competitiveness, the Ministers of Foreign Affairs, Finance, Agriculture, Mines and Energy, Communications, Trade, and Education. Moreover, representatives from other public entities—like the Colombian Institute for the Development of Science and Technology, the

Federation of Regions, the Federation of Municipalities—also make part of the commission. The private sector is represented by the National Business Council and representatives of the Academia. Finally, representatives from the labor unions also make part. Figure 5.1 depicts the organizational structure of the National Competitiveness System.

As aforementioned, the very ambitious goal of transforming Colombia into one of the three most competitive economies in Latin America has been formulated by the National Competitiveness Commission, goal that is supposed to be reached for the year 2032. Within the so-called "Vision 2032," goals have been quantified: to accomplish a high level of income per capita (equivalent to U.S. $18,000), to have a share of 60% of exports comprised of value-added goods and services, and to reduce poverty levels to 15% of the population (Alta Consejería Presidencial para la Competitividad y las Regiones 2010).

The latest version of the National Productivity and Competitiveness Policy, enacted in 2008, is anchored in five "pillars": the development of world-class export sectors, the improvement of productivity, the increase in formalization levels of the economy, the promotion of science, technology and innovation, and to promote competition (CONPES 2008). The progress of the action plans is supposed to be followed through on monitoring indicators, specific targets, and deadlines (CONPES 2008).

The Colombian National Planning Department (*Departamento Nacional de Planeación*), technical entity attached to the Executive Branch which designs the economic and social policies of the country, has also stated the target of boosting the competitiveness of the Colombian economy, by improving productivity levels. Improvements in productivity are expected to generate more employment opportunities, higher income for workers, and an increased welfare of the population (Gómez 2010).

Different mechanisms have been lately discussed for accomplishing the ambitious objective of higher and sustained rates of growth: the further improvement of the business conditions in the country, boosting the so-called "engines of growth," and enhancing the degree of economic formalization have been proposed as possible tools. Moreover, strengthening good governance, and the promotion of science, technology and innovation, are also considered as crucial lines of action. Additionally, the so-called "Internal Agenda for the Productivity and Competitiveness" was formulated, with the objective of defining strategies for taking advantage of the opportunities –and mitigating the risks- associated to the different processes of economic integration. Furthermore, the "High Council for the Competitiveness and Productivity" was established.

The new government that took office in August 2010 expressed its intention of implementing a new National Development Plan, containing policies and programs aimed specifically at increasing the productivity of the "five engines" of growth identified in the plan of government, namely: infrastructure, housing, agriculture, mining and petroleum, and innovation. Furthermore, in the medium term the objective is to continue implementing the country's competitiveness policy, placing

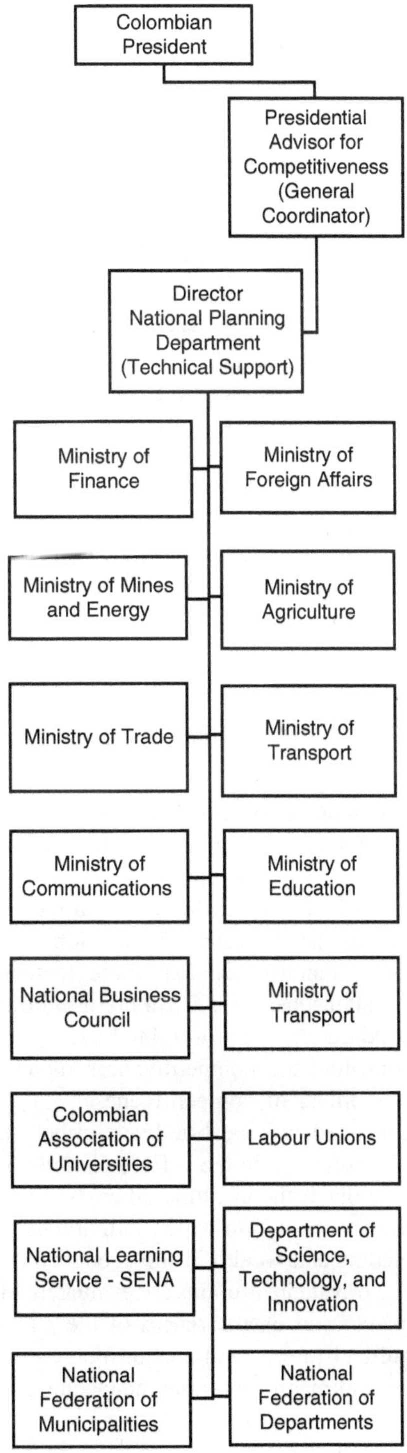

Fig. 5.1 Structure of the Colombian national competitiveness system (Own elaboration, based on information from the Colombian National Competitiveness System)

special emphasis on reducing the levels of informality, achieving higher rates of growth, as well as an enhanced distribution of income (Gómez 2010).

5.3 Measuring Export Competitiveness in Colombia

The current section evaluates the Colombian situation in relation with different factors or criteria of paramount importance for a successful process of export diversification. Based on the methodology of studies like the World Economic Forum's *Global Competitiveness Report* and the International Institute for Management Development's *World Competitiveness Yearbook*, reference is made to the scores and positions that the country has lately obtained in different rankings dealing with competitiveness. The performance of the country is compared to the one of other Latin American countries. The analysis is complemented with the evaluation of other statistics relevant to the field of competitiveness, namely, the macroeconomic environment, productivity levels and hourly compensation costs, logistics performance, infrastructure—transport infrastructure, technologies and communications infrastructure–, human capital, science and technology, and the access to finance.

5.3.1 The Global Competitiveness Index (GCI)

The World Economic Forum's *Global Competitiveness Index* (GCI) aims to capture the microeconomic and macroeconomic foundations of national competitiveness. Recognizing that the elements that explain competitiveness are manifold, Sala-i-Martin et al. (2010, p. 4) argue that many of these assumptions are based on "robust theoretical foundations, and that a vast number of empirical studies have demonstrated that these factors are not mutually exclusive, but in fact, simultaneously true." Taking a multidimensional approach into account, the GCI is constructed as a weighted average of all these components that are believed to constitute the competitiveness of an economy. These factors are the so-called "12 pillars of competitiveness." In what follows, the different criteria that are contained will be briefly described, based on the definition provided by Sala-i-Martin et al. in the WEF's *Global Competitiveness Report*.

Pillar 1, the institutional environment, is defined as the legal and administrative framework within which individuals, firms, and governments interact to generate income and wealth in the economy (Sala-i-Martin et al. 2010). Here, both public and private institutions are evaluated. Pillar 2, infrastructure, makes reference to the quality and extensiveness of the physical infrastructure in a country (e.g. roads, railroads, ports, and air transport). Pillar 3, macroeconomic stability, refers to the general macroeconomic management and performance of the country. Health and primary education, the fourth pillar, deals with the quality and the extensiveness of the provision of health services, as well as the quantity and quality of basic education. Higher education and training, the fifth pillar, captures secondary and tertiary enrollment rates, as well as the quality of that education. Vocational and on-the-job training are considered within this criterion too. The sixth pillar is represented by the goods market efficiency, which is determined by the degree of market competition in the economy, the impediments to business activity, or the restrictions imposed on FDI.

Pillar 7 deals with the labor market efficiency, which is defined in terms of the flexibility to shift workers quickly from one economic activity to another, gender equality issues, and the existence of wage fluctuations without much social disruption (Sala-i-Martin et al. 2010). Pillar 8, financial market sophistication, is evaluated according to criteria such as an effective channeling of resources to those activities with the highest expected rates of return, a system where risks are thoroughly assessed, and properly regulated products. Technological readiness, pillar number 9, aims to capture how swiftly an economy is able to adopt existing technologies, which will allow boosting productivity. Market size, pillar number 10, takes into account both the domestic and foreign markets.

Business sophistication, pillar 11, is defined as the quality of a country's business networks and supporting industries, measured based on indicators of the quality and quantity of local suppliers, the existence of clusters. Finally, pillar 12 is represented by innovation, defined as "the design and development of cutting-edge products and processes to maintain a competitive edge" (Sala-i-Martin et al. 2010, p. 7).

It is also important to mention that for the purpose of the GCI, economies are ranked according to their stage of development. Factor-driven countries are those that primarily compete on the basis of their factor endowments. Efficiency-driven countries must develop more efficient production processes and improve the quality of their products. In the third and most advanced stage, the innovation-driven phase, economies have to compete with new and innovative goods using the most sophisticated production processes (Sala-i-Martin et al. 2010, p. 8).

Another important aspect that should be taken into account when analyzing the GCI is that these 12 "pillars of competitiveness" are grouped into three sub-indexes: the "basic requirements" sub-index is comprised by those factors which are critical for countries in the factor-driven stage (institutions, infrastructure, macroeconomic stability, health and primary education). The "efficiency enhancers" sub-index is composed of those pillars crucial for efficiency-driven countries, namely higher education and training, goods market efficiency, labor market efficiency, financial market sophistication, technological readiness, and market size. Finally, the innovation and sophistication factors sub-index makes reference to the pillars which are crucial for the innovation-driven economies (business sophistication, and innovation). Different weights are assigned to each of these three sub-indexes, according to the country's stage of development:

- For factor-driven economies, 60% of the weight is attributed to basic requirements, 35% to efficiency enhancers, and 5% to innovation and sophistication;
- For efficiency-driven countries, 40% of the weight is attributed to basic requirements, 50% to efficiency enhancers, and 10% to innovation and sophistication;
- For innovation-driven economies, 20% of the weight is attributed to basic requirements, 50% to efficiency enhancers, and 30% to innovation and sophistication.

Data for the calculation of the GCI are obtained from two different sources: international "hard data" sources and the *Executive Opinion Survey* (Browne and Geiger 2010). The latter, which has been conducted for 30 years, was based in the last report on a sample of more than 13.000 surveys conducted in 133 countries (Browne and Geiger 2010, p. 49). The Latin American economies are present in four of the five different categories: Chile, Mexico and Uruguay are the only three nations in the region that are considered to be in a transition from being efficiency-driven economies to innovation-driven economies. Eight countries have been classified as efficiency-driven, and the remaining six are spread between the first category (factor-driven economies) and the second one (transition from one to two). Table 5.1 below shows the classification of the Latin American countries according to their stage of economic development, as defined by the WEF.

At first, the analysis of Colombia's performance in terms of the GCI index can be analyzed in Table 5.2, where the scores for some selected Latin American economies have been included.

Since the first edition of the Global Competitiveness Report (where 75 economies where assessed), some trends can be identified for Latin America. Chile has always ranked first in the region, being the only Latin American country that has accomplished to be included within the list of the "top 30" performers globally. The good scores of that country in different criteria explain Chile's privileged position: its sound macroeconomic management, the efficient and transparent institutions, highly developed infrastructure, and well-functioning goods, labor, and financial markets have been praised by the World Economic Forum

Table 5.1 World economic forum's classification of the Latin American economies, according to their stage of development (World Economic Forum's Global Competitiveness Report 2010)

Factor-driven economies	Transition from one to two	Efficiency-driven economies	Transition from two to three	Innovation-driven economies
Bolivia	Guatemala	Argentina	Chile	N/A
Honduras	Paraguay	Brazil	Uruguay	
Nicaragua	Venezuela	Colombia		
		Costa Rica		
		Ecuador		
		El Salvador		
		Mexico		
		Panama		
		Peru		

N/A Not applicable

Table 5.2 Global competitiveness index 2001–2010, cross-country comparison, Latin American economies (Own elaboration, based on data from the World Economic Forum's Global Competitiveness Reports for the years 2001–2002, 2002–2003, 2007–2008, 2008–2009, and 2009–2010)

	2001–2002 (75 countries)	2002–2003 (74 countries)	2007–2008 (131 countries)	2008–2009 (130 countries)	2009–2010 (133 countries)	2010–2011 (139 countries)
Chile	20	20	26	28	30	30
Panama	53	50	59	58	59	53
Costa Rica	35	43	63	59	55	56
Brazil	46	44	72	64	56	58
Uruguay	42	40	75	75	65	64
Mexico	45	43	52	60	60	66
Colombia	**56**	**52**	**69**	**74**	**69**	**68**
Peru	54	51	86	83	78	73
Argentina	63	58	85	88	85	87
Dominican Republic	50	52	96	98	95	101
Ecuador	73	68	103	104	105	105
Paraguay	72	67	121	124	124	120
Venezuela	68	63	98	105	113	122

(Sala-i-Martin et al. 2010, p. 33). Mexico has traditionally occupied the second position in the region, but it has been replaced by Brazil on the last report's ranking, partially explained by the widespread violence and domestic insecurity that has inflicted that country during the last years.

Brazil, as well as in the case of two of the other "BRICs" (India and China), has significantly improved its competitiveness scores. It has now surpassed Russia in the GCI ranking, and has been approaching the competitiveness levels of China and India. Uruguay, Colombia, and Peru, are other regional economies that have experienced some improvements in their competitiveness scores. Ecuador, Paraguay, and Venezuela have traditionally occupied the last positions not just in the region, but in the world as a whole. This poor performance is explained by their limitations concerning the institutional environment and the lack of good governance standards (Sala-i-Martin et al. 2010).

Within the first Global Competitiveness Report, Colombia occupied the eleventh position among the Latin American economies, behind Chile, Costa Rica, Mexico, Brazil, Uruguay, Argentina, Panama, Peru, El Salvador, and Venezuela. Grave domestic security conditions at the end of the 1990s, when the government faced very complicated challenges to control the national territory, as well as longstanding and widespread internal armed conflict and rampant violence–both political and criminal—undoubtedly had a very important weight on the poor score obtained by Colombia (U.S. Department of State 2002).

Coupled with that, in 1999 the country experienced its first recession in over 60 years, resulting in a decrease in gross domestic product (GDP) of 4.3% and record unemployment of over 18%, and investors confidence was greatly affected by the staggering levels of violence (U.S. Department of State 2002). Despite the very problematic situation in terms of domestic security and macroeconomic conditions at that time, it should nevertheless be pointed out that Colombia has never been included in the lower scores in the region: the country has mostly positioned itself in the middle of the rankings.

In the 2002–2003 edition of the *Global Competitiveness Report*, Colombia started to accomplish positive improvements in its competitiveness rankings. Table 5.2 depicts the evolution of the Latin American economies GCI between 2001 and 2010. The lower scores of all nations– when comparing the first periods (2001–2002 and 2002–2003) and the last periods (2007–2008, 2008–2009, 2009–2010) should be considered cautiously, since the sample of countries increased from 75 countries in 2001 to 139 countries in 2010.

The assessment of Colombia's competitiveness has notably improved during the last years. In the 2009–2010 report, the country improved its position in the raking (up five places), despite of the complex international economic situation. The sounder macroeconomic fundamentals achieved, the significant improvements in domestic security, stabilization and civil pacification, the extensive market size, the sophisticated business sector and the capacity of technology absorption with a "fairly high innovation potential" were important criteria that were taken into account and are considered by the WEF as "notable competitive advantages" (Sala-i-Martin et-al. 2009, p. 35). On the contrary, the poor institutional environment, the great limitations in terms of physical infrastructure, and the inefficient factor markets were mentioned as impediments negatively affecting Colombia's competitiveness (Sala-i-Martin et al. 2009, p. 35).

In the latest 2010–2011 report, Colombia went up another place, and it occupies now position number 7 among the Latin American economies. The strengths of the Colombian economy are recognized again, considering the quality of the macroeconomic environment, the remarkable improvement in social pacification, the sophistication of the business sector, and the technology absorption capacity. But again, it is stressed how the institutional environment, the poor infrastructure standards, and the inefficient and rigid factor markets do not allow Colombia to fully unleash its competitive potential (Sala-i-Martin et al. 2010, p. 36).

Having considered the performance of the GCI for Colombia between 2001 and 2010, it is now important to analyze in a deeper way those factors that, according to the WEF, seriously undermine Colombia's competitiveness.

Table 5.3 shows how Colombia's score for the criteria "public institutions" is one of the most problematic ones. More concerning, this indicator has been constantly decreasing along the last three reports. While it is true that with the exception of Chile and Uruguay, all the Latin American economies do not fare well in this indicator, the poor record of Colombia is rather striking: for the years 2010–2011, Colombia was placed on rank 103 among 139 countries. Factors that make part of this index where ranks are especially worrisome have to do mainly with public institutions: the business costs of terrorism (the country occupies the last position in the world in this indicator, number 139, among 139 countries), organized crime, the burdens of government regulations, favoritism in decision of government officials, and the diversion of public funds are very poorly graded by

Table 5.3 The "12 pillars" of competitiveness: colombian performance, 2007–2010 (Own elaboration, based on data from the World Economic Forum's Global Competitiveness Reports for the years, 2007–2008, 2008–2009, and 2009–2010)

	Pillar	2007–2008 (131 countries)	2008–2009 (130 countries)	2009–2010 (133 countries)	2010–2011 (139 countries)
1	Public institutions	79	87	101	103
2	infrastructure	86	80	83	79
3	Macroeconomic stability	63	88	72	50
4	Health and primary education	64	67	72	79
5	Higher education and training	69	68	71	69
6	Goods market efficiency	85	82	88	103
7	Labor market efficiency	74	92	78	69
8	Financial market sophistication	72	81	78	79
9	Technological readiness	76	80	66	63
10	Market size	30	37	31	32
11	Business sophistication	65	64	60	61
12	Innovation	72	61	63	65

the WEF. On the contrary, the ranks for private institutions in criteria like the ethical behavior of firms or the efficacy of corporate boards get relatively good ranks and are among the best in the Americas.

The quality of the overall infrastructure is another criterion where Colombia gets bad scores, occupying position number 12 in Latin America and number 97 among the whole sample of 139 countries. The poor quality of roads, ports, and railroad infrastructure, have an important weight in that negative rank. Furthermore, in the field of education the country faces important challenges that have been highlighted by the WEF: while primary education quality has been relatively good evaluated, enrollment rates are among the lowest in the Americas (being only inferior in the Dominican Republic, Jamaica, and Paraguay). Tertiary enrollment rates are still insufficient, at levels of 35% in 2009–2010.

As stated before, the goods market efficiency index seeks to evaluate if a country is producing the "right mix" of products and services, considering their supply and demand conditions (Sala-i-Martin et al. 2010). It is related to ensuring a competitive playing field, guaranteeing the minimum obstacles to business activity. In the latest Global Competitiveness Report, from all the ranks obtained by Colombia in the so-called "efficiency-enhancers" criteria, it was precisely in the goods market efficiency pillar where the country gets the worst score. The prevalence of trade barriers (trade-weighted average tariff rate), the total tax rate –which is defined as a combination of profit tax, labor tax, contributions, and other taxes—(World Bank 2010b), the extent and effect of taxation, and the extent of market dominance are elements hindering the efficiency of the goods market in Colombia.

The Labor market efficiency indicator is aimed to capture how swiftly and efficiently are workers reallocated to their most efficient use in the economy. Moreover, it assesses if an appropriate workers incentive system exists in the country, and evaluates gender equality in the business environment. Problematic aspects identified by the WEF in Colombia are related to the relationship between pay and productivity, redundant costs (cost of advance notice requirements, severance payments, and penalties due when terminating a redundant worker, expressed in weekly wages), and the still rigid hiring and firing practices.

The Financial market development indicator evaluates if the country relies on a sound and well-functioning financial sector. The results associated to this pillar are rather mixed: at one side, Colombia gets a good score for the "soundness of banks" criterion, and a quite satisfactory one for the "availability of financial services" and "ease of access to loans" factors. On the contrary, the regulation of securities exchanges and the restriction on capital flows are criteria that the country has to especially pay attention to. The interest rate spread and the national savings rate have also been highlighted as factors that the country should improve.

One important input for the elaboration of the *Global Competitiveness Report* is the *Executive Opinion Survey*, where from a list of 15 factors, respondents are asked to select the five most problematic for doing business in their country. Corruption, tax rates, access to financing, the inefficient government bureaucracy, tax regulations, the inadequate supply of infrastructure, and the restrictive labor regulations were defined as the most problematic factors for doing business in Colombia within the latest edition of the report (Schwab 2010).

5.3.2 The Macroeconomic Context

The importance of the macroeconomic environment for the competitiveness performance of a country is related to the stability that is needed, as a framework for conducting business within an economy. As stated by Sala-i-Martin et al. (2010), it is not possible for an economy to grow in a sustainable without a stable macroeconomic environment: running fiscal deficits, uncontrolled inflation rates, and generally speaking, macroeconomic disarray, affect the economy in a serious manner (Sala-i-Martin et al. 2010, p. 5).

Loser (2008, p. 28) argues that the concept of competitiveness is normally associated to the exchange rate trends of an economy, in comparison with the relative price developments. This is, nevertheless, a very limited perspective that does not take into account other factors of great importance for competitiveness, like productivity, an increasing traded-goods sector, and a stronger balance of payments. Moreover, productivity gains and human capital development, rather than the exchange rate per se, should be considered as the principal factors underpinning competitiveness (Loser 2008).

The macroeconomic environment is also a crucial factor to be considered, when a country is pursuing the goal of export diversification. Brenton et al. (2009, p. 14) stress that in small economies vulnerable to volatile commodity prices or extreme changes in capital inflows, sudden exchange rates appreciations may negatively affect small volumes of exports, due to the so-called "Dutch disease" effects. The latter aspect has been frequently discussed in Colombia during the last years, as the economy has progressively increased its dependence on the export of petroleum and fuels: it is feared that very large revenues expected for the next years could cause a currency appreciation, negatively affecting the so-called "non-traditional exports."

Bebczuk and Berrettoni (2006, p. 8) argue that no unified theoretical framework exists to rely on, when it comes to uncover the macroeconomic drivers of export diversification. However, the return to a new export project depends on the ability of the firms to profitably produce the good, which in turn would respond to both micro and macroeconomic conditions.

With regard to Latin America and its macroeconomic performance, the region has been known for a number of problematic characteristics over the last quarter century: low average rates of growth, high terms of trade volatility, capital flows, fluctuating exchange rates, balance of payment crisis and unemployment are some examples (Loser 2008, p. 27). However, the situation has dramatically changed for many of the Latin American economies during the last years: inflation rates have progressively declined; real exchange rates have showed signs of stabilization, international trade has increased, positive rates of growth have been registered and poverty levels have been reduced (Loser 2008, p. 27). Moreover, the region's resilience with respect to the latest global economic downturn has been recognized: it has been suggested that sounder fiscal management, increased openness, and export diversification did contribute to that positive outcome (World Economic Forum 2010).

In what follows, the macroeconomic environment of Colombia will be assessed, comparing the country's performance to the one of other Latin American economies. The underlying purpose is analyzing to which extent Colombia's macroeconomic performance has favored or hindered the export competitiveness of the country.

On first instance, the *Macroeconomic Environment Index* of the *Global Competitiveness Report* is shown in Table 5.4. Within the 2010–2011 edition, the country that gets the best score in the ranking is Chile (position number 26 in the world), followed by Mexico (position 27), and Panama (position 29). Colombia comes in the fourth place at the regional level, in a higher position than other economies such as Argentina, Ecuador, Peru, and Paraguay, among others.

Table 5.4 Macroeconomic environment index, selected Latin American economies, 2010–2011 (Own elaboration, based on data from the World Economic Forum's Global Competitiveness Report 2010–2011)

Chile	26
Mexico	27
Panama	29
Colombia	**50**
Argentina	54
Ecuador	55
Peru	75
Paraguay	93
Uruguay	107
Brazil	111
Venezuela	113

The quality of Colombia's macroeconomic environment is highlighted in the last edition of the *Global Competitiveness Report*, and is considered as a one of the country's "competitive strengths," along with its market size, business sophistication, technological adoption and innovation enhancement capacities (Sala-i-Martin et al. 2010). Colombia's relatively good position in the macroeconomic environment index is largely explained by its performance on some of the sub-indexes that make part of the overall grade: the country fares good at a regional level in the government budget balance, national savings rate, and country credit rating indicators. In contrast, interest rate spreads, inflation—despite of the significant reduction accomplished during the last years–, and government debt are the sub-indexes where the country gets the lowest scores (World Economic Forum 2010). One first perspective of Colombia's performance is offered by the evolution of its GDP rate of growth for the period 1990–2009. As illustrated in Fig. 5.2, between 1990 and 1996–the first period of the liberalization of the economy– Colombia registered positive rates of growth. In some years, these rates of growth were of more than 5%. From a rate of 3.43% in 1997, a dramatic decrease took place in 1998, to a level of 0.57%. In 1999 the country experienced a severe economic recession, resulting in a contraction of − 4.2%. Different factors explain the economic crisis of the end of the 1990s, such as the currency appreciation, uncontrolled levels of public expenditure, speculative bubbles in the real estate and stock markets, and the sudden contraction of external funding (Kalmanovitz 2004). Moreover, an accelerated expansion of domestic demand, the intensification of the internal armed conflict, political uncertainty, worsening of the terms of trade and turmoil on the international financial markets were all factors that contributed to the grave economic crisis that hit the country at the end of the 1990s (WTO 2006).

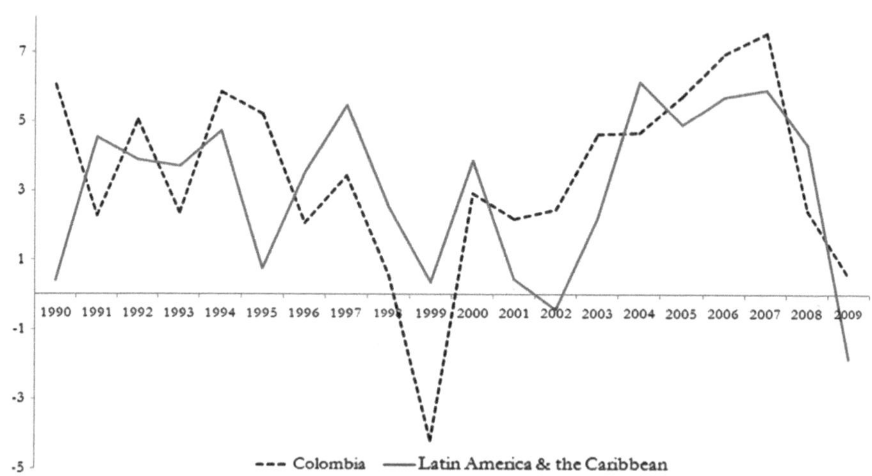

Fig. 5.2 GDP rates of growth (annual percentage), Latin America and the Caribbean and Colombia (Own elaboration, based on data from the World Development Indicators Database)

The economic situation took a positive turn in 2000 and between that year and 2003, positive—but low—rates of growth were registered. It is important to mention that the domestic security conditions at that moment (end of the 1990s, beginning of the 2000s) were extremely unstable and volatile. The Uribe administration, which took office in 2002, undertook important efforts aimed at restoring domestic security and security levels in the country. Very significant improvements in security levels led to an improved level of expectations both of investors and consumers (Kalmanovitz 2004). This was accompanied by a drop in unemployment rates, the growth of exports –especially since 2003—, and a substantial improvement in the terms of trade for some commodities (e.g. petroleum, coal, nickel, gold).

Economic growth has accelerated in Colombia in recent years, due to the increase of investment, the recovery of private consumption, and a favorable external context that has supported the expansion of foreign investment and exports (WTO 2006). For the period 2003–2007, the average rate of growth of Colombia was of 5.90%. This number lies above the average rate of growth for Latin America and the Caribbean within the same period of time, which amounted to 4.97%. Colombian rates of growth were of 4.61% in 2003, 4.66% in 2004, 5.72% in 2005, 6.94% in 2006, and an impressive peak of 7.55% in 2007. The global economic downturn affected the economy, but it can be observed that the country managed to register positive rates of growth even in 2008 and 2009.

In the same line of argumentation, some other developments are worth of commenting: according to the data provided by the World Bank's *World Development Indicators Database*, Colombia has recently performed well in terms of the annual percentage growth of goods and services: in the period 2006–2008, the country's foreign sales increased in levels of 8% in 2006, 11% in 2007, and 7% in 2008. These figures were remarkably higher to the ones registered by other Latin American economies, like Argentina, Brazil, Chile, and Peru. The manufactures exports (as a percentage of merchandise exports) behaved rather good too: after Mexico and Brazil, Colombia registered in the same period of time the highest share of manufactures exports. Whereas in 1990 manufactures exports accounted for 25% of the total merchandise exports, this value peaked to a level of 40% in the year 2007. However, a concerning trend has been developing since 2007: the share of manufactures exports declined to 32% in 2008, and a percentage of 30% was reported by the Colombian Ministry of Trade for 2009.

Furthermore, an increasing trend can be identified for commodities like petroleum and its derivatives and coal: whereas in 1990 fuel exports had a share of 37% of merchandise exports, this participation increased to 47% in 2008 (World Bank 2010). Policymakers, the private sector, and scholars alike have stressed the need to boost the share of manufactures and industrial exports, highlighting that these are the sectors that add the most value and placing special emphasis on the need for employment generation. The challenges are manifold: not only to increase supply, but also to diversify the basket of goods exported and the destination markets –highly concentrated in the United States and Venezuela (Portafolio 2010). This situation makes the country vulnerable to volatility, adverse terms-of-trade shocks, and changes in international demand. Another matter of concern is related to the fact that 91% of Colombian exports are sold just by 6% of the companies that sell abroad (Portafolio 2010). Furthermore, the high-technology exports (as a percentage of manufactured exports) had a share of just 3.75% in 2008, much lower to the ones of Mexico (19%), Brazil (12%), Argentina (9%), or Chile (6%) (World Bank 2010).

Another perspective of Colombia's performance can be obtained by analyzing the inflation and unemployment rates over the period 1990–2009. On first instance, it should be mentioned that Colombia did not experience episodes of hyperinflation or out-of-control inflation, as other Latin American economies did in 1990. In contrast to the rates registered by Peru (7,482%), Brazil (2,948%), Argentina (2,314%) or Uruguay, Colombia was with Mexico one of the countries to register the lowest rates of inflation (see Table 5.5).

In addition to that, it is important to mention that inflation rates in Colombia have progressively declined over the period of time analyzed. From record annual inflation rates of 29% and 30% in 1990 and 1991 respectively, by the middle of the 1990s, it went down to a level of 21%. Since 2000, one-digit inflation rates have been recorded (see Table 5.5). The IMF attributes this to the effective implementation of a new monetary policy strategy (WTO 2006). In the year 2009, the Colombian government accomplished an inflation annual rate of 4.20%. This rate is lower than the one recorded in Uruguay (7.10%), Argentina (6.27%), Mexico (5.30%), Ecuador (5.16%), and Brazil (4.89%). The IMF expects inflation rates in Colombia to remain within the target of 2–4% between 2009 and 2015 (IMF 2010). In contrast, the results obtained in terms of the annual unemployment rate in Colombia are rather mixed. As depicted in Fig. 5.3, a progressive decrease was recorded between 1990 and 1995: from a level of 10.20%, this number decreased to 8.40% in 1994—the lowest level over the period of time analyzed. In 1995, the unemployment rate initiates a path of constant increase, reaching a peak of 20.50% in 2000—right after the economic crisis that hit the country in 1998–1999. The trend has not been stable ever since: from a constant decrease between 2002 and 2005, unemployment rose again in 2006.

One worrisome trend that can be observed is related to the progressive increase of the unemployment rates in Colombia during the last 3 years. In 2009, Colombia exhibited the highest number among the economies included in Table 5.6. It should

Table 5.5 Inflation rates, selected Latin American countries, 1990–2009 (Own elaboration, based on data from the World Development Indicators Database)

	1990	1995	2000	2005	2009
Uruguay	112.53	42.25	4.76	4.70	7.10
Argentina	2,313.96	3.38	−0.94	9.64	6.27
Mexico	26.65	35.00	9.50	3.99	5.30
Ecuador	48.52	22.89	96.09	2.41	5.16
Brazil	2,947.73	66.01	7.04	6.87	4.89
Colombia	**29.15**	**20.89**	**9.22**	**5.05**	**4.20**
Peru	7,481.66	11.13	3.76	1.62	2.94

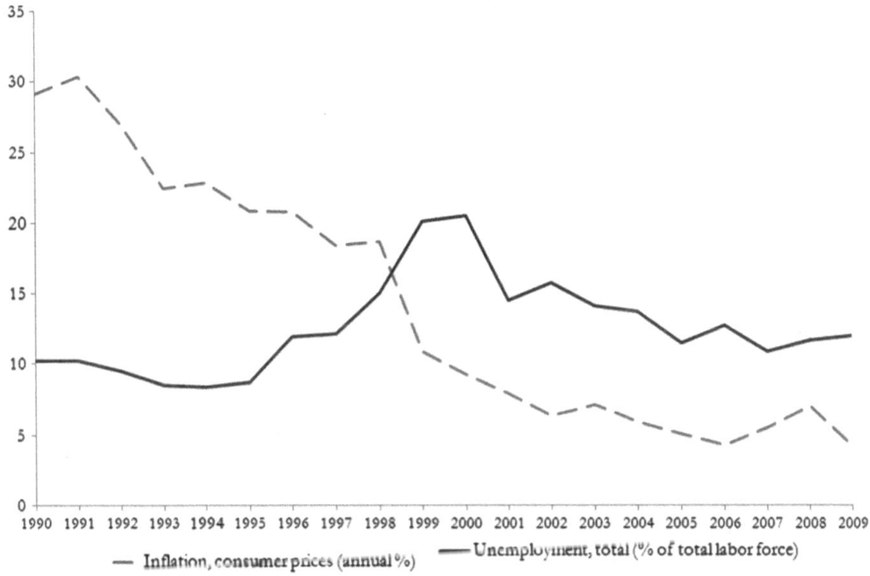

Fig. 5.3 Inflation and unemployment rates in Colombia, 1990–2009 (Own elaboration, based on data from the World Development Indicators Database)

Table 5.6 Total unemployment rates (percentage of total labor force), selected Latin American countries, 1990–2008 (Own elaboration, based on data from the World Development Indicators Database)

	1990	1995	2000	2005	2008
Colombia	**10.20**	**8.70**	**20.50**	**11.50**	**11.70**
Brazil	3.70	6.00	N/A	9.30	7.90
Chile	5.70	4.70	8.30	6.90	7.80
Uruguay	8.50	10.20	13.60	12.20	7.60
Argentina	7.30	18.80	15.00	10.60	7.25
Peru	8.60	7.10	7.40	8.70	N/A
Ecuador	6.10	6.90	9.00	7.90	6.90
Mexico	N/A	6.90	2.60	3.50	4.00

N/A Not Available

also be highlighted how all the economies—with the exception of Colombia, Chile, and Mexico—accomplished to reduce this indicator between 2005 and 2008.

Despite of the fact that the employment situation has improved in Colombia–compared to the situation in 2000–the unemployment rate has stabilized at high levels due to structural factors, such as high labor costs and an excess supply of low-skilled workers (WTO 2006). After the remarkable success of the Uribe administration in terms of domestic security stabilization, significant increases in the rate of economic growth, and important reductions of annual inflation rates, the new government of President Santos has pledged to place a special emphasis on the reduction of unemployment and poverty levels in the country.

As aforementioned, the concept of export competitiveness has also been closely linked to an economy's exchange rates. Loser (2008, p. 27) argues that competitiveness is many times linked to the real exchange rate, the movement in the exchange rate between a country and its trading partners, in comparison with the relative price developments

A first snapshot of Colombia's performance can be taken from the perspective of the real exchange rate. At the end of the 1990s, the important oil discoveries in the country were joined by a massive influx of foreign capitals, factors that decisively contributed to an appreciation of the currency. This was a phenomenon that badly hit the economy, especially the agricultural and manufacturing industries. At that time, analysts talked about the existence of a "Dutch disease" in Colombia, taking into account that a new export rent—petroleum– negatively affected the export of other type of "non-traditional" goods (Kalmanovitz 2004). In 1998, a very complicated juncture of economic recession, a massive outflow of capitals and a substantial reduction in domestic inflation played an important role on the sharp devaluation of the real exchange rate. Afterwards, between 2003 and 2004, a nominal appreciation of the exchange rate was due to the good performance of exports and the larger inflows of capitals (Kalmanovitz 2004).

Over the period 2003–2005, as well as in 2007–2008, an exchange rate appreciation is evident in Colombia, as can be observed in Tables 5.7 and 5.8. The real exchange rate index shows important decreases, offering evidence of a currency appreciation.

Moreover, the evolution of the Colombian Peso exchange rate with relation to the U.S. Dollar is depicted in Fig. 5.4.

Table 5.7 Colombian exchange rates, 1997–2005 (WTO, 2010)

Exchange rates	1997	1998	1999	2000	2001	2002	2003	2004	2005
Representative market rate (annual average: Col$/US$)	1,141	1,427	1,759	2,087	2,299	2,508	2,878	2,626	2,321
Exchange rate variation (December-December)[a]	28.7	19.2	21.5	18.9	2.8	25.0	−3.0	−14.0	−4.4
Real exchange rate index (total trade, December) (increase = depreciation)	94.2	98.3	108.4	118.5	118.4	132.7	131.5	113.6	104.2

[a]A minus sign denotes appreciation; a plus sign, depreciation

Table 5.8 Colombian exchange rates, 2006–2009 (WTO Trade Policy Review, 2010)

Exchange rates	2006	2007	2008	2009
Representative market rate (annual average: Col$/US$)	2,361	2,078	1,968	2,167
Exchange rate variation (December–December)[a]	1.7	−12.0	−5.3	10.1
Real exchange rate index (total trade, December)[b]	104.8	97.3	98.5	90.6

[a]A minus sign denotes appreciation; a plus sign, depreciation
[b](increase = depreciation)

Fig. 5.4 Colombian nominal exchange rate (pesos per U.S. dollar), End of Period, 1990–2009 (Own elaboration, based on data from the IMF's International Financial Statistics Database)

Right now, one of the most important concerns of Colombian policymakers is related to the possible currency appreciation and the associated "Dutch disease" effects that could derive from the increased petroleum exports. There is concern about the increased dependence of the economy on this commodity, as well as the possible effects that the volatility in oil receipts could have for the economy (IMF 2010). The gradual strengthening of the current account balance over the medium term—due to higher oil exports–, and the large investments in exploration, could lead to a further appreciation of the real exchange rate in the future (IMF 2010, p. 19).

Finally, some interesting observations can be made when the Colombian balance of payments is analyzed. A negative balance of trade in goods was recorded in 1997–1998, but since 1999 until 2006, and in 2008–2009, a surplus has been recorded. As stated within the 2006 WTO's *Trade Policy Review* of Colombia, this was initially due to the fall in imports in the context of the economic crisis that affected the economy at the end of the 1990s. Nevertheless, imports have strengthened from 2003 on, along with private investment (WTO 2006, p. 8). The surplus in the trade-in-goods balance of the last years may be explained by the increase of Colombian exports. On the contrary, the services balance has registered a deficit in 1997–2009, mainly because of the important deficit in the transport and financial services accounts (WTO 2006, p. 8).

Despite of the surplus in the balance of trade in goods, when it comes to the overall current account balance, it should be mentioned that Colombia has recorded a deficit since 2001. In 2009, Colombia was –after Brazil and Mexico—the country that registered the largest deficit, as depicted in Table 5.9. When this figure is taken

Table 5.9 Current account balance (billions U.S. dollars) (Own elaboration, based on data from the IMF's World Economic Outlook Database)

	2000	2005	2009
Argentina	−8,955	4,700	8,651
Venezuela	11,853	25,534	8,561
Chile	−0,898	1,449	3,506
Peru	−1,496	1,148	0,248
Panama	−0,689	−0,759	−0,012
Ecuador	0,842	0,356	−0,625
Colombia	**0,764**	**−1,890**	**−5,033**
Mexico	−18,685	−4,549	−5,238
Brazil	−24,225	13,985	−24,334

Table 5.10 Current account balance (% of GDP) (Own elaboration, based on data from the IMF's World Economic Outlook Database)

	2000	2005	2009
Argentina	−3,15	2,57	2,79
Venezuela	10,12	17,72	2,54
Chile	−1,19	1,23	2,17
Peru	−2,81	1,45	0,20
Panama	−5,93	−4,91	−0,05
Mexico	−2,97	−0,54	−0,60
Ecuador	5,28	0,96	−1,09
Brazil	−3,76	1,59	−1,55
Colombia	**0,81**	**−1,31**	**−1,85**

as a percentage of the GDP, Colombia's current account deficit is the largest among the economies included in Table 5.10.

5.3.3 *Productivity and Hourly Compensation Costs*

Labor productivity is defined as output per unit of labor input – persons engaged or hours worked (ILO 2010). The growth in labor productivity may be derived either from an increased efficiency in the use of labor, without more of other inputs, or because each worker works with more of the other inputs, such as physical capital, human capital or intermediate inputs (ILO 2010).

The great challenges in terms of productivity for the economic performance of the Latin American countries are addressed by Pagés (2010). The latter author states that despite of the economic and social advances of the region in the last 15 years (average annual rates of growth of 3.3%, an increase of 1.9% in the income per capita), the growth perspectives in Latin America still lag behind from the ones of other emerging economies. In a study conducted by the Inter-American Development Bank, it was founded that more than the levels of investment, the real "culprit" of the poor economic performance has been the low and sluggish productivity of these economies. The latter, rather than impediments to the accumulation of factors, is proposed as a better explanation for the low levels of income of the

Latin American economies in comparison with the developed economies. It was also found that productivity in Latin America amounts to nearly half of its potential, and it is not catching up the frontier of productivity (Pagés 2010).

The poor performance of the Latin American economies in terms of productivity has been traditionally associated to different factors, such as the very low productivity of the services sector (e.g. logistics, transport, communications), the very large number of small enterprises with very poor productivity records (which account for a large number of the Latin American economies), the proliferation of informal economic activities, the scarce levels of investment in research and development, and the inefficient use of the factors (Pagés 2010).

Compensation costs are considered to be indicators of competitiveness of manufactured goods in world trade (United States Department of Labor 2010). For the International Labor Office, the concept of compensation costs is associated to all those costs incurred by the employer in the employment of labor. It comprises the following items: remuneration for work performed, payments in respect of time paid for but not worked, bonuses and gratuities, the cost of food, drink and other payments in kind, cost of workers' housing borne by employers, employers' social security expenditures, cost to the employer for vocational training, welfare services and miscellaneous items, such as transport of workers, work clothes and recruitment, together with taxes regarded as labor cost (ILO 2010).

The definition of hourly compensation of the U.S. Bureau of Labor Statistics includes hourly direct pay, employer social insurance expenditures, and labor-related taxes. Different to the ILO's definition, this one does not include all labor items, but the ones not included account for no more than 2% of total labor costs (United States Department of Labor 2010). Table 5.11 depicts a comparison of the hourly compensation costs for some selected countries in the Americas. As can be observed, Colombia occupies the third position in South America in terms of the highest hourly compensation costs (after Argentina and Brazil). In the period of time analyzed, compensation costs in Colombia have been higher than the ones in other neighboring economies (such as Peru and Chile) (See Table 5.12).

Table 5.11 Hourly compensation costs in U.S. dollars in manufacturing, selected countries, 1996–2006 (United States Department of Labor, Bureau of Labor Statistics. Figures for Chile, Colombia and Peru: own calculations, based on data from LABORSTA, International Labour Office Database)

Country	1996	2000	2006
United States	22.11	24.63	29.98
Canada	19.01	18.68	29.21
Argentina	7.32	8.05	6.57
Brazil	7.12	4.30	5.98
Colombia	**4.23**	**4.44**	**4.65**
Peru	N/A	4.06	4.16
Chile	4.21	3.77	N/A
Mexico	2.06	3.04	3.71

N/A Information was not available.

Table 5.12 GDP per hour worked (constant 1990 US$ at PPP) (International Labor Organization's Key Indicators of the Labor Market Database (KILM), 2010)

	1990	1995	2000	2005	2008
United States	27	28	31	35	37
Canada	22	24	26	28	28
Argentina	9	12	13	14	16
Chile	10	13	13	14	14
Mexico	9	8	9	9	9
Colombia	**7**	**8**	**8**	**8**	**9**
Brazil	6	6	7	7	7
Peru	4	6	6	7	7

Table 5.13 GDP per hour worked, index (1990 = 100) (International Labour Organization's Key Indicators of the Labour Market Database (KILM), 2010)

	1990	1995	2000	2005	2008
Peru	100	142	145	167	167
Argentina	100	124	140	149	166
Chile	100	135	131	146	145
United States	100	106	118	132	139
Brazil	100	113	118	118	129
Canada	100	109	119	127	128
Colombia	**100**	**108**	**104**	**108**	**124**
Mexico	100	98	102	103	108

One perspective of the productivity of labor in South America can be obtained when considering the GDP per hour worked. For benchmark purposes, the U.S., Canada, and Mexico have been included in the analysis. On first instance, it can be noticed that Colombia's rank is below the ones of Argentina and Chile, but above the ones of Brazil and Peru.

Productivity can also be analyzed on the base of the GDP per hour index. Table 5.13 shows the indexes for some selected countries in South America. The U.S., Canada, and Mexico are included for benchmark purposes.

In Latin America, the record has been rather mixed in terms of productivity growth. When analyzing the periods 1995–2008 and 2000–2008, countries like Argentina, Colombia, Peru, and Chile have performed well. Brazil registered a slight increase in the growth rates, while Mexico's record remained unchanged. Between 2000 and 2008, Colombia registered the highest average annual productivity growth rate (See Table 5.14).

As stated by Daude and Fernández-Arias (2010) the use se of alternative measures of productivity may lead to erroneous conclusions. Increased productivity work does not indicate whether the improvement was derived from a higher educational level of force work, the accumulation of physical capital, or something else. Therefore, the preferred way to measure productivity is the total factor productivity (TFP). It is a comprehensive measure of the efficiency with which the economy can transform their accumulated factors of production in the final product, and takes into account a technological component. It will be increased as

Table 5.14 Labor productivity, average annual growth rates, selected South American countries, 1995–2008 (Labor Productivity Manuscript, International Labour Organization's Key Indicators of the Labour Market Database (KILM), 2010)

	1995–2008	2000–2008
Argentina	2.2	2.1
Brazil	1.0	1.1
Canada	1.2	0.9
Chile	0.6	1.3
Colombia	**1.1**	**2.3**
Mexico	0.7	0.7
Peru	1.2	1.8
United States	2.1	2.1

Table 5.15 Total factor productivity growth for selected Latin American countries (average annual% growth) (Loayza et al. (2004))

	1961–1970	1971–1980	1981–1990	1991–2000
Argentina	0.96	0.24	−2.43	3.05
Brazil	1.88	3.11	−1.43	0.41
Chile	1.24	1.09	1.62	2.81
Colombia	**1.77**	**1.68**	**0.02**	**0.29**
Mexico	1.66	1.25	−1.84	0.42
Paraguay	1.9	5.27	−0.5	−1.12
Peru	1.72	0.04	−3.42	1.55
Uruguay	0.79	1.75	−0.54	1.85
Venezuela	1.97	−2.64	−1.58	−0.18
Average	1.54	1.31	−1.12	0.94

the technological frontier expands and new ideas and technologies are adopted. But the efficiency of the markets, and of the "backbone" services providing them, also influences the TFP (Daude and Fernández Arias 2010, p. 32) (See Table 5.15).

The countries with the most notable performance in terms of TFP growth during the 1990s are Argentina, Chile, Peru, and Uruguay, all of which experienced TFP growth rates above 1% per year in average during this decade. For these countries, TFP growth in the 1990s was higher not only with respect to the 1980s but also the previous decade. A second group comprises countries were average productivity growth was still close to zero during the past decade. This group includes Brazil, Colombia, Mexico, and Venezuela (Loayza et al. 2004). It should be mentioned that the poor TFP records in Colombia of the 1990s came within a context of very unstable domestic security conditions in the country, macroeconomic instability and, later on, a serious economic crisis at the end of that decade.

As stated by Castro et al. (2006), in the second half of the 1990s the performance of Colombia in terms of economic growth was well below expectations, considering the structural reforms introduced at the beginning of that decade that were expected to have a positive impact. At this point, it should be mentioned that studies evaluating the effect of openness and economic integration on the dynamics of productivity levels at manufacturing firms have reported different results. In the case of Mexico, a process of reallocation of resources to more productive industrial activities took place. In Colombia, the opening and liberalization of the economy did not generate such an important reallocation of resources from non-competitive activities towards sectors with a larger comparative advantage as in Mexico (Castro et al. 2006).

Meléndez et al. (2003), cited in Castro et al. (2006), report that the productivity of the Colombian manufacturing sector stagnated and even fell in some industries between 1977 and 1999. Impediments associated to the entry and exit of firms and to the redeployment of labor, and the poor technological levels, are proposed by the authors as possible explanations for that phenomenon. Nevertheless, it is also argued that these findings were mixed and that productivity levels increased for the sectors that were the most exposed to international competition.

TFP levels in Latin America are very diverse among the Latin American economies. The divergence of productivity levels is also registered at the sectoral level (Pagés 2010). In a more recent study conducted by the Inter-American Development Bank for 18 countries, Colombia occupied position number 9 in the rank, after Chile, Costa Rica, The Dominican Republic, Argentina, Uruguay, El Salvador, Mexico, and Brazil (Daude and Fernández-Arias 2010).

Busso et al. (2010) conducts a study aimed to evaluate the productivity performance of Latin American firms and the allocation of resources in the region. Among the most important findings, the authors report that the productivity levels of the companies in the region show a large degree of divergence. Some big companies are very productive, while many small companies show very poor productivity records. They also find out that there is a strong linkage between productivity and size: the more productive firms tend to be larger. Furthermore, it is stated that besides the poor productivity performance, many Latin American companies do not use the labor and capital endowments in the most efficient way.

The productivity gap is especially pronounced in Colombia and Venezuela: in those two countries, the companies that are located in the 90th percentile of productivity show productivity levels that are 500% larger than the ones of companies located in the 10th percentile (Busso et al. 2010). In other Latin American economies, this gap is of approximately 300%. The same study reports large degrees of dispersion in the marginal returns to labor and capital, which could be interpreted as a measure of the inefficiency in the allocation of resources. When the dispersion of marginal products of labor and capital in different firms within a specific sector in some selected countries is conducted, it was founded that the dispersion was higher in Venezuela, Colombia, Uruguay, and Mexico (Busso et al. 2010, p. 96). Taking that into account, it is argued that significant potential gains in productivity could be accomplished by a better allocation of resources between companies.

5.3.4 The Logistics Performance Index

In the year 2007, the World Bank introduced for the very first time the so-called "Logistics Performance Index" (LPI), with the purpose of allowing countries to evaluate and benchmark its performance in the logistics field. The underlying motivation has been to help countries identify the challenges and opportunities they face in trade logistics performance (Arvis et al. 2007). This indicator, based on surveys conducted every 2 years to the private sector and specifically, to professionals related to the field of international freight logistics in 155 countries, was recently updated for the year 2010. It is a weighted average of the country scores in six different areas: efficiency of the clearance process by border control agencies, quality of trade and transport related infrastructure, ease of arranging competitively priced shipments, competence and quality of logistics services, ability to track and trace consignments, and timeliness of shipments in reaching their destination within the expected delivery time (World Bank 2010). The indicator takes into account the logistics environment both at the international and national level.

As stated by Arvis et al. (2007, p. 7)

> Improving logistics performance has become an important development policy objective in recent years because logistics have a major impact on economic activity. Evidence from the 2007 and 2010 LPIs indicates that, for countries at the same level of per capita income, those with the best logistics performance experience additional growth: 1% in gross domestic product and 2% in trade.

In the year 2010, Colombia was ranked 72th in the World Bank's Logistics Performance Index, below Brazil (rank of 41), Argentina (48), Chile (49), Mexico (50), Panama (51), Costa Rica (56), Dominican Republic (65), Peru (67), Honduras (70), and Ecuador (71). In 2007, first year that this indicator was produced, the country ranked 82.

Even though the latest World Bank report recognizes the advance of Colombia between 2007 and 2010 in terms of the implementation of different measures like an interagency single window, the approval of a national logistics action plan, and the establishment of a logistics observatory, still the performance of the country has a long way to go. Especially in the aspects related to infrastructure, international shipments, and the so-called "timeliness" criteria, Colombia needs to undertake important efforts.

The country's position, with respect to other economies in Latin America and the Caribbean, can be appreciated in Table 5.16.

Table 5.16 Logistics performance index, cross-country comparison for selected Latin American countries, 2010 (World Bank, The Logistics Performance Index and its indicators, 2010)

Country	LPI	Customs	Infrastructure	International shipments	Logistics competence	Tracking & tracing	Timeliness
Brazil	3.2	2.37	3.1	2.91	3.3	3.42	4.14
Dominican Republic	2.82	2.51	2.34	2.59	2.42	3.17	3.85
Honduras	2.78	2.39	2.31	2.67	2.57	2.83	3.83
Argentina	3.1	2.63	2.75	3.15	3.03	3.15	3.82
Chile	3.09	2.93	2.86	2.74	2.94	3.33	3.8
Costa Rica	2.91	2.61	2.56	2.64	2.8	3.13	3.71
Mexico	3.05	2.55	2.95	2.83	3.04	3.28	3.66
Ecuador	2.77	2.32	2.38	2.86	2.6	2.84	3.55
Colombia	2.77	2.5	2.59	2.54	2.75	2.75	3.52
Peru	2.8	2.5	2.66	2.75	2.61	2.89	3.38

As stated by the World Bank (2010, p. 3), a competitive network of global logistics is the backbone of international trade. Taking into account theoretical approaches and empirical studies linking better logistics and transport conditions with trade expansion, export diversification, and economic growth, it appears necessary for Colombia to reap the benefits associated with a more modern and advanced logistics sector, which may imply gains in terms of productivity for Colombian exporters.

5.3.5 Infrastructure

It is believed that high-quality infrastructure is part of the process of economic development, and that counting on state- of- the- art infrastructure can positively enhance economic efficiency (Harding 2009). On the contrary, inadequate infrastructure could be a serious impediment to export diversification (Harding 2009). Different empirical studies have tried to capture the possible influence of infrastructure on economic growth. Francois and Manchin (2007) state that infrastructure is a significant determinant not only of export levels, but also of the probability that exports will take place at all. Esfahani and Ramírez (2003) report a substantial contribution of infrastructure services to GDP. A positive effect of investment in transport and communication on economic growth is reported by Easterly and Rebelo (1993). Sánchez-Robles (1998, cited in Canning and Pedroni 1999) argues that there is a positive impact of road length and electricity generating capacity on subsequent economic growth. In the same line of argumentation, Sala-i-Martin et al. (2010) propose that a well developed infrastructure implies different positive effects for a country's economy, like the integration of the market at the domestic level, the connection to the international markets, and the decrease in the effect of distance between regions—lowering the costs for exporters.

In this line of argumentation, Fay and Morrison (2005, p. 5–6) propose that

> Infrastructure affects the investment climate in which firms operate. Good infrastructure contributes to making firms more productive hence more competitive internationally. At the macro-economic level, the performance of infrastructure stock influences total factor productivity (TFP), generally referred to as the only quantifiable measure of competitiveness (Krugman 1994). It is also critical to countries' ability to reap the benefit of trade liberalization as infrastructure is central to the "behind the border" agenda. This is clearly topical in LAC, as trade liberalization continues to advance in many countries.

Both the development and the quality of the infrastructure in Latin America and the Caribbean over the last two decades has lagged behind not just developed nations, but also other developing economies, like the East Asian Tigers or China (Sala-i-Martin et al. 2010). This is due to two different factors: on one hand, public investment in infrastructure was drastically reduced in many of the Latin American economies, as a result of the stabilization policies of the 1990s. On the other hand, the infrastructure investments financed through the so-called "public private partnerships" (PPI) was mainly concentrated in a few countries (Argentina, Brazil,

Table 5.17 Infrastructure indexes for selected Latin American countries, 2010–2011 (World Economic Forum's Global Competitiveness Report 2010–2011)

	Infrastructure		Transport infrastructure		Electricity and telephony infrastructure	
Country	Rank	Score	Rank	Score	Rank	Score
Chile	40	4.69	37	4.56	48	4.83
Panama	44	4.53	46	4.15	44	4.92
Uruguay	53	4.29	75	3.54	42	5.03
Brazil	62	4.02	67	3.76	65	4.28
Guatemala	66	3.9	76	3.48	64	4.31
Mexico	75	3.74	57	3.96	92	3.51
Argentina	77	3.63	89	3.17	73	4.08
Costa Rica	78	3.62	111	2.78	59	4.45
Colombia	**79**	**3.59**	**101**	**2.94**	**68**	**4.24**
Honduras	85	3.51	82	3.30	88	3.73
Peru	88	3.47	94	3.08	84	3.86

Chile, Colombia, Peru, and Mexico) and a few sectors (telecommunications, energy, and transport) (Sala-i-Martin et al. 2010).

A first glance at the situation of Colombia in infrastructure can be obtained by evaluating the position of the country according to the infrastructure index of the *Global Competitiveness Report.* Table 5.17 depicts the ranks and scores included within the 2010–2011 report, organized according to the integrated infrastructure index (columns 2 and 3). As can be observed, Chile is the leader in the integrated infrastructure ranks in Latin America, followed by Panama, Uruguay, and Brazil. Colombia, together with Costa Rica, Honduras, and Peru, occupy the last positions on the list. Within the infrastructure index, Colombia is especially poorly graded in terms of the quality of the port infrastructure, the quality of railroads infrastructure, and the quality of roads (Porter and Schwab 2008). The situation of the country seems much better, when it comes to electricity and telephony infrastructure.

5.3.5.1 Transport Infrastructure

In a study conducted in 2009 by Salin and Mello for the U.S. Department of Agriculture, it is found that transportation costs are greater obstacles to overcome for the American exporters in the Colombian market than tariffs. The authors report that if the U.S.-Colombia Free Trade Agreement is ratified, American exporters should take into account the lack of infrastructure in the country, well as the implicit security costs in some regions of the country, and that natural barriers (such as the mountain terrain of the Andes) impede direct connection between the most important industrial centers and the maritime ports (Salin and Mello 2009, p. 2).

Colombia is one of the countries in Latin America with the lowest standards in terms of roads infrastructure. To put things in perspective, one should consider that developed nations tend to have 100% of its roads fully paved. Developing Asian

Table 5.18 Roads paved (percentage of total roads), selected Latin American countries, 1990–1998 (Own elaboration, based on data from the World Development Indicators Database)

	1990	1995	1998
Mexico	35	31	34
Argentina	29	29	30
Panama	32	34	28
Latin America & Caribbean	22	22	23
Ecuador	13	13	19
Chile	14	16	18
Colombia	**12**	**9**	**14**
Peru	10	11	13
Brazil	10	9	10

economies vary in that figure: for instance, 100% in Hong Kong or Singapore, 71% in China, and 48% in Vietnam (World Bank 2010). Table 5.18 illustrates the situation for some selected Latin American countries (comparable statistic were just available for the period 1990–1998). It can be noticed that the percentage of paved roads is significantly much lower in Latin America, being Mexico (34%) and Argentina (30%) the countries with the largest share in the region. Colombia, with just 14%, is one of the countries positioned at the bottom of the list.

In a study conducted for the United Nations' Economic Commission for Latin America (ECLA, or CEPAL by its Spanish acronym), Fainboim and Rodríguez (2000) state that Colombia is one of the countries with the poorest road infrastructure in Latin America. Besides the very low percentage of roads paved, they report that the coverage of roads in the country is of approximately 100 m/km^2, below the Latin American average of 118 m/km^2. Moreover, while Costa Rica has 1,059 km of paved roads per million inhabitants, Argentina 858, and Mexico 820, Colombia only has 310 km.

Despite the great limitations in coverage and quality of road infrastructure, road transport is the most important mode of transportation in Colombia. In 1997, 95% of passenger transport and 92% of freight were moved by road (Fainboim and Rodríguez 2000, p. 24). The small share that remained was dominated by air transport. As far as the river transport is concerned, it is "virtually nonexistent." Furthermore, transport is concentrated on the network of roads that provide access to the main capital cities (Fainboim and Rodríguez 2000, p. 24).

Another indicator that demonstrates the inadequate standards of the road infrastructure in Colombia is the road density, defined as kilometer of road per squared kilometer. of land area. In the year 2004, the *World Development Indicators Database* reported that the United States had 70 km/km^2, Brazil 20, Mexico 18, and Colombia only 16.

Table 5.19 depicts the conditions of some selected Latin American countries in terms of railways. Argentina, Brazil, and Mexico are the countries with the largest number of total route-kilometers. In contrast, Colombia is the country with the scarcest coverage. Between 1990 and 2008, total route –kilometers decreased from 2,532 to 1,663. The latter fact is explained by the abandonment and the lack of investments in the railways infrastructure –currently, only 47% of the total track miles are in service through concessions granted by the government to private

Table 5.19 Rail lines (total route-kilometers), selected Latin American countries (Own elaboration, based on data from the World Development Indicators Database)

	1990	1995	2005	2008
Argentina	34,059	0	35,753	35,753
Brazil	4,916	4,651	29,314	29,817
Mexico	20,351	20,688	26,662	26,677
Chile	6,916	0	7,928	5,898
Peru	1,611	1,609	2,177	2,020
Colombia	**2,532**	**1,800**	**2,137**	**1,663**

Table 5.20 Air transport, freight (million ton-kilometers) (Own elaboration, based on data from the World Development Indicators Database)

	1990	1995	2000	2005	2006
Brazil	1,082	1,582	1,728	1,531	1,412
Colombia	**464**	**498**	**601**	**1,092**	**1,051**
Chile	419	775	1,312	1,054	1,028
Mexico	143	156	310	390	457
Argentina	214	177	297	133	125
Peru	26	35	54	139	112
Panama	3	9	22	37	36
Costa Rica	39	44	79	10	10
Ecuador	63	32	15	5	6

railroad companies (Salin and Mello 2009). A large number of track kilometers are inactive or abandoned (Salin and Mello 2009). Besides that, it should be mentioned that railways are concentrated in the Andean departments of the national territory (Cárdenas et al. 2005).

Finally, it is important to clarify that the railroad system in Colombia is mostly used for hauling just a few specific products, like coal, cement, steel, scrap iron, grains, and coffee (Cáceres et al. 2006).

In contrast, the airport infrastructure in Colombia is one of the most extensive ones in Latin America. Cárdenas et al. (2005) argue that the number of airports in Colombia suggests that there is a wide coverage at the national level. They also state that air transport in the country has functioned as sort of a substitute to road transport in many isolated areas, like the Amazons, where practically no roads exist. The assessment of the air transport freight (defined in million ton-kilometers), confirms the latter argument. From the group of countries included in Table 5.20, Colombia was after Brazil the second country to mobilize the largest amount of tons per kilometer. It can be observed that the value is much larger to the ones of Mexico, Argentina, Peru, Panama, Costa Rica, and Ecuador.

In terms of number of passengers carried, Colombia is also one of the most important countries from the group of economies included in Table 5.21. It comes in the third place, after Brazil and Mexico. This figures support the argument of Cárdenas et al. (2005) too, concerning the relatively good development of the air transport infrastructure in Colombia.

Table 5.21 Number of passengers carried by air transport, selected Latin American countries, 1990–2008 (Own elaboration, based on data from the World Development Indicators Database)

	1990	1995	2000	2005	2008
Brazil	19,149,600	20,196,100	31,287,784	37,661,733	58,763,225
Mexico	14,341,300	14,968,800	20,894,205	21,857,658	18,825,976
Colombia	**5,266,700**	**7,863,300**	**8,568,734**	**9,984,424**	**12,338,706**
Chile	1,363,600	3,197,200	5,174,876	5,939,020	8,021,939
Peru	1,816,200	2,508,300	1,595,268	4,332,223	6,184,410
Argentina	5,369,100	6,641,700	8,915,627	6,938,436	6,147,290
Ecuador	762,500	1,670,900	1,318,518	2,011,004	2,926,821
Costa Rica	467,000	870,400	877,833	953,217	1,023,665

Colombia's general maritime cargo trade has been administered by four public ports: Barranquilla, Cartagena, and Santa Marta on the Atlantic coast and Buenaventura on the Pacific coast (Gaviria 1998). In 1993, these ports were concessioned to societies established under company law, which are responsible for contracting with port operators for the use of facilities and supervising the facilities' use (Gaviria 1998). This movement towards the privatization of port services was planned as a strategy for improving the ports' productivity, and for decreasing the fees to users (Gaviria 1998). According to the Colombian National Planning Department, movement of goods trough ports has increased considerably: Between 2002 and 2008, the volume of tons transported by sea increased by 64% (Departamento Nacional de Planeación 2009, p. 4). Hence, there is a great necessity in the country of undertaking serious efforts to improve the ports infrastructure.

The Colombian government faces significant challenges with relation to the maritime ports infrastructure, ranging from the lack of highways connecting the terminals with the main economic centers, the necessity to increase the depth of some ports (for receiving larger vessels), and congestion at the ports (Salin and Mello 2009). Nevertheless, it should be mentioned that this is not the situation of all the maritime ports in the country: the Port of Cartagena (Caribbean Sea) is a natural port and one of the most efficient in Latin America (Salin and Mello 2009, p. 7).

On the other hand, it should be mentioned that the transport of goods by river in Colombia is very limited, and mainly focused on some specific products, like petroleum and coal (Ospina 2004). Cargo movement in the country's waterways has not increased in recent years, being shifted to the transport of goods by road (Cáceres et al. 2006). Even though the river is in many isolated regions the only mode of transport and that the passenger demand is important, the available infrastructure is extremely limited. There are, for instance, no passenger terminals.

Furthermore, currently no incentives are offered to attract private investment, which is badly needed for upgrading the fluvial infrastructure (Cáceres et al. 2006). In 2005, the inland waterway system moved less than 3% of Colombian general cargo and received less than 2% of the Colombian transportation budget allocation (Salin and Mello 2009). Additional problems associated to the transport of goods by river in Colombia have to do with the limited navigability, the lack of connections

Table 5.22 Quality of port infrastructure, WEF (1 = extremely underdeveloped to 7 = well developed and efficient by international standards) (Own elaboration, based on data from the World Development Indicators Database)

	2007	2008	2009
United States	5,81	5,87	5,67
Canada	5,71	5,78	5,61
Panama	5,65	5,71	5,54
Chile	4,85	4,94	5,36
Latin America & Caribbean	3,45	3,51	3,75
Mexico	3,26	3,31	3,67
Argentina	3,20	3,33	3,64
Ecuador	2,82	2,86	3,34
Colombia	**2,72**	**2,87**	**3,21**
Peru	2,36	2,34	2,66
Brazil	2,63	2,52	2,65

between the rivers and the main industrial centers, and the absence of investments in dredging and channel improvements (Salin and Mello 2009).

The Quality of Port Insfrastructure Index, another indicator included within the World Economic Forum's *Global Competitiveness Report*, offers another perspective of the current status of the port infrastructure in Colombia. As illustrated in Table 5.22, Colombian scores are among the lowest in Latin America, and are far behind the region's average grade.

5.3.5.2 Information and Communication Technologies (ICT) Infrastructure

As stated by Colecchia and Schreyer (2001), economic growth can be achieved based on an increased or improved use of labor and capital or through a rise in multi-factor productivity (MFP). Furthermore, it has been founded that another factor that enhanced growth in some economies is related to the information and communication technologies (ICT). Sala-i-Martin et al. (2010, p. 7) argue that ICT should be considered as the "general purpose technology" of our time, considering the critical spillovers to the other economic sectors and their role as industry-wide enabling infrastructure.Hence, ICT access and usage should be considered as crucial enablers for a country's general technological readiness. One of the "competitive strengths" that the 2010 *Global Competitiveness Report* identifies in Colombia has precisely to do with its technological readiness. The ability shown by the country to successfully adopt technology and enhance innovation is praised within the last edition of the report.

In terms of the so-called *Technological Readiness Index*, Colombia is one of the most competitive countries in Latin America, according to the World Economic Forum. Chile has always been the leader in the region, followed by Uruguay, and Brazil (see Table 5.23). Colombia is currently placed in the fourth position, surpassing other countries such as Mexico, Argentina, Peru, and Venezuela. Ecuador and Paraguay are the less competitive nations.

Table 5.23 Technological readiness index, selected Latin American countries, 2007–2011 (Own elaboration, based on data from the World Economic Forum's Global Competitiveness Report)

	2007–2008	2008–2009	2009–2010	2010–2011
Chile	42	42	42	45
Uruguay	67	64	51	50
Brazil	55	56	46	54
Colombia	76	80	66	63
Mexico	60	71	71	71
Argentina	78	76	68	73
Peru	80	87	77	74
Venezuela	79	86	91	90
Ecuador	100	104	102	107
Paraguay	128	119	103	116

Table 5.24 Internet users (per 100 people) (Own elaboration, based on data from the World Development Indicators Database)

	1998	1999	2000	2001	2002	2003	2004	2005	2006	2007	2008
United States	31	37	44	50	60	63	66	70	71	74	76
Canada	25	36	42	45	62	64	66	68	70	73	75
Colombia	**1**	**2**	**2**	**3**	**5**	**7**	**9**	**11**	**15**	**28**	**38**
Brazil	1	2	3	5	9	13	19	21	28	31	38
Chile	2	4	17	19	19	25	28	31	34	31	32
Ecuador	0	1	1	3	4	4	5	6	7	15	29
Argentina	1	3	7	10	11	12	16	18	21	26	28
Panama	3	4	7	7	9	10	11	11	17	22	27
Peru	1	2	3	8	9	11	12	17	23	25	25
Mexico	1	2	5	7	11	15	17	19	20	21	22

One of the indicators used in the *Global Competitiveness Report* to evaluate the countries in terms of their technological readiness is the number of internet users. An important trend observed in the country is the very significant increase in this indicator during the last years, especially since 2005. Colombia, together with Brazil, are the two economies in the region with the largest numbers of internet users per 100, as can be observed in Table 5.24.

Two other indicators that show the degree of orientation of the Colombian economy towards ICTs are the ones concerning the exports of the country of ICT goods and ICT services. As illustrated in Table 5.25, Mexico is by far the leader in the region: within 1998–2008, on average, 22% of its total goods exports have been comprised of ICT goods exports. Except for Mexico and Brazil—the latter country with a much lower share of 3,1% on average–, for all the selected Latin American economies shown in Table 5.25, less than 1% of their total goods exports are comprised of ICT goods exports. In Colombia, this share has on average amounted to 0, 2%.

In contrast, between 1998 and 2007, Colombia registered the largest share of ICT services exports as a share of the total services exports: 8,6% on average.

Table 5.25 ICT goods exports (% of total goods exports) (Own elaboration, based on data from the World Development Indicators Database)

	1998	1999	2000	2001	2002	2003	2004	2005	2006	2007	2008
Mexico	21,0	22,3	23,0	24,0	22,6	21,8	22,0	20,5	21,4	19,6	20,9
Brazil	2,3	3,1	4,6	4,5	4,0	3,2	2,4	3,4	3,2	2,0	1,8
Argentina	0,5	0,6	0,7	0,8	0,7	0,4	0,5	0,5	0,6	0,6	0,5
Ecuador	0,0	0,1	0,0	0,0	0,1	0,1	0,1	0,2	0,4	0,3	0,2
Colombia	**0,1**	**0,1**	**0,2**	**0,2**	**0,3**	**0,3**	**0,4**	**0,3**	**0,3**	**0,2**	**0,2**
Chile	0,2	0,2	0,2	0,2	0,2	0,2	0,1	0,1	0,1	0,1	0,2
Peru	0,1	0,2	0,4	0,2	0,2	0,1	0,2	0,2	0,1	0,1	0,1
Panama	0,0	0,0	0,0	0,1	0,5	0,1	0,2	0,1	0,0	0,0	0,0

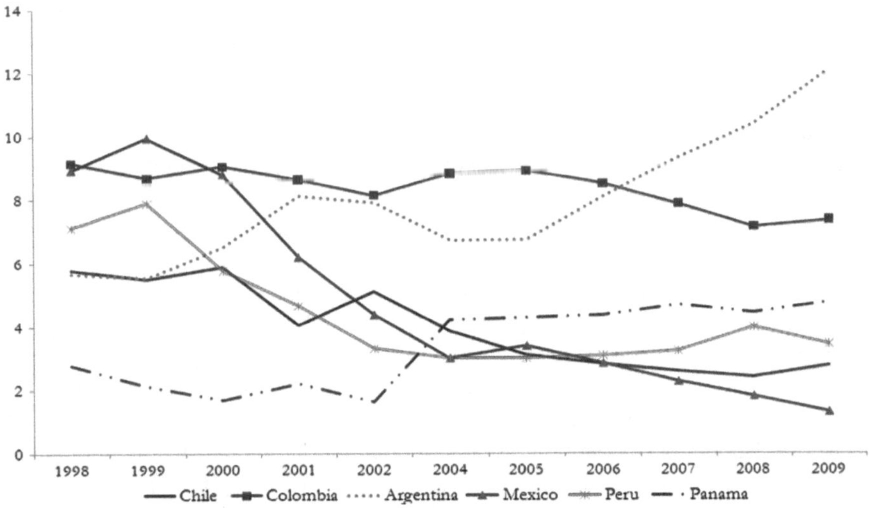

Fig. 5.5 ICT service exports (percentage of service exports, balance of payments) (Own elaboration, based on data from the World Development Indicators Database)

In second place came Argentina, with a share –on average—of 7,1%, and then Mexico and Chile (5,3% and 4,3% respectively). These trends can be observed in Fig. 5.5.

5.3.6 Technology Absorption, Research, and Development

Technology is a factor of paramount importance for determining a country's competitiveness in the global economy (Knight and Marques 2008). As stated by De Ferranti et al. (2003, p. 1),

> Over the last 50 years, the world has increasingly become divided into two clubs—those of the rich and poor countries. What is most striking is that the increasing bimodal distribution of income is due not to concentration of the factors of production, such as capital, but rather

of knowledge. The North has continued to generate new technologies that statistical studies suggest drive at least half of economic growth, while most of the South has been unable to take full advantage of them. Latin America for the most part finds itself in the less desirable club.

The trend is of special concern since the newly industrialized countries of Asia (NICs)—as well as other countries, such as Finland, that are closer to the Latin American and Caribbean countries in resource endowments—were able to achieve dramatic technology-driven increases in living standards across the same period.

Latin American nations, for which time series data is available, have not made significant progress in closing the technology gap that separates them from the world's technological leaders (Marques and Oliveira 2006). The latter authors place special emphasis on three important aspects concerning technological change: first of all, it is an integrated process related to the innovative behavior and the accumulation of technological capabilities in firms. Secondly, it derives from the capability of firms both to manage and generate innovation, as well as to diffuse technological knowledge (Freeman 1987, cited in Knight and Marques 2008). To develop that capability, the interaction with other firms, research institutions, universities, and funding institutions is required. Thirdly, the quantity and quality of technological development largely stems from government policies, which have a great influence. Besides these mechanisms, the specific endowments of an economy and the environment which serves as its framework may also exert a great influence on the industrial development of a nation. Indicators like the technological readiness index or the innovation index contained within the *Global Competitiveness Index*, as mentioned by Knight and Marques (2008), point out to the evident technological gap between Latin America and the developed nations.

For instance, in the 2010–2011 *Global Competitiveness Report* Panama and Chile are the best positioned countries in the region, in terms of the technological readiness index, at places 41 and 45 respectively. Even though the ranks of other countries such as Uruguay, Costa Rica, Brazil and Colombia are not bad, still the region lags far behind the developed nations and the developing Asian economies.

On the other hand, the *Networked Readiness Index* (NRI), developed jointly by the *Institut Européen d'Administration des Affaires* (INSEAD) and the WEF aims to capture the economies' preparedness to leverage ICT advances for increased competitiveness and development (Dutta and Mia 2010). It aims to measure the degree to which a national environment contributes to ICT development and diffusion, the extent to which the main stakeholders—individuals, business sector, and the government—are prepared to use ICT, and the actual use of ICT by these stakeholders (Dutta and Mia 2010). It is based on 68 variables, combining both hard data and the results of the World Economic Forum's *Executive Opinion's Survey*.

The performance of Latin America countries is relatively varied with respect to the NRI. Only Chile and Costa Rica are placed among the "top 50" performers. Following these two leaders, a first tier of economies that are relatively well placed for the region's standards are Uruguay, Panama, Colombia, Brazil, and Mexico. The second tier of nations is composed by Argentina, Peru, Paraguay, Ecuador, and Venezuela, which lag behind, as illustrated in Fig. 5.6.

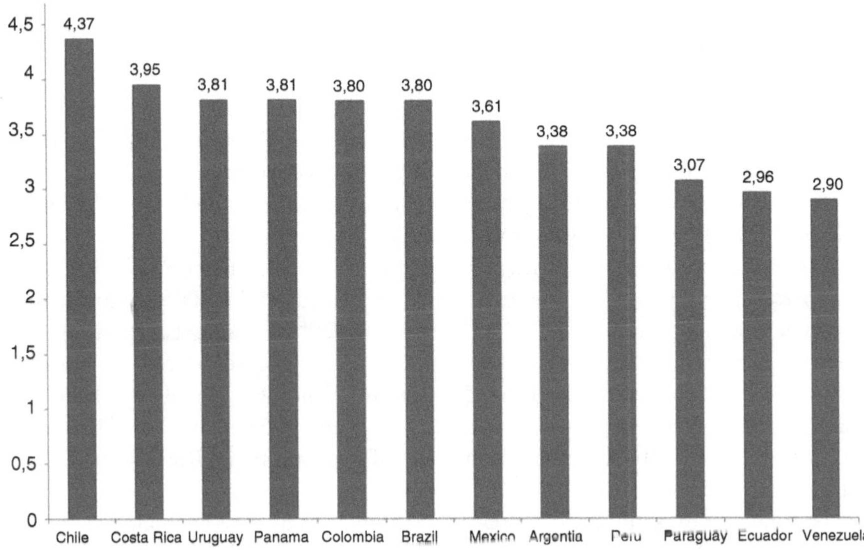

Fig. 5.6 Networked readiness index (scores), 2009–2010, selected Latin American countries (Own elaboration, based on data from the Global Information Technology Report, 2010–2011)

Table 5.26 Regional totals for research and development expenditure, 2002 and 2007 (UNESCO (Institute for Statistics) and the World Bank's World Development Indicators Database)

	% World		% of GDP	
	2002	2007	2002	2007
World	100.0	100.0	1.7	1.7
Developed countries	82.9	75.9	2.2	2.3
Developing countries	17.0	23.9	0.8	1.0
Less-developed countries	0.1	0.1	0.2	0.2
Regions				
Americas	40.4	37.6	2.1	2.1
North America	37.8	34.7	2.6	2.6
Latin America and the Caribbean	**2.6**	**2.9**	**0.6**	**0.6**
Europe	30.3	27.3	1.7	1.6
Africa	0.9	0.9	0.4	0.4
Asia	27.1	32.7	1.5	1.6
Oceania	1.4	1.6	1.7	2.1

In Table 5.26, a comparison of the research and development expenditures for different regions in the world is illustrated, for the years 2002 and 2007. The Americas contributed with a share of 37.6% of the global R&D expenditure in 2007: 34.7% from North America, and just 2.9% from the Latin American and Caribbean. This is a strikingly small figure that pales in comparison to the ones of North America, Asia, and Europe. After Africa, Latin America and the Caribbean is the region with the smallest GDP contribution to R&D (0.6%). These figures support the argument of De Ferranti et al. (2003, p. 7), who argues that LAC countries have not given innovation, science, and technology a central role in their development strategies until very recently.

Another indicator of the technological gap in LAC can be obtained when assessing the percentage of researchers. As depicted in Table 5.27, the Americas contributed with a share of 25.8% to the total number of world researchers in 2007: 22.2% of that contribution proceeded from North America (United States, Canada), and just 3.6% of the share came from the LAC.

Colombia is one of the countries at the bottom of the list, when R&D expenditure as a percentage of GDP is analyzed at a global scale. In 2005, high-income countries invested, on average, 2.35% of its GDP in R&D. Latin American countries invested 0.66% of its GDP, while Colombia registered a share of 0.18%. As can be observed in Table 5.28 below, Colombia has always been the country with the lowest levels of investment, between 1996 and 2007. Furthermore, the country has actually decreased the amount of expenditure on R&D in the period of time analyzed.

The trends of expenditure in R&D in Colombia can also be evaluated based on the number of researchers per million inhabitants. The expenditure on R&D, as well as the quality of scientific output, is strongly associated within any country to a

Table 5.27 Percentage of researchers per region, 2002 and 2007 (UNESCO (Institute for Statistics) and the World Bank's World Development Indicators Database)

	% of World researchers	
	2002	2007
World	100.0%	100.0%
Developed countries	69.7%	61.6%
Developing countries (excl. less developed countries)	29.8%	37.9%
Less-developed countries	0.5%	0.5%
Americas	28.1%	25.8%
North America	25.2%	22.2%
Latin America and the Caribbean	**2.9%**	**3.6%**
Europe	31.9%	28.4%
Africa	2.3%	2.3%
Asia	35.7%	41.4%
Oceania	2.1%	2.1%

Table 5.28 Research and development expenditure as a percentage of GDP, selected Latin American countries (UNESCO (Institute for Statistics) and the World Bank's World Development Indicators Database)

	1996	2000	2004	2007
Argentina	0.42	0.44	0.44	0.51
Brazil	0.72	1.02	0.90	1.10
Chile	0.53	0.53	0.68	N/A
Colombia	**0.30**	**0.12**	**0.16**	**0.16**
Cuba	0.38	0.45	0.56	0.44
Mexico	0.31	0.37	0.40	0.37
Panama	0.33	0.38	0.24	0.20

N/A information not available

Table 5.29 Researchers per million inhabitants, selected Latin American countries (UNESCO (Institute for Statistics) and the World Bank's World Development Indicators Database)

	1998	2002	2006	2007
Argentina	704	692	896	980
Brazil	N/A	401	620	657
Chile	402	440	N/A	N/A
Mexico	216	305	341	353
Venezuela	49	70	146	163
Panama	162	97	N/A	144
Colombia	**80**	**126**	**142**	**126**

N/A information not available

well-trained group of scientists (ESCAP 2009). In 2005, Singapore had 5,575 researchers per million inhabitants, the United States 4,584, and Canada 4,156 (World Bank 2010). In the case of the selected countries included in Table 5.29 the one with the largest number has traditionally been Argentina, followed by Brazil, Mexico, Venezuela, and Panama. Colombia registered an important increase between 1998 and 2002, but the trend has remained stable ever since. Colombia occupies the last position of the list for the year 2007, as can be observed below.

Tiffin and Bortagaray (2008) argue that R&D investment in Latin America is very low, compared to the levels of developed nations. Based on a time series analysis of the evolution of publications and patents over the period 1986–2002, they report to different trends: concerning publications, despite of the still low percentage of the Latin American publications within the total number of publications, there has been a constant and rapid increase since the last decade. On the contrary, they report that Latin American-held US patents have increased at a much slower rate than publications (Tiffin and Bortagaray 2008, p. 122). The latter fact is considered by the authors as a concerning phenomenon, since this figures imply that much of the research knowledge is not oriented to product development.

The innovation potential of Colombia can also be assessed taking into account the evolution of the patent applications, based on the statistics provided by the World Intellectual Property Organization (WIPO). Figure 5.7 illustrates the trends of six Latin American countries, including Colombia. First, it is important to notice that Brazil has traditionally been, by far, the leading country in terms of innovation: in 2000, Brazilians registered 3,660 patents and in 2005, that number peaked to 4,708. Nevertheless, a very significant decrease can be observed between 2005 and 2008. Mexico and Chile are the second and third most important innovators, registering a positive trend of growth in the number of patent applications.

The situation in Argentina remains practically stable. Panama, while still not approaching the numbers of the other economies, increased its number of applications from 19 in 2000 to 106 in 2008. On the contrary, patent applications by Colombians decreased from 79 in 2000 to 68 in 2008. Furthermore, it should be stressed that Colombia was the worst performer in 2008. Mexico took the lead with 1,178 patent applications, closely followed by Brazil with 1,173. Chileans

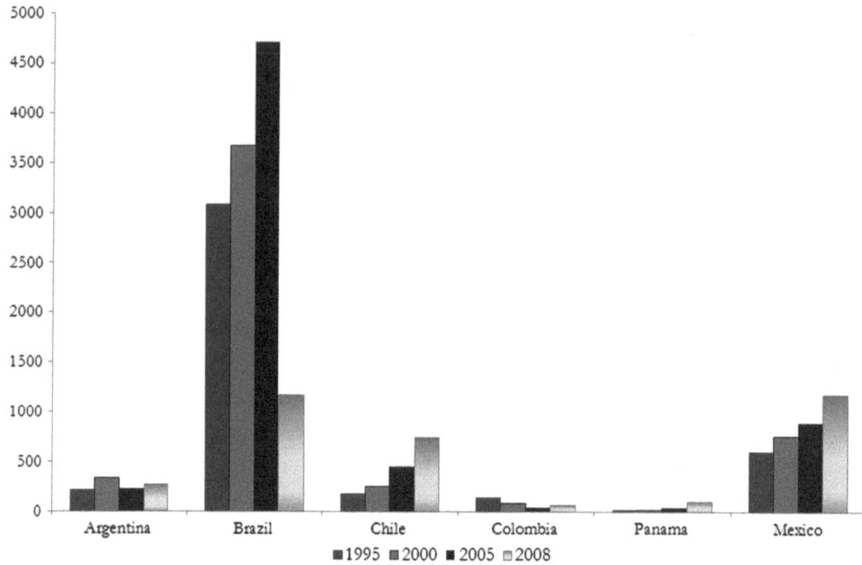

Fig. 5.7 Patent applications by country of origin, 1995–2008 (Own elaboration, based on data from the World Intellectual Property Organization (WIPO) Statistics Database)

registered 743 applications, Argentineans 269, Panamanians 106, and Colombians only 68.

5.3.7 Human Capital: Education Attainment Levels and Quality

It has been suggested that one of the factors of paramount importance for an economy to be competitive is related to not just to the education attainment levels, but to the quality of its education as well. In that line of argumentation, Puryear and Ortega (2008, p. 45) emphasize that good education enhances workers' skills, promotes growth, reduces poverty, and provides an important foundation for the institutions and good governance that are needed.

Sala-i-Martin et al. (2010, p. 5) state that in addition to health, the quantity and quality of basic education received by a country's population exerts an impact on the efficiency of its workers. Individuals with little or inadequate formal education will not be able to adapt to more advanced production processes and techniques. In addition to this, it has been proposed that for those economies that want move up the value chain and produce sophisticated, value-added goods and services, quality higher education and training is of the utmost importance. Within the *Global Competitiveness Report*, the so-called "fifth pillar of competitiveness"—higher education and training—deals both with enrollment rates and the quality of the secondary and tertiary education (Sala-i-Martin et al. 2010, p. 5).

As stated by Barro (1992, p. 1), different theoretical models of economic growth, like those of Nelson and Phelps (1966); Lucas (1988); Becker et al. (1990); Rebelo (1991); and Mulligan and Sala-i-Martin (1992), have stressed the role of human capital in the form of educational attainment. Furthermore, empirical studies have provided evidence in favor of a positive linkage between human capital and growth. Barro (1992, p. 15) reports that countries starting with a higher level of educational attainment grow faster. The effects would be related to the positive effect of human capital on physical investment, the negative effect of human capital on fertility, and an additional positive effect on growth for given values of investment and fertility (Barro 1992, p. 15).

Mankiw et al. (1992) suggest that growth is enhanced by investing in human capital. Firms investing in capital, but also employing educated, healthy and skilled workers, will count on productive labor, and capital and technology will be used in a more efficient manner (ESCAP 2001). Mattoo (2009, p. 164) argues that some services sectors, like business services, banking, and telecommunications, are more skill intensive than most goods production. Skill intensity is defined by the author as the share of the total workforce that has a tertiary education. Hence, human capital is a critical source of comparative advantage for the export of this kind of services.

Puryear and Ortega (2008) report that in Latin American countries, education participation levels have increased during the last years: more children attend school and stay longer, contributing to an increasingly educated labor force. Moreover, most of the national governments have taken measures aimed to establish national education standards, and to introduce national testing systems. Nevertheless, student learning in the region "remains low and inadequate for the needs of modern societies" (Puryear and Ortega 2008, p. 46). Despite of the significant progress in enrollment rates and years of schooling for children, Latin America lags behind other developing regions, like East Asia and Eastern Europe (Puryear and Ortega 2008). The average worker in Latin America attains far less than a complete high school education (Puryear and Ortega 2008, p. 47).

In their study conducted for the World Bank, De Ferranti et al. (2003) report some staggering figures concerning education in Latin America. While it is recognized that some positive developments have taken place over the last two decades, such as an increase in the average years of schooling or the enrollment rates at the primary level, the same cannot be affirmed for education at the secondary and tertiary levels. The authors report an overall deficit of approximately 20% points in net secondary enrollment and 10% points in gross tertiary enrollment given its average income level. On the contrary, East Asia has surpluses of more than 17% and 5% points respectively (De Ferranti et al. 2003, p. 3). The problem of education in Latin America is not just a problem of enrollment rates, but also, of quality standards, inefficient expenditure on education, and inequality to its access (Puryear and Ortega 2008). Sánchez Páramo and Schady (2003b) state that many Latin American countries show large education deficits, and a highly inequitable distribution of educational attainment.

A first snapshot of Colombia's performance in human capital at the regional level may be obtained looking at the *Global Competitiveness Report's* Health and

Table 5.30 Health and primary education index: selected Latin American countries, 2010–2011 (Own elaboration, based on data from the Global Competitiveness Report 2010–2011)

	Health and primary education (fourth pillar)	Primary education enrollment rates (sub-index)	Higher education and training (fifth pillar)
Costa Rica	22	1	43
Uruguay	47	35	40
Argentina	60	22	55
Mexico	70	29	79
Chile	71	65	45
Ecuador	75	43	92
Panama	76	26	82
Colombia	**79**	**92**	**69**
Venezuela	86	91	68
Brazil	87	68	58
Peru	92	64	76

Primary Education Index, which has been defined as one of the *12 Pillars of Competitiveness*. Colombia is placed in position number 8 among 11 economies in the region. Within this overall index, one of the sub-indexes that plays an important role for Colombia's position in the ranking is associated to the score that the country gets for primary education enrollment rates: among the selected countries, Colombia occupies the last position, as depicted in Table 5.30.

Interestingly, Colombia's position slightly improves concerning the fifth pillar of competitiveness, namely, the *Higher Education and Training Index*, where Colombia is placed at number 7 among the same number of countries.

Different indicators may be analyzed at the moment of evaluating the performance of Colombia in terms of education at the regional level. On first instance, the literacy rates can be assessed. According to the UNESCO Data Center's Statistics for the year 2008, the literacy rate of Colombia was of 93.4%. While the figure may appear optimistic, it should be noted that this figure is below the rates of Chile (98.6%), Uruguay (98.2%), Argentina (97.7%), Costa Rica (96%) and Panama (93.5).

At the primary level, Colombia is placed at the ninth position in Latin America: while in Panama or Mexico (at the top of the list), the net enrollment rate is of 98%, in Colombia it is of 90%, lower than in Honduras (97%) Guatemala (95%), Peru (94%), Brazil (94%), El Salvador (94%), and Nicaragua (92%).

At the secondary level, Colombia's enrollment rate (71%) is the fourth in the region, after Brazil (82%), Peru (75%), and Mexico (72%). The World Bank praises the gains that have been accomplished in secondary enrollment and completion rates: between 1991 and 2006, this rate nearly doubled and secondary completion increased by 67% between 1985 and 2005. Nevertheless, serious problems with retention levels at the higher grades persist, and although many students advance to secondary school, the graduation rate is considered to be low (World Bank 2008, p. 2).

In 2010, 35% of the Colombian population of tertiary age was effectively enrolled. Hence, Colombia was placed in the ranking of the *Global Competitiveness*

Report after Venezuela (79%) Argentina (68%), Uruguay (64%), Chile (52%), Panama (45%), Ecuador (42%), and Bolivia (38%). It should also be mentioned that there is a significant inequality in Colombia in terms of enrollment and completion rates: on average, poorer departments show lower enrollment rates than do wealthier departments, as well as a large urban-rural gap (World Bank 2006, cited in World Bank 2008). While the country has made significant progress in the tertiary age enrollment rates (from 23% in 1999 to 35% in 2008), this participation is still very low, both at the global and regional level.

Table 5.31 shows the evolution of another indicator, namely, the total public spending on education, as a percentage of the GDP. For the year 2006 (latest year for which comparable statistics are available), Colombia was the fifth country among the ones included in table in terms of the total public spending on education. It should also be observed that the share decreased between 2002 and 2006.

In the year 2006, the Colombian expenditure per student in primary education, as a percentage of the GDP per capita, was of 13%. While this percentage is inferior to the one registered in Mexico and Argentina, Table 5.32 shows that it was larger than the figure exhibited in Latin America on average.

In the same period of time –for which comparable statistics are available— Colombia's expenditure per student at the secondary level, as a percentage of its GDP per capita, was of 10,9%. This figure lies above the Latin American and Caribbean percentage. Nevertheless, the contribution has been decreasing since 2004 (See Table 5.33).

In addition to enrollment rates and public expenditure levels, one factor of the utmost importance for assessing Colombia's educational standards is the quality of the education. In 2006, the country participated for the very first time in the *Program for International Student Assessment* (PISA), with five other Latin American

Table 5.31 Total public spending on education (percentage of GDP) (Own elaboration, based on data from the World Development Indicators Database)

	2002	2004	2006
Brazil	3.78	4.01	4.95
Mexico	5.30	4.87	4.83
Costa Rica	5.07	4.89	4.65
Argentina	4.02	3.78	4.51
Colombia	**4.50**	**4.20**	**3.90**
Chile	4.23	3.67	3.19
Peru	2.97	2.83	2.55

Table 5.32 Expenditure per student, primary (% of GDP per capita) (Own elaboration, based on data from the UNESCO Data Center)

	2004	2005	2006
Mexico	13,4	13,8	13,4
Argentina	11,3	12,0	13,2
Colombia	**16,3**	**15,6**	**13,0**
Chile	12,7	12,0	11,1
Latin America & Caribbean (Average)	11,3	12,0	11,0
Peru	7,0	6,6	7,2

Table 5.33 Expenditure per student, secondary (% of GDP per capita) (Own elaboration, based on data from the UNESCO Data Center)

	2004	2005	2006
Argentina	15,7	19,6	20,3
Mexico	14,1	14,8	13,8
Chile	14,1	13,2	12,4
Colombia	**15,7**	**14,6**	**10,9**
Latin America & Caribbean	13,6	13,1	10,7
Peru	9,3	8,8	9,2

Table 5.34 Expenditure per student, tertiary (% of GDP per capita) (Own elaboration, based on data from the UNESCO Data Center)

	2004	2005	2006
Mexico	37,2	37,9	35,4
United States	23,5	23,4	25,4
Colombia	21,2	19,6	18,8
Chile	15,4	11,6	11,7
Peru	12,1	9,0	10,9

countries: Argentina, Brazil, Chile, Mexico, and Uruguay. Colombian students scored lower on reading, mathematics, and science than most countries in the Pisa 2006 Assessment. Nevertheless, it should be observed that the other countries in the region also scored lower than most countries in the sample. Colombia's performance among lower middle-income countries was found to be roughly average in reading, but it fell below average in mathematics and science. Besides that, the country's performance in mathematics and to a lesser extent in science fell short of the expected performance in those subjects based on its per capita GDP (World Bank 2008, p. 46).

From a regional perspective, it was concluded that Colombia performed roughly average in reading and below average in mathematics and science (World Bank 2008). Moreover, Colombia and Mexico exhibited high equity and low quality in their education systems (World Bank 2008). Chile fell roughly at the international average for equity, whereas it scored higher than most countries regionally on quality (World Bank 2008).

5.3.8 Access to Finance

The "eight pillar of competitiveness" is measured by the so-called *Financial Market Development Index.* Within this pillar, the WEF assesses the functioning and quality of an economy's financial sector. Sala-i-Martin et al. (2010, p. 7) define an efficient financial sector as one that allocates the resources to their most productive uses. Having the support of sophisticated financial markets, as well as guaranteeing the necessary risk management, is also evaluated (Sala-i-Martin et al. 2010, p. 7). Smith et al. (2008, p. 79) stress that "resilient, and far-reaching banking systems go in hand with higher growth and income equality." Hence, banks should be understood "as institutions with the function of converting income and savings into investment and productivity gains" (Smith et al. 2008, p. 79). The performance of a country's financial system—composed of banks, stocks and bond markets, and regulating agencies—is considered as one the factors of the greatest importance for an efficient functioning of the economy (Weil 2009).

The *Financial Market Development Index* is comprised of a set of sub-indexes, measuring both the efficiency and trustworthiness of a country's financial sector. The criteria that are evaluated in the first category have to do with the availability and affordability of financial services, the financing through the local equity market, the ease of access to loans, venture capital availability, and the restrictions imposed to capital flows (WEF 2010). The confidence in the system is supposed to be captured by the soundness of banks, the regulation of securities exchanges, and the legal rights index (WEF 2010). At this point, it should be highlighted that all the scores that make part of this indicator are based on the results of the *Executive Opinion Survey* that the WEF conducts. Only one indicator, namely the one concerning the "legal rights index," is derived from so-called "hard data." Panama and Chile are the region's leaders in terms of financial development, followed by Peru and Brazil: the well-developed financial markets of these four countries are praised by the World Economic Forum (WEF 2010). On the contrary, Venezuela and Argentina are graded with the lowest scores in terms of financial development.

With regard to the *Financial Market Development Index*, Colombia occupies an intermediate position in Latin America, as shown in Table 5.35. The regulation of securities exchanges and the restriction on capital flows are the sub-indexes where Colombia gets the lowest scores. Furthermore, it is interesting to mention that within the *Executive Opinion Survey*, from a list of the 15 most problematic factors for doing business, access to finance came in the third position, after corruption and tax rates (WEF 2010). On the other hand, the soundness of banks and the availability of financial services are two factors that are well graded within the survey.

Another study conducted by the World Economic Forum, the *Financial Development Report 2009*, also makes reference to Colombia's main weaknesses in terms of financial development. The development level of the financial markets (especially the foreign exchange and equity markets), as well as the access to finance, are some of the most problematic issues that limit Colombia's competitiveness (WEF 2009).

Table 5.35 Financial market development index, selected Latin American economies, 2010 (Own elaboration, based on data from the Global Competitiveness Report 2010)

Country	Rank
Panama	21
Chile	41
Peru	42
Brazil	50
Uruguay	70
Colombia	**79**
Mexico	96
Paraguay	97
Ecuador	115
Argentina	126
Venezuela	132

5.4 Concluding Remarks

The "competitiveness debate" is far from over. On one hand, Krugman (1994) warns about the "dangerous obsession" and "pervasive rhetoric" associated to the concept of competitiveness, underscoring that the "idea that a country's economic fortunes" are linked to its performance on world markets is a hypothesis that – as an empirical matter- "is flatly wrong" (Krugman 1994, p. 30). For Krugman national productivity, rather than competition in the world's marketplace, is the one leading to higher living standards. Other authors, such as Klein, propose a multidimensional approach where competitiveness is determined by relative prices. In turn, these are determined based on the unit cost (wage rate), productivity, profit margins and the exchange rate. Another point of view attempting to provide a definition links the concept of competitiveness to world market shares. In that line of argumentation, Cheptea et al. (2005) state that the gains or losses of world market shares by individual countries could be considered as an indicator of their trade competitiveness. Market share growth, in turn, depends also on structural factors. The market share growth of an economy will be influenced by its geographical and sectoral specialization too.

A survey of the concept of competitiveness should not miss Porter's well-known concept of "competitive advantage," the latter being associated to the ability of a country's firms to use their resources competitively in the global market. This argument proposes that a nation's "competitive advantage" is represented by the value and/or the rate of growth of the national product, in comparison to other relevant competitors. Supporters of this strand of the literature argue that it is of paramount importance for any economy to constantly improve its competitiveness, being the export strategy a very important aspect. This position also defends the argument that the government's intervention is needed for creating a competitive advantage in growth sectors.

The concepts of trade competitiveness and export competitiveness have also been proposed: ensuring the quality of institutions that promote trade, relying on the market to determine prices, and addressing market failures where possible, are here of utmost importance. Consequently, it is argued that the improvement of export competitiveness is dependent from the incentives regime (guaranteeing that domestic resources are channeled to the most productive sectors and firms), the cost reduction of the so-called "backbone" services (e.g. energy, telecommunications, customs services, transport and logistics, security), and the implementation of pro-active policies supporting trade (export and investment promotion entities, agencies to support innovation and clustering, and mechanisms geared towards limiting the costs of adjustment) (Brenton et al. 2008).

The term "competitiveness" has been increasingly incorporated in the Colombian governmental agenda. In 1999, Colombia's "National Productivity and Competitiveness Policy" was launched, gathering different strategies and efforts previously undertaken since the beginning of the 1990s. In 2008, this policy was upgraded, being now grounded in five "pillars": the development of world-class export sectors, the improvement of productivity, the increase in formalization levels of the economy, the promotion of science, technology and innovation, and the promotion of competition (CONPES 2008). Targets, deadlines, and monitoring indicators are being developed to follow the progress of the action plans. The so-called "National Competitiveness System" (*Sistema Nacional de Competitividad*), launched in 2006, represents the institutional framework that aims to coordinate the different actions related to the productivity and competitiveness levels of the economy.

Colombian policymakers have formulated the ambitious goal of turning the country into one of the three most competitive economies in Latin America for the year 2032—as stated in Chap. 5, Colombia is currently ranked number 7 in the region. The recent performance of Colombia in some of the most well-known international rankings—like the World Economic Forum's *Global Competitiveness Report*, the World Bank's *Doing Business Report*, and the IMD's World Competitiveness Yearbook—shows that the country has made significant improvements, principally in the fields of domestic security and internal pacification, the macroeconomic fundamentals, the consolidation of a sophisticated business sector, and an increasing capacity of technology absorption. The country's so-called "technological readiness," as defined by the WEF, is one of the best in Latin America. In addition to the WEF's indicator, criteria such as the number of Internet users, or the ICT services exports of the country, provides further evidence of Colombia's relatively good ICT infrastructure status.

Another positive aspect that should be mentioned is that the regulatory environment for the operation of business has been recognized by the World Bank's 2010 *Doing Business Report* as the best in Latin America, in a scale that intends to measure the ease of doing business. Moreover, the country has been considered as one of the most progressive ones in the last three reports. Likewise, the ranks for private institutions of the WEF in criteria like the ethical behavior of firms or the efficacy of corporate boards get relatively good grades and are among the best in the Americas. Other "competitive strengths" of the country are related to its market size, and the "fairly high" innovation potential, as defined by the WEF.

There are, however, a number of factors that do not allow Colombia to fully unleash its potential and that will have to be addressed, if the aforementioned goal of increasing Colombian productivity and export competitiveness levels wants to be accomplished. First, it has been stressed that one of the most problematic aspects negatively affecting Colombia's performance is related to its public institutional environment. In this case, the business costs of terrorism and organized crime still carry a very important weight and negatively affect the Colombian competitive position in international rankings. The burdens of government regulations, the favoritism in decision of government officials, and the diversion of public funds are other limitations associated to the institutional environment.

The endowment and quality of the Colombian transport infrastructure is another factor that clearly undermines the economy's productivity. The figures and statistics analyzed demonstrate that Colombia is one of the countries in Latin America with the lowest standards in terms of roads infrastructure, both in terms of coverage and quality. The latter is particularly concerning; taking into account that road transport is precisely the most important freight transportation system in the country. Transport of goods by river practically does not exist, and railways are underutilized and concentrated in a few regions of the country. In contrast, the Colombian airport infrastructure is one of the most extensive ones in Latin America.

Colombia's maritime trade, concessioned in 1993 to societies under company law, has effectively increased its efficiency. However, there is a great need for more and better road connections between these ports and the main industrial centers. The necessity to increase the depth of some ports has also been proposed as an urgent priority, taking into account the growing movement of goods that has taken place in the last years. Generally speaking, very significant investments are needed to upgrade the country's transport infrastructure. As will be addressed in the next chapter, studies conducted demonstrate that the Colombian economy needs investments in transport infrastructure between 5.5% and 6% of its GDP to boost economic growth and improve the competitiveness of Colombian export products (Flórez 2010). In sharp contrast, in the period 1993–2008, investment in public infrastructure had a share of only 0.6% of the country's GDP.

Investment in R&D is strikingly low in Colombia. As an illustration, in 2005 high-income countries invested–on average–2.35% of its GDP in R&D. Latin American countries invested 0.66% of their GDP, while Colombia registered a share of only 0.18%. Furthermore, the country has actually decreased the amount of expenditure on R&D in the period 1996–2007. Other indicators demonstrate the gravity of the situation, like the very low number of researchers per million inhabitants—one of the lowest in Latin America–, and the very scarce number of patent applications.

In terms of human capital, the figures and statistics analyzed reveal that the country has registered significant progress in terms of literacy rates, as well as basic primary and secondary education attainment levels. However, at the secondary education level serious problems are evident with respect to retention levels and graduation rates. Tertiary enrollment rates are among the lowest in Latin America. Other problems afflicting the human capital situation are related to the significant inequality between urban richer areas and rural poorer areas in terms of enrollment rates, as well as the poor scores obtained in the 2006 version of the Program for International Student Assessment (PISA). Regarding the latter, it should be mentioned that Colombian students scored lower on reading, mathematics, and science than most countries evaluated in the assessment.

In terms of the access to finance, the Colombian competitive performance is rather mixed. On one hand, the different indexes and studies surveyed point to the necessity of reforming the regulation of securities exchanges. The restrictions on capital flows are a limitation too. On the other hand, the soundness of banks and the availability of financial services are seen as strengths of the Colombian economy.

Chapter 6
Enhancing Colombia's Export Diversification: A Normative Approximation, with an Emphasis on the European Union's Market

Why do some economies find it easier to diversify from traditional to nontraditional products and keep the progression rolling along? We get a better handle on this question by turning it on its head and asking why diversification is not a natural process and how it can easily be derailed.

(Dani Rodrik, *One Economics Many Recipes: Globalization, Institutions, and Economic Growth*, 2007, p. 103)

Chronic civil wars explain some countries' underdevelopment. Colombia has a very professional and high-quality civil service and exemplary economic management. Yet Colombia's history since independence has been plagued by civil wars or violent insurgencies...Gabriel García Márquez had his fictional character Colonel Aureliano Buendía continually start new civil wars in his tragicomedy "One Hundred Years of Solitude."

(William Easterly, *The Elusive Quest for Growth: Economist's Adventures and Misadventures in the Tropics*, 2002, p. 210).

The trend towards export concentration not just in Colombia, but in Latin America as a whole, has been remarked on several times in the current research study. According to the World Bank, 52% of the region's exports were composed of commodities in the past decade. In contrast, commodity exports in dynamic developing regions—East Asia and the Pacific—represented a share of only 30% (The Economist 2010). The main motivation of this chapter is to take a look at different policies and mechanisms that could spur export diversification in Colombia, placing a special emphasis on the opportunities and challenges associated with an increased level of trade with the EU.

Section 6.1 reviews the pros and cons that would imply shifting from the current unilateral, non-reciprocal mechanism that frames the commercial relations, to a bilateral reciprocal one. Section 6.2 discusses some policy recommendations and suggestions: for that purpose, this section capitalizes on reports and studies that have been conducted at the international level, and explains how these recommendations could be useful for boosting Colombia's export diversification.

J.F. Mejía, *Export Diversification and Economic Growth*, Contributions to Economics, DOI 10.1007/978-3-7908-2742-2_6, © Springer-Verlag Berlin Heidelberg 2011

6.1 Towards a Strengthened EU-Colombia Trade Relation: From the *GSP Plus*, to the FTA

Since 1991, Commercial relations between the European Union and Colombia have been framed by unilateral schemes of preferences. These trade mechanisms, initially called the *Andean Generalized System of Preferences* and later on the *Special Incentive Arrangement for Sustainable Development and Good Governance* (known as *GSP Plus*), have been granted by the EU as a special support to the Andean countries–Bolivia, Colombia, Ecuador, Peru and Venezuela–in their fight against the production and trafficking of illegal drugs. In addition to the tariff reductions, the mechanism includes the possibility of regional cummulation of origin within the so-called "group two"–Bolivia, Colombia, Costa Rica, Ecuador, El Salvador, Guatemala, Honduras, Nicaragua, Panama, Peru, and Venezuela (European Commission 2010c). Coupled with the political motivations, the EU has also expressed its objective of promoting industrialization and export diversification in the beneficiary countries, as well as enhancing economic growth. Last but not least, political considerations, as well as human right and sustainable development concerns, have been mentioned as motivations behind the agreement (De Gucht 2010).

Colombia is nowadays one of the 16 beneficiary countries included in the EU's *GSP* that have been granted additional preferences under the *GSP Plus* until the year 2015. These nations get these additional benefits, taking into account that they fulfill the so-called "vulnerability" criteria. This means that these countries are considered as "vulnerable," either due to their size or to the degree of concentration of their exports to the EU's market. In the latter case, concentration is defined by the EU as "meaning that the five largest sections of its GSP-covered imports to the Community must represent more than 75% of its total GSP-covered imports" (European Commission 2005). In the case of Colombia, this share is 78.3%. Furthermore, these 16 beneficiary countries must demonstrate that they have ratified and implemented 27 international conventions, dealing with different topics like human rights, good governance, sustainable development and labor conditions, among others (European Commission 2005).

6.1.1 Opportunities for Colombia from an Amplified Commercial Relation

6.1.1.1 General Considerations

The European Union and Colombia launched free trade negotiations in 2007 with the objective of signing a bilateral reciprocal FTA, which were concluded in May 2010 within the framework of the fourth EU-Latin America and Caribbean Summit in Madrid. Different arguments have been exposed by the Colombian government in explaining that decision.

First of all, the importance of the EU's market–both in terms of its dimension and purchasing power–has been frequently stressed. In that line of argumentation, the EU's role as Colombia's main trading partner for some of its "traditional" export products, as well as for some of its "non-traditional" ones, has been highlighted. Hence, increasing the level of certainty for Colombian exporters is considered a crucial priority. Second, the inclusion of a larger number of goods than the ones included within the GSP Plus, as well as services—which are not covered by that unilateral scheme of preferences—has also been emphasized.

Moreover, the prominent role of the FDI proceeding from the EU has also been underscored: that regional block is Colombia's second most important source of foreign investment, after the United States. The country is nowadays one of the most important recipients of the EU's FDI in Latin America, after Brazil, Mexico, and Chile (Delegación de la Unión Europea en Colombia 2010). The main sectors that have been benefitted by the EU's capitals are the petroleum sector, followed by the mining and quarrying sector, financial services, manufacturing and retail (Delegación de la Unión Europea en Colombia 2010). Furthermore, it has been suggested that important opportunities could be derived for "non-traditional" export sectors, such as apparel, processed food, and leather products, among others.

The Colombian government has cited the experience of Chile, as a sort of "benchmark" and with the objective of illustrating the possible positive effects that could be derived from the FTA with the EU. It has been stated that between 2003–when the Chile-EU agreement came into force – and 2008, Chilean exports to that regional block increased by 238%, growing from USD $5,086 to $17,200 million. The accomplishment in terms of diversification of the export basket has also been underscored (Ministerio de Comercio, Industria y Turismo 2010).

6.1.1.2 Improved Market Access

Among the positive considerations for Colombia derived from the signature of a FTA with the EU, one should consider the following points:

In first instance, the improved market access conditions for some Colombian export products—compared to the current benefits offered within the GSP Plus–, as well as the inclusion of FDI provisions and the liberalization of services, may be regarded as more advanced and far-reaching trade cooperation mechanism between Colombia and the European Union.

In that sense, it should be mentioned that for some Colombian industrial sectors, one important benefit associated with the EU-Colombia FTA is related to the relative relaxation of the stiff rules of origin that under the current *GSP Plus* negatively affect sectors like the petrochemical and plastics industry, textiles, and apparel. As will be discussed later, it has been precisely suggested that the strict rules of origin have not allowed not only Colombia, but also the other Andean countries, to gain a better access to the EU's market.

Among the improved market access conditions for some specific products, it is worth mentioning that tariffs for bananas, one of the principal Colombian "traditional" exports, will be significantly reduced to 75 €/t as of 2020–nowadays, the tariff is 176 €/t (El Colombiano 2010). With regard to sugar, new market access would be opened, by establishing a quota of 62,000 t (De Gucht 2010). Furthermore, the country is expecting benefits for the export of some specific products, like tobacco, beef, fruits and vegetables, and food preparations. Products that are not covered by the current GSP Plus—e.g. beef and rice—would be included within the FTA. Moreover, the duty-free access for 99.9% of Colombian industrial products is also contemplated. The services liberalization has also been proposed as an opportunity for Colombia, especially in some areas of interest—such as call centers, data processing, and design services (Ministerio de Comercio, Industria y Turismo 2010).

On the EU's side, the agreement is expected to bring benefits in different areas, such an increased market access for major agricultural products and processed agricultural products—e.g. milk powder, cheese, whey, pork meat, cereals, olive oil, wines and spirits—which are of crucial interest for the EU's agricultural sector (De Gucht 2010). Moreover, the free market access for all of industrial products—within a period of 10 years for the European products—has also been emphasized (De Gucht 2010).

As will be commented later, there are nevertheless serious concerns in Colombia with respect to the access of the EU's agricultural products, and concerns have been expressed over the possibility that some sectors could be "crowded out" by the foreign competition.

6.1.1.3 Addressment of Trade Diversion Concerns

A second issue to consider is related to the fact that other countries in the region either have already signed a Free Trade Agreement with the EU—Mexico, and Chile—, or are looking forward to doing it in the future—Central American countries, Mercosur. Not joining a FTA could therefore lead to a disadvantageous situation for Colombian exporters, and to trade diversion effects.

6.1.1.4 Solution to Problems Associated to the *GSP Plus*

It has been suggested that the EU-Colombia FTA would overcome two important limitations of the current *GSP Plus*, namely its temporary character, and the so-called "graduation mechanism." Regarding the former, it should be mentioned that these preferences have to be continuously renewed, and that there is no guarantee that they will be, indeed, be granted in the future. Consequently, it could be considered that for Colombian exporters, "to level the playing field" with the EU in a permanent and stable manner, could eventually lead to greater incentives for companies to invest and improve their productivity, since they will be able to forecast their activities in the long term.

Concerning the second limitation, the so-called "graduation mechanism," the *GSP Plus* explicitly contemplates the possibility of "graduating" sectors as soon as they reach a certain level of "competitiveness." The latter means that those sectors, as a result of their improved position with respect to the EU's market, lose their preferential access. This controversial mechanism is presented by the EU as a sign of the "increased export success" of the sector involved (European Commission 2004). The "graduated" sectors are determined, each year, by the EU's Commission. Both the temporary character of the *GSP Plus*, as well as the "graduation mechanism," could negatively affect Colombian export sectors. Hence, the signature of an EU-Colombia FTA could overcome those obstacles.

6.1.2 Challenges Associated to the Entrance into the FTA

6.1.2.1 Inter-Sectoral Adjustments

One important challenge linked to the participation in an EU-Colombia FTA is that domestic sectors that could be "crowded out" by the international competition. Whereas inter-sectoral adjustment is considered as normal and necessary for the emergence of new sectors, policymakers should be aware of the potential job losses, and the costs associated with finding and taking up a new one (Brenton et al. 2008). Consequently, providing the new unemployed people with different types of support, like implementing adjustment assistance policies, the provision of new training and skills, the connection of employers and the unemployed, and the shift to the expanding sectors are absolutely necessary. Coupled with that, actions have to be taken to provide support to the unemployed people that would lose their sources of income.

Throughout the negotiation process, some Colombian sectors have expressed their concerns about joining a FTA with the EU. Special attention has drawn the case of the dairy sector, which fiercely opposes the agreement. Many small and medium-sized Colombian dairy farmers fear the loss of jobs for approximately 400,000 families, a situation that would present daunting social problems in some rural regions of the country. Representatives from the dairy industry have expressed their objection to the agreement, arguing that they will not be able to compete with the European dairy sector (Borkan 2010).

In closing the negotiations, the Colombian government admitted the serious threat that would be imposed on the dairy sector, but noted that it should be seen as a "sacrifice for the gains expected for other sectors of the economy" (Borkan 2010). On the other hand, the Colombian government argued that it took the necessary precautions to protect the dairy sector: the effective protection for the industry will be for 20 years, and Colombian policymakers have expressed their expectation that the dairy sector could improve its competitiveness within that period of time. Different policies have been announced for improving the productivity and upgrading the productive capacity of this sector.

Other sectors that have been critical of the agreement, like the workers unions, argue that the agreement will not contribute to the diversification of Colombian exports in the EU market, taking into account the very strict rules of origin, as well as the competition in manufactures of other developing nations such as China and India. This position defends the argument that Colombian exports will not diversify from the very "traditional" products currently exported to the EU and that, consequently, a FTA is not needed (Arroyave 2010).

6.1.2.2 A Free Trade Agreement is not Synonymous to an Unlimited Free Market Access

The consideration about market access cannot be restricted, in a shallow manner, just to tariff reductions. Rules of Origin (RoO), as stated by Carrère et al. (2010), exert a significant effect on market access, taking into account the costs that exporters have to incur in order to comply with those requirements. The latter authors conduct a study about the possible effects of an EU-ASEAN FTA, currently under negotiation. Based on empirical measures, their main research question is linked to the issue of how much market access these countries can expect from entering an FTA with the EU. One of their most interesting findings is that "market access is further eroded once rules of origin (RoO), necessary to satisfy originating status under any FTA, are taken into account" (Carrère et al. 2010, p. 58). These RoO are therefore, very important criteria that should be observed by Colombia in its negotiations with the EU.

Moreover, the experience of other developing nations has shown that preference margins for many products currently exported are rather small and therefore, the liberalization undertaken within the FTA would not imply significant benefits in terms of tariffs reductions. In addition to that, for those products where the margins of preference are substantial, stiff rules of origin may restrict the access of those goods (Brenton et al. 2008).

Finally, one important aspect that is worth mentioning is that the agreement includes a clause that provides for its suspension in the event of a serious violation of human rights, and evaluation mechanisms are mentioned within a section dealing with the commitment to human rights. As expressed by the EU's Trade Commissioner himself, the threshold for unilateral suspension of the EU-Colombia agreement, compared to previous agreements signed, is "significantly lower" (De Gucht 2010). While all the EU agreements on trade or cooperation with third countries contain such a clause, this is nevertheless an issue to be carefully considered by the Colombian administration, taking into account the still challenging situation of the country when it comes to the human rights situation.

6.1.2.3 The Recurrent Under-Utilization of the Commercial Preferences

In Chap. 4, it was mentioned that one striking fact associated with the EU's *GSP Plus* is related to the low degree of utilization both by Colombian and Andean exporters. For the particular case of Colombia, it is striking to notice that the country has been exporting only 17% of the products covered during the last few years. This has been subject of debate at different levels, taking into account that the unilateral scheme of preferences is considered to be generous, and that the benefits are offered to approximately 7,200 products (Koetsenruijter 2006). The EU has frequently stated that the reason behind this contradictory outcome is related to the poor level of competitiveness of many export goods, especially industrial products and manufactures.

The Commission of the EU has expressed that the *GSP Plus* aims to stimulate industrialization and diversification process in the beneficiary countries (European Commission 2004).

Moreover, an important underlying motivation for granting the *GSP Plus* has been to support the Andean nations in their fight against the production of illegal crops, motivating these economies to export alternative goods and promoting their economic and social development. However, almost 20 years have passed, and the objective of diversification of exports has not been accomplished yet.

Different reasons have been proposed for the low degree of utilization of the preferences, and for the failure in diversifying the Colombian export basket to the EU. Nieto (2002) argues that the inadequate trade specialization, the very concentrated structure of exports, and the low productivity levels, seem to be factors to explain that situation. He further states that the preferential regime has not contributed to an improvement of the export basket, either in terms of an enlarged degree of diversification, or quality enhancements. The Generalized System of Preferences granted by the EU, according to Nieto, has not been effective in boosting the exports of products different to primary products. Furthermore, it has been argued that the EU's global imports have shown a greater dynamism towards products which are not offered by the Andean countries (Nieto 2002).

Another line of argumentation is related to the temporary character of the commercial preferences and the uncertainty associated with their possible renewal, which would have failed to provide long-term motivations that firms need to invest (Guerra et al. 2009). The recurrence of protectionism, in new ways, has also been proposed (Guerra et al. 2009).

In one way or another, the big question that remains is if shifting from a unilateral, non-reciprocal to a bilateral scheme of preferences could play an important role in promoting the diversification of Colombian exports to the EU.

One important consideration that should be taken into account is that passing from a unilateral, non-reciprocal scheme of preferences to a FTA is not synonymous to a permanent unlimited free access to the EU's market. One example to bear in mind is the case of agricultural products. Despite the fact that Colombia cannot pose serious threats to the EU's Common Agricultural Policy, and that similarly to

Chile, it is mainly interested in exporting tropical fruits and vegetables and canned processed food, it is evident that a set of mechanisms that make part of FTAs could be used to limit Colombian agricultural exports (Moehler 2007). Protective mechanisms ranging from exceptions to tariff reductions, tariff rate quotas (TRQs) and safeguard clauses, which can be both applied to agricultural and industrial products, have to be considered (Moehler 2007).

6.1.2.4 The Need for Aid for Trade and Technical Assistance

Entering a Free Trade Agreement, per se, does not lead to a greater level of export competitiveness. The experience of the country with the GSP and the GSP Plus demonstrates that, whereas these mechanisms have exerted a positive influence in promoting trade with the EU, Colombian exports continue to show a path of concentration with that market. In the year 2008, 85% of the country's exports to the EU were comprised of primary products–especially coffee, oil and coal. On the other hand, industrial exports have not significantly increased since these mechanisms were granted to the country, and the share of industrial exports has stalled at levels between 13% and 15%. This evidence suggests that commercial preferences, by themselves, are not sufficient for boosting Colombia's exports to the EU's market.

These reciprocal agreements have to be consistent with national development strategies, as stated by Brenton et al. (2008). An improved market access, the elimination of tariffs, and services liberalization are not the only topics to consider when these agreements are signed between developed and developing economies, as is the case of the FTAs between the EU and Andean nations. For the agreement to be beneficial for Colombia and to effectively contribute to promoting economic growth, the country has to previously work on establishing the foundations that will allow the country to be competitive in the EU's market. In other words, it is of paramount importance to establish the adequate trade policy environment, to fully reap the benefits of liberalization with the EU. It is here that the concept of aid for trade comes into question.

Within the framework of the Uruguay Round Agreements and the associated multilateral liberalizations, the difficulties of developing nations for successfully participating in more open markets have been frequently discussed. It has been recognized that some common features explain the lackluster performance of many developing nations in terms of export growth and export diversification. The OECD (2006, p. 21) argues that in these countries "governments, institutions and enterprises often lack capacities, e.g. information, policies, procedures, institutions and/or infrastructure, to compete effectively in global markets." Hence, it would be necessary to support these nations, so that they can "take full advantage of the opportunities that are provided through international trade" (OECD 2006, p. 21). Aid for trade appears as an alternative, consisting of different mechanisms, like technical assistance to improve trade and negotiation capacities, as well as supporting "supply-side" capacities that may include support for infrastructure, education, health, and the environment, which are considered as elements of the utmost importance for enhancing export competitiveness (OECD 2006). From the analysis undertaken in Chap. 5, it appears evident that the country requires support in fields like upgrading the physical infrastructure, reforming institutions, and building productive capacities.

A crucial element to be considered is that Colombia faces serious limitations in areas such as the provision of physical infrastructure, the high costs of the so-called "key backbone services"—transport, logistics, finance–, the poor institutional environment, and the inefficient factor markets pose serious limitations to Colombia's export competitiveness. Taking that into account, it appears logical to consider the necessity of mechanisms like "aid for trade."

6.2 Policy Recommendations to Promote Export Diversification in Colombia

Based on a set of indicators, indexes and studies, the analysis conducted in Chap. 5 showed that the most problematic aspects that negatively affect both export diversification and export competitiveness in Colombia are currently related to its institutional environment, physical infrastructure, logistics and transport availabilities, human capital endowments, and R&D levels. In what follows, the aim of the chapter is to analyze some policy recommendations that have been proposed and that could be useful in tackling these problems. While the present research project places a special emphasis on the EU's market, the lines of action and mechanisms proposed are applicable to the trade with any market in the world.

6.2.1 Reforming the Public Institutional Environment

As discussed in the previous chapter, the institutional environment has been identified by the World Bank as one of the factors that most seriously hinders the competitiveness of the Colombian economy. To make things worse, this indicator has been constantly decreasing in the last three reports. However, it should be said that this is a phenomenon that is not exclusive to Colombia: with the exception of Chile and Uruguay, all the Latin American economies get poor scores in terms of the institutional environment. For the particular case of Colombia, the most problematic aspects are related to the public institutions. Conversely, the ranks for private institutions in criteria like the ethical behavior of firms or the efficacy of corporate boards get relatively good rankings and are among the best in the Americas, as mentioned in Chap. 5.

Positive institutional developments should be recognized in Colombia. The World Bank's latest *Doing Business* Report, which measures business regulations and their enforcement across 183 economies, ranked Colombia in first place at the Latin American level. Within this classification, Colombia occupies a better position than other countries known for being leaders in the regional rankings, such as Chile and Uruguay.

This score was granted based on the so-called *Ease of Doing Business Index*, which tries to capture if the country's regulatory environment is conducive to businesses. Factors like the protection of investors, trading across borders, or enforcing contracts are evaluated within that indicator. Colombia is also recognized as one of the ten most progressive reformers in the world, taking into account the implementation of positive changes in eight of the ten areas considered by the World Bank (CONPES 2008).

The good performance of the institutional framework that surrounds the private economic activity is not joined by a transparent and efficient public institutional environment. Rodrik (2007, p. 154), citing Lin and Nugent (1995), defines institutions "as a set of humanly devised behavioral rules that govern and shape the interactions of human beings, in part by helping them to form expectations of what other people will do."

Institutions are related to aspects like the property rights system, the regulatory framework that controls corruption and fraud and enhances competition in the market, the rule of law, good governance, and social and political institutions that are able to handle social conflicts (Rodrik 2007). In Colombia, the most relevant problems at the institutional level that need to be addressed are closely linked to social conflicts: income inequality, the lack of social insurance institutions, and social divisions are very problematic factors. To illustrate this point, it should be mentioned that within the 2009 *Human Development Report*, Colombia's GINI Index, from a regional perspective, is placed below the ones of Chile, Argentina, Uruguay, Mexico, Costa Rica, Venezuela, Panama, and Brazil.

Moreover, the same report states that 64% of the Colombian population lives below the national poverty line, which is after Haiti and Bolivia, the worst position in the whole Latin American region. Social inequality and corruption are factors that play a pivotal role in explaining terrorism, narcotrafficking, and criminality. This is reflected in the poor grades that the country gets in the WEF *Global Competitiveness Report*, in relation with criteria like the business costs of terrorism—where Colombia occupies the last position in the world, despite the very significant improvements in domestic security and pacification since 2002—and organized crime.

Rodrik (2007) makes reference to a set of different institutions that serve as a kind of framework for the market to properly function. Property rights, regulatory institutions, macroeconomic stabilization institutions, social insurance institutions, and conflict management institutions are proposed as mechanisms that should perform regulatory and stabilizing functions in a market economy. From the analysis undertaken in Chap. 5, and taking into account the current political and social juncture of the country, one important recommendation to formulate has to do with the urgent necessity of strengthening the country's efforts in the enhancement of social insurance and conflict management institutions.

As far as social insurance is concerned, the Colombian situation is no different to the other Latin American nations that resorted to a free market approach in the 1990s, but seriously pondered the necessity for promoting social insurance institutions and safety nets (Rodrik 2007). This is particularly challenging, taking into account the striking levels of income inequality in the country. Concerning conflict management, an ethnically diverse and economically unequal society as the Colombian one, in the words of Rodrik (2007), are the seeds for social conflict that divert resources from the most economically productive activities, and generates uncertainty.

Easterly (2002), citing the work of Svensson (2000), argues that countries that are both commodity dependent and ethnically divided are more prone to corruption, since the different groups will try to reap as much as possible from the commodity revenues. This has, as well, been a problem present in Colombia and that must be seriously considered by policymakers, especially in the light of the petroleum and fuels *bonanza* that the country is experiencing, which is expected to last for some years.

Based on the aforementioned conditions of the country, some policy recommendations could be made. The first one has to do with giving a much stronger emphasis to the promotion of institutions in the fields of corruption, social insurance, and conflict management. Other fields where actions are urgently required are related to improving the extent and effects of taxation–Colombia is one of the countries in the world with the highest total tax rate, the latter being defined by the WEF as the amount of taxes and mandatory contributions payable by a business in the second year of operation, expressed as a share of commercial profits (World Economic Forum 2010b). Other priority lines of action include addressing the problem of the inefficiency of the judiciary system, as well as enforcing the rule of law.

6.2.2 Upgrading the Transport Infrastructure and Logistics System

Different studies, indexes, and reports provide evidence of the poor level of the Colombian physical infrastructure. This is clearly a paradoxical aspect, taking into account that other Latin American nations with lower GDP levels which are classified in lesser stages of development are favored by a better infrastructure than Colombia. In a preliminary manner, it may be inferred that the most important underlying reason for the lack of investment in infrastructure is related to the large expenditures that have been destined for security and internal pacification purposes. As mentioned in the previous chapter, the situation is particularly worrying with regard to the transport infrastructure, and more specifically, concerning the coverage and quality of the road infrastructure. In addition to that, fluvial transport practically does not exist, railways are scarce and concentrated in some specific regions, and the quality of ports has been graded as one of the lowest in Latin America. The lack of an efficient articulation of the different transport modes—multimodal transport–, as well as the absence of specialized logistics platforms, are problematic factors that are required to be addressed too (CONPES 2008).

In stark contrast, the ICT infrastructure is considered as one of Colombia's "competitive strengths." Moreover, it is important to underscore that Colombia's social infrastructure endowment in areas like basic household services—water, sanitation—is high compared to the Latin American region, as well as in terms of electricity (World Bank 2004).

Consequently, the current status of the infrastructure in the country takes its toll on the export competitiveness of Colombian companies. It is, therefore, an urgent priority to significantly improve the level of investment in the so-called "productive infrastructure." An important upgrade and maintenance of the railway infrastructure is needed, coupled with a more extensive coverage at the national level, as well as the offering of incentives aimed at a more extensive utilization—in order to broaden the variety of goods carried by this mode of transportation, currently limited to some primary goods, like coal and coffee. Fluvial transport requires important investments in dredging and multimodal transport facilities (World Bank 2004). As far as maritime ports are concerned, better land connections, as well as the upgrade of the facilities –which would allow the handling of larger volumes of trade—are required. In addition to that, multimodal transportation has to be significantly improved (World Bank 2004). Taking into account the huge amount of the investment needed, it has been proposed that these projects should be co-financed with the private sector (World Bank 2004).

Price (2008, p. 163) argues that logistics "is a powerful economic enabler, one of the fundamental building blocks of external and internal trade." The author further states that nations like Germany or the United States, thanks to its supply chain efficiency, obtain important economic benefits from their logistical strengths (Price 2008). In contrast, as mentioned previously, Colombia's performance in criteria such as the quality of trade and transport related infrastructure, competitively priced shipments, and the quality of logistics services leaves much to be desired. According to a study conducted by the International Finance Corporation (IFC), the cost of exporting in Colombia—measured in terms of cost per container—amounted to $1,770 USD in 2009, which was the highest value in Latin America, after Venezuela. In comparison, this cost in Germany amounted to $872 (World Bank and International Finance Corporation 2010).

The great need for investment and upgrading both in the productive infrastructure endowment and in the logistics system is a daunting task to be faced by the Colombian government, when it comes to boosting its export competitiveness. As in the case of infrastructure, because of the high costs associated to it, an important priority is related to motivating private investment in the logistics services, which should be joined by the public investment, as proposed by Price (2008).

Colombian policymakers are aware of these problems. In 2008, the National Logistics Policy (*Política Nacional de Competitividad*) was enacted. It makes reference to different strategies to be implemented for the development of a national logistics system in Colombia, which should enhance the productivity and competitiveness of the economy. While the policy makes reference to infrastructure, it places special emphasis on the facilitation of the freight transport logistics and the distribution of goods, which suffer from bottlenecks in Colombia. The reduction of the transport and logistics costs is also recognized as a very important priority (CONPES 2008).

Very important lines of action that have been recently launched, and that should be strengthened, have to do with the establishment of an institutional environment conducive to the coordination of policies and actions in the field of infrastructure and logistics. Taking into account the multiplicity of actors involved, both at the public and private level, the recent creation of the Committee for the Facilitation of Trade, Logistics, and Transport (*Comité para la facilitación de la logística y el transporte*, COMIFAL), a technical agency attached to the national competitiveness institutional framework, is a positive development.

Public investment in infrastructure should be a first concern for the national government. In a study conducted by the National Planning Department of Colombia, in the period 1993–2008 the public investment in transport infrastructure had a share of 0.6% of the country's GDP. This is a strikingly low figure: other studies suggest that the Colombian economy needs investments in transport infrastructure between 5.5% and 6% of its GDP to boost economic growth and improve the competitiveness of Colombian export products (Flórez 2010). In order to build a proper multimodal system, it has been estimated that investments in the maritime, fluvial and aerial infrastructure should be approximately 2% of the GDP (Flórez 2010).

6.2.3 Improving the Human Capital's Availability and Quality

Despite the significant progress that Colombia has made during recent years in terms of literacy rates and primary education enrollment rates, the country still has a long way to go to improve both education attainment levels and quality standards. The analysis conducted in Chap. 5 evidenced a number of limitations, like the still insufficient enrollment rates—especially low at the secondary and tertiary levels–, the inequalities between rural and urban areas, and the poor scores of the country in the PISA 2006 assessment, where Colombian students showed weaknesses in mathematics and sciences. The argument of Puryear and Ortega for the whole Latin American region (2008, p. 46) describes the Colombian situation well: student learning in the country does not meet the requirements of modern societies, and lags behind other developing nations.

While it is true that the educational gap seriously limits not just the Colombian, but the Latin American competitiveness as a whole, attention must be paid to the fact that the educational upgrading must be balanced, as stated by De Ferranti et al. (2003). This means that once after having accomplished significant improvements in basic education attainment, the emphasis should be placed now on increasing the opportunities of access to the secondary and tertiary levels. And, following the argumentation of De Ferranti et al., the educational offer should be harmonious with the stage of the country's technological development: while it is appropriate to increase the opportunities to get a tertiary-level education, a balanced transition asks for the stress to be placed mostly on improving the access and completion rates at the secondary level. A balanced "skills upgrading" and educational transition, like the one undertaken in the NICs or Finland, seems to be the most adequate and reasonable solution.

As mentioned in Chap. 5, empirical studies suggest that one of the most important determinants of comparative advantage in the services sector is related to human capital endowments. Colombia aspires to diversify its export offer, including tourism, professional, and business service within its basket. Some of these sectors, as expressed by Mattoo (2009), are more skill-intensive than most goods. And many of these services require people that have completed a tertiary education, aspect that has to be considered in the country. Brazil and India are countries whose experience speaks in favor of promoting the creation of institutions of higher learning: the significant increase in the output of business services of these two nations seems to be related to the bigger importance given to skill-generating institutions in these two nations (Mattoo 2009, p. 170).

Rodrik (2007) formulates an argument that should be carefully considered, namely, that the problem of poor human capital levels in developing countries may be caused by a low demand for schooling. This sounds rather paradoxical, taking into account that the traditional approach is to believe that the problem of scarce human capital endowments should be addressed by increasing the educational offer. But if there is an environment where the lack of opportunities pushes down the return to education, the propensity to acquire learning will be low. Consequently, as proposed by De Ferranti et al. (2003), the right policies will be designed by understanding first where the bottlenecks are located. The Latin American experience, according to the latter authors, suggests that "while the opportunity costs for sending a child to primary schools is thought to be low, this is not the case for children of secondary school age" (De Ferranti et al. 2003, p. 87). In addition to that, the rate of return to secondary education is low in Colombia (De Ferranti et al. 2003, p. 88).

As far as the tertiary education is concerned, different policies could be considered, which have been previously proposed in different studies. Increasing the efficiency of the public universities, as well as facilitating the access to the private universities (either through scholarships or student loan programs), are policy actions have been suggested (Sánchez-Páramo and Schady 2003a). It is concerning that within Colombia's National Competitiveness Policy; no reference is made to the necessity of improving attainment levels at the secondary and tertiary levels. In contrast, one positive aspect is related to the fact that enhancing the quality of the system is stressed, when proposing a broader implementation of the so-called "education based on competences."

6.2.4 *Making Research, Development, and Innovation a Priority*

Even at the regional level, Colombia lags behind in terms of research and development expenditure as a percentage of the GDP. Besides that, the number of researchers per million inhabitants is one of the lowest in Latin America. Consequently, the country exhibits a very poor performance in patent applications and publications, as explained in the previous chapter.

Rodrik (2007) argues that it is the demand side the one that limits innovation in the developing world, and not the supply side. He defends the idea that the demand for innovation is low because entrepreneurs perceive new activities as having a low profitability. This, in turn, leads to a lack of demand of trained scientists and engineers. One interesting policy approach suggested by Rodrik (2007) is that the government may play a positive role, in helping the entrepreneurs to get the information they need about which new activities could be produced at a low cost and be profitable enough. Information externalities that limit self-discovery should be addressed by promoting investments in new, "non-traditional" industries, as has been the case in countries like Taiwan.

Guasch (2003, p. 134) defends the idea that "the process of knowledge acquisition and diffusion is plagued by market and coordination failures," making public intervention a justifiable option. All around the world, countries with successful innovation experiences have relied on coordination mechanisms and the provision of funds to spur innovation.

Klinger and Lederman (2009, p. 101) make reference to a market failure that can be detrimental to innovation. An "inside-the-frontier innovation"—that is, the production of a new export product that is not a novel invention, but is new within a country's export basket–, while creates valuable social knowledge, leads to imitation. The latter implies that first movers are not able to fully appropriate the value of their investments in discovery, which in turn leads to underinvestment in experimentation. Based on this consideration and an empirical analysis, the authors propose that "public support for experimentation in new sectors and activities may be warranted" (Klinger and Lederman 2009, p. 108). However, this support should not be based on increased barriers to entry, since imitation allows the socialization of the discoveries.

As well as in previous sections, it must be recognized that the Colombian government is aware of this problem, and recognizes that the poor levels of research, development, and experimentation in the country represent a serious hindrance to an increased productivity of the economy. Colombia needs to make very important efforts, if it wants to overcome this grim situation. First of all, the national government needs to make R&D a crucial priority within the national strategies, as other developing nations—like the Asian Tigers—already did. Only until 2008 did Colombian policymakers launch—for the very first time–a national policy for the support of research and innovation. The country is a latecomer in relation to other regional economies, such as Brazil and Chile. What has been suggested by Knight and Marques (2008) for Latin America as whole, should be observed in Colombia: much more people with a Doctoral formation are required as well as researchers, and these people should have a much bigger participation within the country's workforce.

R&D investments need urgently to be increased. In that sense, experiences like the Brazilian one—where taxes on the exploitation of natural resources have been invested in sectoral funds that promote R&D–could be pondered (Knight and Marques 2008). As mentioned before, Colombia is experiencing petroleum and commodities *bonanzas*, and the positive trends of commodity prices are expected to persist. This type of mechanism could be considered in Colombia, with the objective of allocating more resources to R&D activities, but R&D investments should be undertaken, considering the availability of human capital in the country. Linkages between the private sector, innovation-related institutions, and universities should be strengthened, and stronger incentives should be offered to firms in order to motivate investments in R&D.

Finally, it should be said that both the improvements in human capital and the increased efforts in R&S should go hand in hand, since they complement each other. No innovation can take place without the skilled workforce needed.

Appendix

Table A.1 List of empirical studies surveyed-trade and growth, exports diversification and growth (Own Elaboration)

Author	Year	Main research question	Methodology	Data
Arkolakis, Costinot, and Rodríguez-Clare	2010	Do new sources of gains from trade lead to larger gains from trade?	Analysis of trade models.	N.A
Madsen	2009	Does openness have an influence on total factor productivity (TFP) growth and per capita growth?	Simple Regressions.	16 OECD countries, period 1870–2006.
Kohli	2009	Do nations that open their economies, and keep government's role to a minimum, experience rapid economic growth?	Case studies of India, Brazil, Nigeria and South Korea.	N.A.
Krishna and Levchenko.	2009	Why do less developed countries tend to experience higher output volatility?	Regressions.	Industry-level data, 459 manufacturing sectors, 1970–1997.
Agosin	2006	Is there a particular kind of export growth which can result in sustained growth both in exports and GDP?	Regressions, empirical model of growth.	Cross section data for 1980–2003. Sample of Asian and Latin American countries.
Ben Hammouda et al.	2006	Can diversification be a framework to formulate development	Statistical model for the determinants of diversification.	Panel data, sample of 18 African countries, 1996–2001.

(continued)

J.F. Mejía, *Export Diversification and Economic Growth*, Contributions to Economics,
DOI 10.1007/978-3-7908-2742-2,

Table A.1 (continued)

Author	Year	Main research question	Methodology	Data
		strategies for African economies?	Panel econometrics.	
Bebczuk and Berrettoni	2006	How does the macroeconomic environment foster or inhibit export diversification, as measured by the Herfindahl index?	Cross country regressions. Case study, firm-level export diversification in Argentina.	69 sectors, 56 countries, period 1962–2002.
Hausmann et al.	2006	Does the mix of goods that a country produces have important implications for its economic growth?	An index of the *income level of a country's exports* is constructed. Cross-section and panel analysis, instrumental variables specifications and country fixed effects.	1992–2003 period. Two datasets, consisting of more than 5.000 individual commodities.
Wälde and Wood	2004	Does the empirical and theoretical literature unambiguously support, from an efficiency perspective, the case for liberalization?	Literature Review.	N.A.
United Nations - ESCAP	2004	Is there a relationship between GDP growth rates and exports, and export diversification?	Test of the *export-led growth hypothesis*, based on the simple ordinary least squares method and the standard Granger causality technique. Analysis of export performance, using export concentration and diversification indexes.	Bangladesh, Myanmar, Nepal, Malaysia (1972–1996).
Lemoine and Ünal	2004	Is China's foreign trade performance explained by its involvement in the	Case analysis, China's trade by stages of production and by	1997–1999.

(continued)

Table A.1 (continued)

Author	Year	Main research question	Methodology	Data
		international segmentation of production processes?	technology content.	
Lederman and Maloney	2003	Does the trade structure have an influence on economic growth? Which are the influences of natural resource abundance, export concentration and intra-industry trade?	*Herfindahl* index, share of natural resources exports in total exports, *Grubel-Lloyd* index. GMM system estimator.	Cross sectional and panel data, 1975–1999, 65 countries.
Wacziarg and Welch	2003	Does outward orientation lead to economic growth?	Regressions of growth. Cross-sectional and panel econometrics.	Cross-country database of trade indicators such as tariffs, non tariff barriers, and other measures of trade restrictions -as well as policy liberalization dates- for 1970–1999, 118 countries.
Stanley and Bunnag	2001	Have diversification programs, both in the agricultural and manufacturing sectors, led to more stable earnings in Central America?	Analysis of instability and concentration statistical indices. OLS multivariate regression techniques with country-specific dummy variables. Fixed effects regression specification for the panel data set available.	Time series and panel data, 1974–1995. Guatemala, Costa Rica, El Salvador, Honduras.
Al-Marhubi	2000	Does export diversification promote economic growth?	Cross-country growth regressions. OLS estimations.	Cross-country sample, 91 countries, period 1961–1988.
Frankel and Romer	1999	What is the effect of international trade on income?	Countries' geographic characteristics are used to obtain instrumental variables estimates	Two samples: full set of 150 countries covered by the Penn World Table. Second sample is

(continued)

Table A.1 (continued)

Author	Year	Main research question	Methodology	Data
			of trade's impact on income. Cross-country regressions of income per person on international trade and country size by instrumental variables (IV) are conducted, and compared with ordinary least-squares (OLS) estimates of the same equations.	the 98-country sample used by N. Gregory Mankiw et al. (1992).
Cramer	1999	Which has been the experience of Mozambique, when processing commodities for export?	Literature review, case analysis.	N.A.
Feenstra et al.	1998	Are changes in export variety correlated with the growth in total factor productivity (TFP)?	Sectoral regressions.	1975–1991, data for South Korea and Taiwan, 16 sectors. The product variety of these two countries is measured using data on their exports to the U.S.
Amin Gutiérrez de Piñeres and Ferrantino.	1997	Is there a link between diversification, export growth and aggregate development?	The relation between exports and growth in Chile is analyzed by constructing several measures of diversification and structural change in that country. Using these measures, a number of relationships among the structure of exports, export growth, Chilean growth, and world	Two-digit export data for Chile, period 1962–1991.

(continued)

Table A.1 (continued)

Author	Year	Main research question	Methodology	Data
			growth is tested. Causality tests.	
Amin Gutiérrez de Piñeres and Ferrantino.	1997	Has a long-run trend toward export diversification been present in Latin America?	Stylized facts analysis (export specialization index, cumulative export experience function, traditionality index) of export diversification and structural change in exports.	Data on merchandise exports, period 1962–1993, for Argentina, Brazil, Chile, Colombia, Mexico and Venezuela.
Levine and Renelt	1992	Are the existing empirical studies that analyze the relationship between long-run growth rates and a variety of economic policy, political, and institutional indicators, robust?	Extreme bounds analysis. Cross-country growth regressions.	Period 1960–1989. 119 countries, excluding major oil exporters.
Ali et al.	1991	Is there a relationship between the degree of export diversification and export performance?	Case study approach. Analysis of export performance measures.	1961–1987, Malawi, Tanzania and Zimbabwe.
Taylor	1988	Is trade liberalization an optimal development strategy?	Literature review. Stylized facts analysis.	N.A.
Love	1983	Are earnings from manufactures more stable than earnings from primary products? Does diversification reduce the covariances between earnings from different pairs of products?	Analysis of covariances.	Ten basic SITC commodity groups. Two periods: 1959–1968 and 1969–1978. 24 countries.

N.A Not Applicable

Table A.2 Trade performance of the fresh food export sector in Colombia, 2004–2008 (Data from the International Trade Centre)

Fresh food (SITC Rev. 3, Sector 1)	2004	2005	2006	2007	2008
Value of exports (in thousand US$)	2,627,171	3,546,258	3,734,561	4,511,905	5,210,913
Share in national exports (%)	16%	17%	15%	15%	14%
Share in world market (%)	0.77%	0.95%	0.91%	0.93%	0.89%
Market diversification (N° of equivalent markets)	4	5	5	5	6

Table A.3 Trade performance of the processed food export sector in Colombia, 2004–2008 (Data from the International Trade Centre)

Processed food (SITC Rev.3, Sector 2)	2004	2005	2006	2007	2008
Value of exports (in thousand US$)	949,633	1,053,969	1,191,801	1,331,809	1,493,457
Share in national exports (%)	6%	5%	5%	4%	4%
Share in world market (%)	0.28%	0.29%	0.29%	0.27%	0.25%
Market diversification (N° of equivalent markets)	9	10	10	10	8

Table A.4 Trade performance of the wood products export sector in Colombia, 2004–2008 (Data from the International Trade Centre)

Wood products (SITC Rev.3, Sector 3)	2004	2005	2006	2007	2008
Value of exports (in thousand US$)	343,183	391,476	466,029	608,854	691,407
Share in national exports (%)	2%	2%	2%	2%	2%
Share in world market (%)	0.14%	0.15%	0.17%	0.19%	0.21%
Market diversification (N° of equivalent markets)	8	8	8	5	4

Table A.5 Trade performance of the textiles export sector in Colombia, 2004–2008 (Data from the International Trade Centre)

Textiles (SITC Rev.3, Sector 4)	2004	2005	2006	2007	2008
Value of exports (in thousand US$)	319,894	356,123	382,841	628,003	857,930
Share in national exports (%)	2%	2%	2%	2%	2%
Share in world market (%)	0.17%	0.18%	0.18%	0.27%	0.36%
Market diversification (N° of equivalent markets)	6	6	6	3	2

Table A.6 Trade performance of the chemicals export sector in Colombia, 2004–2008 (Data from the International Trade Centre)

Chemicals (SITC Rev.3, Sector 5)	2004	2005	2006	2007	2008
Value of exports (in thousand US$)	1,616,981	1,885,984	2,144,069	2,556,218	3,083,890
Share in national exports (%)	10%	9%	9%	9%	8%
Share in world market (%)	0.16%	0.16%	0.16%	0.17%	0.18%
Market diversification (N° of equivalent markets)	10	11	10	10	10

Table A.7 Trade performance of the leather and leather products export sector in Colombia, 2004–2008 (Data from the International Trade Centre)

Leather and leather products (SITC Rev.3, Sector 6)	2004	2005	2006	2007	2008
Value of exports (in thousand US$)	189,190	203,779	239,589	466,399	672,596
Share in national exports (%)	1%	1%	1%	2%	2%
Share in world market (%)	0.21%	0.20%	0.21%	0.36%	0.48%
Market diversification (N° of equivalent markets)	8	8	8	3	2

Table A.8 Trade performance of the basic manufactures export sector in Colombia, 2004–2008 (Data from the International Trade Centre)

Basic Manufactures (SITC Rev.3, Sector 7)	2004	2005	2006	2007	2008
Value of exports (in thousand US$)	1,400,111	1,729,482	2,292,894	3,014,846	2,406,968
Share in national exports (%)	8%	8%	9%	10%	6%
Share in world market (%)	0.20%	0.21%	0.22%	0.24%	0.17%
Market diversification (N° of equivalent markets)	11	9	10	11	10

Table A.9 Trade performance of the non-electronic machinery export sector in Colombia, 2004–2008 (Data from the International Trade Centre)

Non-electronic machinery (SITC Rev.3, Sector 8)	2004	2005	2006	2007	2008
Value of exports (in thousand US$)	198,956	198,510	234,753	294,649	445,000
Share in national exports (%)	1%	1%	1%	1%	1%
Share in world market (%)	0.02%	0.02%	0.02%	0.02%	0.03%
Market diversification (N° of equivalent markets)	7	8	7	7	5

Table A.10 Trade performance of the IT and consumer electronics export sector in Colombia, 2004–2008 (Data from the International Trade Centre)

IT & Consumer Electronics (SITC Rev.3, Sector 9)	2004	2005	2006	2007	2008
Value of exports (in thousand US$)	55,555	56,067	54,060	39,757	49,564
Share in national exports (%)	0%	0%	0%	0%	0%
Share in world market (%)	0.01%	0.01%	0.01%	0.00%	0.00%
Market diversification (N° of equivalent markets)	3	2	3	4	3

Table A.11 Trade performance of the electronic components export sector in Colombia, 2004–2008 (Data from the International Trade Centre)

Electronic components (SITC Rev.3, Sector 10)	2004	2005	2006	2007	2008
Value of exports (in thousand US$)	207,367	285,346	389,992	598,794	667,096
Share in national exports (%)	1%	1%	2%	2%	2%
Share in world market (%)	0.03%	0.04%	0.04%	0.06%	0.06%
Market diversification (N° of equivalent markets)	6	5	4	4	3

Table A.12 Trade performance of the transport equipment export sector in Colombia, 2004–2008 (Data from the International Trade Centre)

Transport equipment (SITC Rev.3, Sector 11)	2004	2005	2006	2007	2008
Value of exports (in thousand US$)	449,032	725,049	840,916	1,275,060	722,693
Share in national exports (%)	3%	3%	3%	4%	2%
Share in world market (%)	0.04%	0.07%	0.07%	0.09%	0.05%
Market diversification (N° of equivalent markets)	2	2	2	2	3

Table A.13 Trade performance of the clothing export sector in Colombia, 2004–2008 (Data from the International Trade Centre)

Clothing (SITC Rev.3, Sector 12)	2004	2005	2006	2007	2008
Value of exports (in thousand US$)	867,683	907,581	962,083	1,350,992	1,221,893
Share in national exports (%)	5%	4%	4%	5%	3%
Share in world market (%)	0.36%	0.35%	0.33%	0.41%	0.35%
Market diversification (N° of equivalent markets)	3	3	4	3	3

Table A.14 Trade performance of the miscellaneous manufacturing export sector in Colombia, 2004–2008 (Data from the International Trade Centre)

Miscellaneous manufacturing (SITC Rev.3, Sector 13)	2004	2005	2006	2007	2008
Value of exports (in thousand US$)	555,619	653,080	743,925	991,884	1,029,275
Share in national exports (%)	3%	3%	3%	3%	3%
Share in world market (%)	0.08%	0.09%	0.09%	0.10%	0.10%
Market diversification (N° of equivalent markets)	8	7	7	5	5

Table A.15 Trade performance of the minerals export sector in Colombia, 2004–2008 (Data from the International Trade Centre)

Minerals (SITC Rev.3, Sector 14)	2004	2005	2006	2007	2008
Value of exports (in thousand US$)	6,372,726	8,564,085	9,879,278	11,516,709	18,040,409
Share in national exports (%)	38%	40%	41%	38%	48%
Share in world market (%)	0.53%	0.52%	0.48%	0.51%	0.59%
Market diversification (N° of equivalent markets)	3	3	3	3	3

References

Acemoglu D, Zilibotti F (1997) Was prometheus unbound by chance? risk, diversification, and growth. J Polit Econ 105(4):709–751

Aghion P, Howitt P (1998) Endogenous growth. MIT Press, Cambridge, MA

Agosin MR (1999) Trade and growth in Chile. CEPAL Rev 68:79–100

Agosin MR (2006) Trade and growth: why Asia grows faster than Latin America, vol 1. Inter-American Development Bank, Washington DC

Agosin MR (2007) Export diversification and growth in emerging economies. Working Papers, University of Chile, Department of Economics, pp 1–35

Agostino M, Aiello F, Cardamone P (2008) Evaluating the impact of non-reciprocal trade preferences using gravity models. Appl Econ. doi:10.1080/00036840802314614

Aiello F, Demaria F (2010) Do trade preferential agreements enhance the exports of developing countries? Evidence from the EU GSP. Munich Pers RePEc Arch 20093:1–32

Ali R, Alwang J, Siegel PB (1991) Is export diversification the best way to achieve export growth and stability? A look at three African countries. Pollcy, Research, and External Affairs, Working Papers, Agriculture Operations, Agriculture Operations Division, Southern Africa Department, Africa Regional Office, 1–44

Al-Marhubi F (2000) Export diversification and growth: an empirical investigation. Appl Econ Lett 7(9):559–562

Alta consejería presidencial para la competitividad y las regiones (2010) Sistema nacional de competitividad, Retrieved March/04, 2010, from http://www.snc.gov.co/Es/Institucionalidad/Paginas/SNC.aspx

Amemiya T, MaCurdy TE (1986) Instrumental-variable estimation of an error components model. Econometrica 54:869–881

Amurgo-Pacheco A, Pierola M (2008) Patterns of export diversification in developing countries: intensive and extensive margins. World bank policy research working paper 4473:1–32

Anderson JE (1979) A theoretical foundation for the gravity equation. Am Econ Rev 69:106–116

Anderson JE, van Wincoop E (2003) Gravity with gravitas: a solution to the border puzzle. Am Econ Rev 93(1):170–192

Arkolakis C, Costinot A, Rodríguez-Clare A (2010) New trade models, same old gains? *NBER*. http://www.econ.ceu.hu/download/BESS/26Mar10.pdf. Accessed 14 Dec 2009

Arroyave R (2010) El tratado de libre comercio con la Unión Europea: El cierre de la tenaza que ahoga nuestro desarrollo nacional, Retrieved July/14, 2010, from http://www.bilaterals.org/spip.php?article17656

Arvis J, Mustra MA, Ojala L, Shepherd B, Saslavsky D (2007, 2010) Connecting to compete: trade logistics in the global economy. The World Bank, Washington DC

Balassa B (1971) The structure of protection in developing countries. Johns Hopkins University Press, Baltimore

Balassa B (1977) Export incentives and export performance in developing countries: a comparative analysis. World bank staff working paper 248:1–84
Balassa B (1978a) Export incentives and export performance in developing countries: a comparative analysis. Rev World Econ 114(1):24–61
Balassa B (1978b) Exports and economic growth: further evidence. J Dev Econ 5(2):181–189. doi:10.1016/0304-3878(78)90006-8
Balassa B (1981) The newly industrializing developing countries after the oil crisis. World Bank Reprint Series, (190):142-194. http://www-wds.worldbank.org/external/default/WDSContentServer/WDSP/IB/2001/01/24/000178830_98101903354510/Rendered/PDF/multi_page.pdf
Balassa B (1985) Exports, policy choices, and economic growth in developing countries after the 1973 oil shock. J Dev Econ 18(1):23–35, http://www.elsevier.com/wps/find/journaldescription.cws_home/505546/description#description
Baldwin RE (1992) Measuring dynamic gains from trade. J Polit Econ 100(11):162–174
Baldwin R Taglioni D (2006) Gravity for dummies and dummies for gravity equations. NBER Working Paper Series (Working Paper 12516), pp 1–31
Baldwin RE, Forslid R (2000) Trade liberalisation and endogenous growth: a q-theory approach. J Int Econ 50(2):497–517, http://www.elsevier.com/wps/find/journaldescription.cws_home/505552/description#description
Baltagi BH (2008) Econometric analysis of panel data, 4th edn. John Wiley & Sons Ltd., Chippenham, Wiltshire, UK
Barkai H (1969) A formal outline of a smithian growth model. Q J Econ 83(3):396–414, http://www.mitpressjournals.org/loi/qjec
Barro RJ (1992) Human capital and economic growth. Proceedings, Federal Reserve Bank of Kansas City, 199–230
Barro RJ, Sala-i-Martin X (1995) Economic growth. McGraw-Hill, New York
Batra A (2004) India's global trade potential: the gravity model approach. Indian Council for Research on International Economic Relations, Working Paper 151:1–38
Baum CF (2006) An introduction to modern econometrics using stata. Stata Press, College Station, Texas, USA
Bebczuk RN, Berrettoni ND (2006) Explaining export diversification: an empirical analysis. Unpublished manuscript. Retrieved 10 Dec 2009, from http://www.depeco.econo.unlp.edu.ar/doctrab/doc65.pdf
Becker GS, Murphy KM, Tamura R (1990) Human capltal. fenlllty, and economlc growth. J Polit Econ 98:12–37
Belke A, Spies J (2008) Enlarging the EMU to the east: what effects on trade? Empirica 35(4):369–389
Ben Hammouda H, Karingi SN, Njuguna AE, Sadni-Jallab M (2006) Diversification: towards a new paradigm for Africa's development, vol 35. United Nations Economic Commission for Africa
Ben-David D (1993) Equalizing exchange: trade liberalization and income convergence. Q J Econ 108(3):653–679
Bergstrand JH (1985) The gravity equation in international trade: some microeconomic foundations and empirical evidence. Rev Econ Stat 67(3):474–481
Bergstrand JH (1989) The generalized gravity equation, monopolistic competition, and the factor-proportions theory in international trade. Rev Econ Stat 71:143–153
Bergstrand JH (1990) The Heckscher-Ohlin-Samuelson model, the Linder Hypothesis and the determinants of bilateral intra-industry trade. Econ J 100:1216–1229
Bernard AB, Bradford Jensen J (1999) Exceptional exporter performance: cause, effect, or both? J Int Econ 47(1):1–25. doi:10.1016/S0022-1996(98)00027-0
Berry A, Thoumi F (1977) Import substitution and beyond:Colombia. World Dev 5(1/2):89–109

Berthélemy J, Söderling L (1999) The role of capital accumulation, adjustment and structural change for economic take-off: empirical evidence from African growth episodes. Technical Papers 150:4–38

Bertinelli L, Salins V, Strobl E (2006) Export diversification and price uncertainty in sub-saharan Africa and other developing countries: a portfolio theory approach. Unpublished manuscript.

Besedes T, Prusa TJ (2007) The role of extensive and intensive margins and export growth. NBER Working Paper 13628:1–31

Bhagwati J (1958a) Immiserizing growth: a geometrical note. Rev Econ Stud 25(3):201–205

Bhagwati J (1958b) International trade and economic expansion. Am Econ Rev 48(5):941–953

Bhagwati J (1978) Anatomy and consequences of exchange control regimes. Publishing Company for NBER, Cambridge

Blomstrom M, Kokko A (2001) Foreign direct investment and spillovers of technology. Int J Technol Manage 22(5–6):435–454

Bonaglia F, Fukasaku K (2003) Export diversification in low-income countries: an international challenge after doha. OECD Development Centre Working Papers, (209) http://dx.doi.org/10.1787/043266813306

Borkan B (2010) Dairy industry to protest colombia-EU FTA signing. Retrieved August/10, 2010, from http://colombiareports.com/colombia-news/news/9770-dairy-farmers-launch-final-protest-ahead-of-eu-fta-signing.html

Brenton P, Newfarmer R (2009) Watching more than the discovery channel to diversify exports. In: Newfarmer R, Shaw W, Walkenhorst P (eds) Breaking into new markets: emerging lessons for export diversification. The World Bank, Washington DC, pp 111–124

Brenton P, Hoppe M, Newfarmer R (2008) Economic partnership agreements and the export competitiveness of Africa. World Bank, Policy Research Working Paper 4627:1–27

Brenton P, Newfarmer R, Shaw W, Walkenhorst P (2009) Breaking into new markets: overview. In: Brenton P, Shaw W, Walkenhorst P (eds) Breaking into new markets: emerging lessons for export diversification. Washington DC: The World Bank, pp 1–35

Browne C, Geiger T (2010) The executive opinion survey: capturing the views of the business community. In: Schwab K (ed), The global competitiveness report 2010–2011 (pp. 49–57). Geneva: World Economic Forum

Brun J, Carrère C, Guillaumont P, de Melo J (2005) Has distance died? Evidence from a panel gravity model. The World Bank Economic Review 19(1):99–210

Busso M, Madrigal L, Pagés C (2010) Productividad desde los cimientos: Empresas y asignación de recursos. In: Pagés C (ed) La era de la productividad: Como transformar las economías desde sus cimientos. Inter-American Development Bank, Washington DC, pp 79–107

Caballero C (2010) Que sea una bendición, no una maldición, Portafolio, [online]. Available at: http://www.portafolio.co/archivo/cronologico/2010/010/05/?pagina=126680. Accessed on 4 June 2010

Cáceres D, Mojica A, Escobar M, Guio G (2006) Diagnóstico del sector transporte. Ministerio de Transporte, República de Colombia, Bogotá

Cafiero JA (2005) Modelos gravitacionales para el análisis del comercio exterior. Revista Del CEI Comercio Exterior e Integración 4:76–89

Canning D, Pedroni P (1999) Infrastructure and long run economic Growth. Consulting Assistance on Economic Reform II, Discussion Papers 57:1–41

Cárdenas M, García C (2004) El modelo gravitacional de comercio y el TLC entre colombia y Estados Unidos. Working Paper Series, Fedesarrollo 27:1–37

Cárdenas M, Gaviria A, Meléndez M (2005) La infraestructura de transporte en colombia. Fedesarrollo & Universidad de Los Andes, Bogotá

Carrère C (2006) Revisiting the effects of regional trade agreements on trade flows with proper specification of the gravity model. Eur Econ Rev 50(2):223–247. doi:10.1016/j.euroecorev.2004.06.001

Carrère C, de Melo J, Tumurchudur B (2010) Disentangling market access effects of preferential trading arrangements with an application for ASEAN members under an ASEAN–EU FTA. World Econ 33(1):42–59

Castro CA, Perilla JR, Gracia JO (2006) El comercio internacional y la productividad total de los factores en colombia. Archivos De Economía, Dirección De Estudios Económicos, Departamento Nacional De Planeación 307:1–15

Central Intelligence Agency – CIA (2010) CIA-the world factbook. Retrieved February/12, 2010, from https://www.cia.gov/library/publications/the-world-factbook/geos/xx.html

Chacholiades M (1990) International economics. McGraw-Hill, New York

Chapman R, Biggs T, Bertrand T, Watts M, Robertson J, Zerby J (2003) Nepal: trade and competitiveness study. Washington D.C.: World Bank

Cheptea A, Gaulier G, Zignago S (2005) World trade competitiveness: a disaggregated view by shift-share analysis. CEPII 23:1–47

Choudhry MT (2009) Determinants of labor productivity: an empirical investigation of productivity divergence. University of Groningen, Department of Economics, pp 1–21

Cipollina M, Salvatici L (2010) The trade impact of the European Union agricultural preferences. J Econ Policy Reform 13(1):87–106

Clerides SK, Lach S, Tybout JR (1998) Is learning by exporting important? micro-dynamic evidence from colombia, mexico, and morocco. Q J Econ 113(3):903–947

Colecchia A, Schreyer P (2001) ICT investment and economic growth in the 1990s: is the United States a unique case? a comparative study of nine OECD countries. OECD Science, Technology and Industry Working Papers 7:1–32

Consejo Superior de Comercio Exterior, República de Colombia (2004) Agenda para la integración dinámica de colombia en el mundo. Bogotá D.C.

Consejo Nacional de Política Económica y Social (CONPES), República de Colombia (2006) Institucionalidad y principios rectores de política para la competitividad y productividad. Bogotá, D.C.: Departamento Nacional de Planeación

Consejo Nacional de Política Económica y Social (CONPES), República de Colombia (2010) Informe de seguimiento a la política nacional de competitividad y productividad, ley 1253 de 2008, vol 3668. Bogotá: Departamento Nacional de Planeación

Consejo Nacional de Política Económica y Social (CONPES) (2008) Política nacional de competitividad y productividad. Bogotá D.C.

Correia LJ (2008) The determinants of colombian exports: an empirical analysis using the gravity model, Revista Desarrollo y Sociedad, Universidad de Los Andes-Cede

Cramer C (1999) Can Africa industrialize by processing primary commodities? The case of Mozambican cashew nuts. World Dev 27(7):1247–1266. doi:10.1016/S0305-750X(99)00053-4

Daude C, Fernández-Arias E (2010) La productividad agregada: la clave para el desarrollo de América Latina. In: Pagés C (ed) La era de la productividad: como transformar las economías desde sus cimientos. Inter-American Development Bank, Washington DC, pp 32–53

De Ferranti D, Perry G, Gill I, Guasch JL, Maloney W, Sánchez-Páramo C, Schady N (2003) Closing the gap in education and technology. Washington DC, World Bank

De Gucht K (2010) On the EU trade agreement with Colombia and Peru. European Commission, Brussels

Deardorff AV (1995) Determinants of bilateral trade: does gravity work in a neoclassical world? NBER (Working Paper 5377) pp 1–28

Deardorff AV (1998) Determinants of bilateral trade: does gravity work in a neoclassical world? In: Frankel JA (ed) The regionalization of the world economy. University of Chicago Press, Chicago, pp 7–32

Delegación de la Unión Europea en Colombia (2010) Inversión extranjera directa, Retrieved July/21, 2010, from http://ec.europa.eu/delegations/colombia/eu_colombia/trade_relation/foreign_direct_investment/index_es.htm

Departamento Nacional de Planeación (2009) Cómo va colombia en competitividad? DNP, Bogotá
DeRosa DA (2008) Gravity model analysis. In: Hufbauer G, Brunel C (eds), Maghreb regional and global integration: a dream to be fulfilled (pp. 45–68). Washington D.C.: Institute for International Economics
Dijkstra T (2001) Export diversification in Uganda: developments in non-traditional agricultural exports. African Studies Centre, Working Paper 47:1–126
Dixit AK, Stiglitz JE (1977) Monopolistic competition and optimum product diversity. Am Econ Rev 67:297–308
Dollar D (1986) Technological innovation, capital mobility, and the product cycle in north-south trade. Am Econ Rev 76(1):177–190
Dollar D (1992) Outward-oriented developing economies really do grow more rapidly: evidence from 95 LDCs, 1976–1985. Econ Dev Cult Change 40(3):523–544
Dunning JH (1992) The competitive advantage of countries and the activities of transnational corporations UNCTAD
Durand M, Simon J, Webb C (1992) OECD's indicators of international trade and competitiveness. OECD Economics Department Working Papers 120:1–51
Dutta S, Mia I (2010) Global information technology report 2009–2010: ICT for sustainability. World Economic Forum, Geneva
Easterly W (2002) The elusive quest for growth. MIT Press, Cambridge, MA
Easterly W, Levine R (2002) Tropics, germs, and crops: how endowments influence economic development. Unpublished manuscript
Easterly W, Rebelo S (1993) Fiscal policy and economic growth: an empirical investigation. J Monetary Econ 32:417–458
Eaton J, Kortum S (2002) Technology, geography, and trade. Econometrica 70(5):1741–1779
Eaton J, Eslava M, Kugler M, Tybout J (2008) The margins of entry into export markets: evidence from colombia. In: Helpman E, Marin D, Verdier T (eds) The organization of firms in a global economy. Harvard University Press, Cambridge, MA, pp 231–272
Edwards S (1992) Trade orientation, distortions and growth in developing countries. J Dev Econ 39(1):31–57, http://www.elsevier.com/wps/find/journaldescription.cws_home/505546/description#description
Edwards S (1993) Openness, trade liberalization, and growth in developing countries. J Econ Lit 31(3):1358–1393, http://www.aeaweb.org/jel/
Edwards S (1998) Openness, productivity and growth: what do we really know? Econ J 108 (447):383–398
Edwards S, Steiner R (2000) On the crisis hypothesis of economic reform: Colombia 1989–91. Cuadernos De Economía 37(112):445–493
Egger P (2002) An econometric view on the estimation of gravity models and the calculation of trade potentials. World Econ 25(2):297–312
El Colombiano (2010) Bajaron los aranceles al banano en la Unión Europea. El Colombiano, Medellín
Esfahani HS (1991) Exports, imports, and economic growth in semi-industrialized countries. J Dev Econ 35(1):93–116
Esfahani HS, Ramírez MT (2003) Institutions, infrastructure, and economic growth. J Dev Econ 70:443–477
European Commission (2004) El sistema de preferencias generalizadas de la unión europea. European Commission, Brussels
European Commission (2005) GSP – the new EU preferential terms of trade for developing countries. http://www.europa-eu-un.org/articles/fr/article_4337_fr.htm. Accessed July 2010
European Commission (2010) Regions: Latin america. Retrieved 10 August 2010, from http://ec.europa.eu/trade/creating-opportunities/bilateral-relations/regions/latin-america-caribbean/
European Commission (2010) EU launches major new trade relationship with Latin America. European Commission, Brussels

European Commission (2010) Generalyzed system of preferences, Retrieved July/14, 2010, from http://ec.europa.eu/taxation_customs/customs/customs_duties/rules_origin/preferential/article_781_en.htm
Evenett SJ, Keller W (2002) On theories explaining the success of the gravity equation. J Polit Econ 110(2):281–316
Evenett SJ, Venables AJ (2002) Export growth in developing countries: market entry and bilateral trade flows. University of Bern Working Paper, pp 1–42
EEAS (European External Action Service) (2010) European Union external action, Republic of Colombia. Retrieved 28 Jul 2010, from http://www.eeas.europa.eu/colombia/index_en.htm
Fainboim I, Rodríguez CJ (2000) El desarrollo de la infraestructura en colombia en la década de los noventa. Documentos De Investigación, CEPAL Naciones Unidas, (002490), 1–80
Fay M, Morrison M (2005) Infrastructure in Latin America and the Caribbean: recent developments and key challenges. World Bank, Washington, D.C
Feder G (1983) On exports and economic growth. J Dev Econ 12(1–2):59–73. doi:10.1016/0304-3878(83)90031-7
Feenstra RC, Taylor AM (2008) International economics, 1st edn. Worth, New York
Feenstra RC, Madani D, Yang T, Liang C (1998) Testing endogenous growth in South Korea and Taiwan. NBER Working Paper Series 6028:1–25
Feenstra RC, Markusen JR, Rose AK (2001) Using the gravity equation to differentiate among alternative theories of trade. Can J Econ Rev Can Economique 34(2):430–447
Flórez D (2010) Infraestructura tendrá un mayor protagonismo en la economía. Bogotá, Portafolio
Francois J, Manchin M (2007) Institutions, infrastructure, and trade. World Bank Policy Research Working Paper 4152:1–38
Frankel JA, Romer D (1999) Does trade cause growth? Am Econ Rev 89(3):379–399
Frankel JA, Wei S (1993) Trade blocs and currency blocs. NBER Working Paper Series, (4335)
Freeman C (1987) Technology and economic performance: lessons from japan. Pinter, London
Garay LJ (2004) De la sustitución de las importaciones a la apertura. In: Colombia: Estructura industrial e internacionalización 1967–1996. Edición virtual, Banco de la República, Bogotá
Gaviria J (1998) Port privatization and competition in Colombia. Public Policy Priv Sect 167:1–4
Glick R, Rose AK (2002) Does a currency union affect trade? The time-series evidence. Eur Econ Rev 46(6):1125–1151
Goldberg P, Pavcnik N (2005) Trade, wages, and the political economy of trade protection: Evidence from the colombian trade reforms. Journal of International Economics 66(1):75–105
Gómez HJ (2010) Productividad es la receta del crecimiento del país. Retrieved July/30, 2010, from http://www.portafolio.co/archivo/documento/CMS-7851340
GRECO (Grupo de estudios del crecimiento económico colombiano) (2002) Exportaciones no tradicionales de Colombia. In: El crecimiento económico colombiano en el siglo XX. Banco de la República, Bogotá
Grossman GM, Helpman E (1991) Innovation and growth in the global economy. MIT Press, Cambridge, MA
Grubel HG, Lloyd P (1975) Intra-industry trade: the theory and measurement of international trade in dfferentiated products. MacMillan, London
Guasch JL (2003) Technological transitions and elements of technology policy. In: De Ferranti D, Perry G, Gill I, Guasch JL, Maloney W, Sánchez-Páramo C, Schady N (eds) Closing the gap in education and technology. World Bank, Washington DC, pp 133–169
Guerra M, López A, de la Fé López M (2009) Intercambio comercial unión europea-comunidad andina 1997–2007. Revista Facultad De Ciencias Económicas 17(2):133–150
Gutiérrez A, de Piñeres S, Ferrantino M (1997a) Export diversification and structural dynamics in the growth process: the case of Chile. J Dev Econ 52(2):375–391. doi:10.1016/S0304-3878(96)00446-4
Gutiérrez A, de Piñeres S, Ferrantino M (1997b) Export diversification trends: some comparisons for Latin America. Int Exec 39(4):465–477

Haddad M, Fane G, Nuansavanh K, Brenton P, Schuler P (2006) Building export competitiveness in laos: background report. Washington D.C.: World Bank

Harrison A, Hanson G (1999) Who gains from trade reform? Some remaining puzzles. J Dev Econ 59:125–154

Hanratty DM, Meditz SW (eds) (1988) Colombia: a country study. GPO for the Library of Congress, Washington DC

Harding T (2009) Infrastructure and diversifying through better products. In: Newfarmer R, Shaw W, Walkenhorst P (eds) Breaking into new markets: emerging lessons for export diversification. World Bank, Washington, D.C, pp 237–254

Harding T, Javorcik BS (2007) Note on the effect of FDI on export diversification in central and eastern europe. Unpublished manuscript. Retrieved 7 Dec 2009, from http://siteresources.worldbank.org/INTEXPCOMNET/Resources/Javorcik,_Note_on_the_Effect_of_FDI_on_Export_Diversification_in_Central_and_Eastern_Europe.pdf

Hausman JA, Taylor WE (1981) Panel data and unobservable individual effects. Econometrica 49:1377–1398

Hausmann R, Klinger B (2006) Structural transformation and patterns of comparative advantage in the product space. CID Working Paper (128)

Hausmann R, Hwang J, Rodrik D (2006) What you export matters. Discussion Pap Ser 5444:1–14

Hausmann R, Hwang J, Rodrik D (2007) What you export matters. Journal of Economic Growth 12(1):1–25

Helleiner GK (1986) Outward orientation, import instability and african economic growth: an empirical investigation. In: Lall S, Stewart F (eds) Theory and reality in development: essays in honour of Paul Streeten. Macmillan, London, pp 139–153

Helpman E, Krugman P (1985) Market structure and foreign trade. Increasing returns, imperfect competition, and the international economy. MIT Press, Cambridge, MA

Helpman E, Melitz MJ, Rubinstein Y (2008) Estimating trade flows: trading partners and trading volumes. Q J Econ 123(2):441–487

Herzer D, Nowak-Lehmann F (2004) Export diversification, externalities and growth. Discussion Papers, (99)

Hofman AA (2001) Long run economic development in latin america in a comparative perspective: proximate and ultimate causes (8), 1–43

Holmes J, Amin Gutiérrez de Piñeres S, Curtin K (2009) Guns, drugs, and development in Colombia. Austin: University of Texas Press

Howitt P (2000) Endogenous growth and cross-country income differences. Am Econ Rev 90 (4):829–846

Hummels D, Klenow P (2005) The variety and quality of a nation's exports. Am Econ Rev 95 (3):704–723

Imbs J, Wacziarg R (2003) Stages of diversification. Am Econ Rev 93(1):63–86

International Labour Office (ILO) (2010) LABORSTA internet. Retrieved June/7, 2010, from http://laborsta.ilo.org/applv8/data/c6e.html#n1

International Monetary Fund (IMF) (2010) IMF country report, Colombia. IMF, Washington DC

International Trade Center (2009) Trade competitiveness map. http://www.trademap.org. Accessed 15 June 2010

International Trade Centre (ITC) (2007) The trade performance index: technical notes. Market Analysis Section, International Trade Center, Geneva

Irwin DA (2000) How did the United States become a net exporter of manufactured goods? NBER Working Paper Series, (7638)

Johnston J, DiNardo J (1997) Econometric methods, 4th edn. New York: McGraw-Hill/Irwin

Kalmanovitz S (2004) Recesión y recuperación de la economía colombiana. Nueva Sociedad 192:98–116

Kavoussi RM (1984) Export expansion and economic growth: further empirical evidence. J Dev Econ 14(1):241–250. doi:10.1016/0304-3878(84)90052-X

Keller W (2000a) Do trade patterns and technology flows affect productivity growth? World Bank Econ Rev 14(1):17–47
Keller W (2000) Geographic localization of international technology diffussion. NBER Working Paper Series (7509). http://www.nber.org/papers/w7509
Klein LR (1988) Components of competitiveness. Science 241(4863):308–313
Klinger B, Lederman D (2009) Diversification, innovation, and imitation of the global technological frontier. In: Newfarmer R, Shaw W, Walkenhorst P (eds) Breaking into new markets: emerging lessons for export diversification. World Bank, Washington, D.C., pp 101–110
Knight PT, Marques RA (2008) Closing the technology gap. In: Haar J, Price J (eds) Can Latin America compete? Confronting the challenges of globalization. Palgrave Macmillan, New York, pp 99–119
Koetsenruijter A (2006) Evolución de las relaciones comerciales colombia-unión europea. Bogotá: Delegación de la Comisión Europea para Colombia
Kohler U, Kreuter F (2005) Data analysis using stata, 2nd edn. Stata Press, College Station, Texas
Kohli A (2009) States and economic development. Brazilian J Polit Econ 29(2):212–227
Kohli I, Singh N (1989) Exports and growth: critical minimum effort and diminishing returns. J Dev Econ 30(2):391–400. doi:10.1016/0304-3878(89)90011-4
Krishna P, Levchenko AA (2009) Comparative advantage, complexity and volatility. NBER Working Paper Series 14965:1–29
Krueger AO (1978) Foreign trade regimes and economic development: liberalization attempts and consequences. Ballinger Publishing Company for NBER, Cambridge
Krugman P (1979a) A model of innovation, technology transfer, and the world distribution of income. J Polit Econ 87(2):253–266
Krugman PR (1979b) Increasing returns, monopolistic competition, and international trade. J Int Econ 9(4):469–479, http://www.elsevier.com/wps/find/journaldescription.cws_home/505552/description#description
Krugman PR (1979c) Increasing returns, monopolistic competition, and international trade. J Int Econ 9(4):469–479, http://www.elsevier.com/wps/find/journaldescription.cws_home/505552/description#description
Krugman P (1994) r. A dangerous obsession, Competitiveness
Krugman PR, Obstfeld M (2006) International economics: theory and policy, 7th edn. Pearson Addison Wesley, Boston
Laursen K (1998) Revealed comparative advantage and the alternatives as measures of international specialisation. DRUID working paper (98–30):1–17
Lall S (1998) Exports of manufactures by developing countries: emerging patterns of trade and location. Oxford Rev Econ Pol 14(2):54–73
Leamer E, Stern R (1970) Quantitative international economics. Allyn and Bacon, Boston
Leamer EE, Levinsohn J (1995) International trade theory: the evidence. In: Grossman G, Rogoff K (eds) The handbook of international economics. North-Holland, Elsevier
Lederman D, Maloney WF (2003) Trade structure and growth. Policy Research Working Paper (3025)
Lederman D, Özden Ç (2007) Geopolitical interests and preferential access to U.S. markets. Econ Polit 19(2):235–258
Lee J (1995) Capital goods imports and long-run growth. J Dev Econ 48(1):91–110. doi:10.1016/0304-3878(95)00015-1
Lee HY, Ricci LA, Rigobon R (2004) Once again: is openness good for growth? NBER Working Paper Series (10749):1-28. http://www.nber.org/papers/w10749
Leibenstein H (1966) Allocative efficiency vs. "X-efficiency". Am Econ Rev 56(3):392–415, http://www.jstor.org/stable/pdfplus/1823775.pdf
Lemoine F, Ünal D (2004) Assembly trade and technology transfer:The case of china. World Dev 32(5):829–850
Levchenko AA (2007) Institutional quality and international trade. Rev Econ Stud 74(3):791–819, http://www.blackwellpublishing.com/journal.asp?ref=0034-6527

Levchenko AA, di Giovanni J (2006) Openness, volatility and the risk content of exports. Paper presented at the (86)

Levine R, Renelt D (1992) A sensitivity analysis of cross-country growth regressions. Am Econ Rev 82(4):942–963, http://www.aeaweb.org/aer/

Lin JY, Nugent JB (1995) Institutions and economic development. In: Behrman J, Srinivasan TN (eds) Handbook of economic development. Elsevier, (pp. 2301–2370). Amsterdam: Elsevier

Linneman H (1966) An econometric study of international trade flows. North-Holland, Amsterdam

Loayza N, Fajnzylber P, Calderón C (2004) Economic growth in Latin America and the Caribbean: stylized facts, explanations, and forecasts. Central Bank of Chile, Working Papers 265:1–150

Loser C (2008) The macroeconomic environment of competitiveness. In: Haar J, Price J (eds) Can Latin America compete? Confronting the challenges of globalization. Palgrave MacMillan, New York, pp 27–43

Love J (1983) Concentration, diversification and earnings instability: some evidence on developing countries' exports of manufactures and primary products. World Dev 11(9):787–793. doi:10.1016/0305-750X(83)90091-8

Lucas RE (1988) On the mechanics of development planning. J Monetary Econ 22:3–42

MacDonald JM (1994) Does import competition force efficient production? Rev Econ Stat 76(4):721–727

Maddison A (1991) Economic and social conditions in Latin America, 1913–1950. In: Urrutia M (ed) *Long-term trends in latin american economic development* (). Johns Hopkins University Press for the Inter-American Development Bank, Baltimore

Madsen JB (2009) Trade barriers, openness, and economic growth. South Econ J 76(2):397–418, http://www.utc.edu/Outreach/SouthernEconomicAssociation/southern-economic-journal.html

Mahon J Jr (1992) Was Latin America too rich to prosper? structural and political obstacles to export-led industrial growth. J Dev Stud 28(2):241–263

Maloney WF (2002) Missed opportunities: innovation and resource-based growth in Latin America. World Bank Policy Research Working Paper 2935:1–40

Mankiw G, Romer D, Weil D (1992) A contribution to the empirics of economic growth. Q J Econ 107(2):407–437

Manzano O, Rigobon R (2001) Resource curse or debt overhang. NBER Working Paper Series (8390)

Marques RA, Oliveira G (2006) Sectoral system of innovation in Brazil: reflections about linkages and the accumulation of technological capabilities experienced by SME suppliers to the aeronautic industry. Unpublished manuscript

Martin W, Mitra D (2001) Productivity growth and convergence in agriculture versus manufacturing. Econ Dev Cult Change 49(2):403–422

Martínez-Zarzoso I, Suárez-Burguet C (2005) Transport costs and trade:Empirical evidence for latin american imports from the european union. Int Trade Econ Dev 14(3):353–371

Martínez-Zarzoso I, Cantavella M, Fernández JI (2003) Estimación y aplicaciones de una ecuación de gravedad para el comercio atlántico de la unión europea. Información Comercial Española, ICE: Revista De Economía 806:23–32

Matsuyama K (1992) Agricultural productivity, comparative advantage, and economic growth. J Econ Theory 58(2):317–334. doi:10.1016/0022-0531(92)90057-O

Mattoo A (2009) Exporting services. In: Newfarmer R, Shaw W, Walkenhorst P (eds) Breaking into new markets: emerging lessons for export diversification. The World Bank, Washington DC, pp 161–182

Mazumdar J (1996) Do static gains from trade lead to medium-run growth? J Polit Econ 104(6):1328–1337

Meléndez M, Seim K, Medina P (2003) Productivity dynamics of the colombian manufacturing sector. Documentos CEDE, Universidad De Los Andes 23:1–45

Melitz MJ (2003) The impact of trade on intra-industry reallocations and aggregate industry productivity. Econometrica 71(6):1695–1725, http://www.econometricsociety.org
Michaely M (1977) Exports and growth: an empirical investigation. J Dev Econ 4(1):49–53. doi:10.1016/0304-3878(77)90006-2
Michaely M, Papageorgiou D, Choksi A (1991) Liberalizing foreign trade. Blackwell, Oxford
Ministerio de Comercio, Industria y Turismo, República de Colombia (1999) Plan estratégico exportador 1999–2009. Bogotá D.C.
Ministerio de Comercio, Industria y Turismo, República de Colombia (2010) ABC del acuerdo comercial con la unión europea. Bogotá: Ministerio de Comercio, Industria y Turismo
Ministerio de Comercio, Industria y Turismo, República de Colombia (2010) Colombia y la unión europea, 2010, from http://www.tlc.gov.co/eContent/newsdetail.asp?id=4166&idcompany=37
Ministerio de Relaciones Exteriores de Colombia (2010) Europa. http://www.cancilleria.gov.co/wps/portal/espanol/!ut/p/c1/04_SB8K8xLLM9MSSzPy8xBz9CP0os_jQsKAwo2AXYwN3P3NDA0-zIDcDf0dnQ4sgQ6B8JJK8v2-QqYFRmI9ZoJersRFQJQHdfh75uan6BbkR5QCoxd1J/dl2/d1/L2dJQSEvUUt3QS9ZQnB3LzZfVVZSVjJTRDMwR0xTQzBJNjdTQU9DTTEwMDA!/?WCM_GLOBAL_CONTEXT=/wps/wcm/connect/WCM_MENUPRINCIPAL_MRE/menu+principal/relaciones+internacionales/bilaterales/europa/europa. Accessed June 2010
Ministerio de Comercio, Industria y Turismo, República de Colombia (2006) Por el cual se organiza el sistema administrativo nacional de competitividad y se dictan otras disposiciones. Bogotá, D.C.
Misas G (2001) De la sustitución de importaciones a la apertura económica.la difícil consolidación industrial. In: Misas G, Corredor C (eds) Desarrollo económico y social en colombia, siglo XX. Universidad Nacional de Colombia, Facultad de Ciencias Económicas, Bogotá, pp 111–134
Moehler R (2007) EU bilateral and regional trade agreements:Impacts on the CAP. EuroChoices 6(2):28–35
Moreno A, Posada H (2006) Evolución del comercio intraindustrial entre las regiones colombianas y la comunidad andina, 1990–2004:un análisis comparativo. Munich Personal RePEc Archive 4936:1–37
Moschos D (1989) Export expansion, growth and the level of economic development: an empirical analysis. J Dev Econ 30(1):93–102. doi:10.1016/0304-3878(89)90052-7
Mulligan CB, Sala-i-Martin X (1992) Some empirical evidence on two-sector models of endogenous growth. Unpublished manuscript
Neary JP (2009) Putting the 'new' into new trade theory: Paul krugman's nobel memorial prize in economics. Scand J Econ 111(2):217–250, http://www.blackwellpublishing.com/journal.asp?ref=0347-0520
Nelson RR, Phelps ES (1966) Investment in humans, technological diffusion, and economic growth. Am Econ Rev Pap Proc 56:69–75
Ng F, Yeats A (2005) What can Africa expect from its traditional exports? World Bank, Africa Region Working Paper Series 26:1–84
Nieto JA (2002) Exportación andina hacia la Unión Europea: Índices de especialización comercial y cuotas de mercado 1995–2000. Revistas ICE 802:173–194
Nilsson L (2002) Is the roadmap from Lome to Cotonou correct? Appl Econ 34(11):439–452
Ocampo JA, Villar L (1992) Trayectoria y vicisitudes de la apertura económica colombiana. Pensamiento Iberoamericano 21:165–186
OECD (2006) Aid for trade: making it effective. OECD, Paris
Orozco AM (2002) Colombia, la unión europea y el SGP andino. Unpublished manuscript.from www.mincomercio.gov.co/econtent/. . ./Colombia_UEySGPAndino.ppt
Ospina G (2004) Colombia: Desarrollo económico reciente en infraestructura. Washington D.C.: World Bank
Oughton C (1997) Competitiveness policy in the 1990s. Econ J I07:1486–1503
Pagés C (ed) (2010) La era de la productividad: Como transformar las economías desde sus cimientos. Inter-American Development Bank, Washington DC

Pérez R (2006) Are the economic partnership agreements a first-best optimum for the african caribbean pacific countries? J World Trade 40(6):999–1019
Plümper T, Troeger V (2007) Efficient estimation of time-invariant and rarely changing variables in finite sample panel analyses with unit fixed effects. Polit Anal 15(2):124–139
Por El Cual Se Organiza El Sistema Administrativo Nacional De Competitividad y Se Dictan Otras Disposiciones, Decree 2828U.S.C. (2006).
Portafolio (2010) Colombia no despega en exportaciones per cápita. Retrieved September/22, 2010, from http://www.portafolio.co/archivo/documento/CMS-7929943
Porter M, Schwab K (2008) The global competitiveness report 2008–2009. World Economic Forum, Geneva
Poyhonen P (1963a) A tentative model for the volume of trade between countries. Welwirtschaftliches Arch 90(1):93–99
Poyhonen P (1963b) Toward a general theory of international trade. Ekonomiska Samfundets Tidskrift 16(2):69–78
Prebisch R (1950) The economic development of Latin America and its principal problems. United Nations, New York
Press S (2009) Stata longitudinal-data panel-data reference manual, release 11. Stata Press, College Station, Texas, USA
Price J (2008) Logistics: the software that drives an economy. In: Haar J, Price J (eds) Can Latin America compete? Confronting the challenges of globalization. Palgrave Macmillan, New York, pp 163–174
Puryear J, Ortega T (2008) Coveting human capital: is Latin American education competitive? In: Haar J, Price J (eds) Can Latin America compete? Confronting the challenges of globalization. Palgrave Macmillan, New York, pp 45–62
Quah D, Rauch JE (1990) Openness and the rate of economic growth. Working Paper, University of California San Diego
Rajapatirana S (1998) Colombian trade policies and the 1996 WTO trade policy review. World Econ 21(4):515–527. doi:10.1111/1467-9701.00145
Ram R (1985) Exports and economic growth: some additional evidence. Econ Dev Cult Change 33(2):415–425
Ram R (1987) Exports and economic growth in developing countries: evidence from time-series and cross-section data. Econ Dev Cult Change 36(1):51–72, http://www.journals.uchicago.edu/EDCC/home.html
Rebelo S (1991) Long-run policy analysis and long-run growth. J Polit Econ 99(3):500–521
Reinhart C, Wickham P (1994) Commodity prices: cyclical weakness or secular decline? Int Monetary Fund Staff Pap 41(2):175–213
Relaciones bilaterales colombia - europa (2010) Retrieved July/2010, 2010, from www.cancilleria.gov.co
Rigobon R, Rodrik D (2004) Rule of law, democracy, openness, and income: estimating the interrelationships. NBER Working Paper Series, (10750):1–28. http://www.nber.org/papers/w10750
Rivera-Batiz L, Romer PM (1991) Economic integration and endogenous growth. Q J Econ 106(2):531–555, http://www.mitpressjournals.org/loi/qjec
Rodríguez F, Rodrik D (1999) Trade policy and economic growth: A Skeptic's guide to the cross-national evidence. NBER Working Paper Series 7081:1–80
Rodrik D (2007) One economics, many recipes: globalization, institutions, and economic growth. Princeton University Press, New Jersey
Rodrik D, Subramanian A, Trebbi F (2004) Institutions rule: the primacy of institutions over geography and integration in economic development. J Econ Growth 9:131–165
Romer PM (1990a) Endogenous technological change. J Polit Econ 98(5):S71–S102, http://www.journals.uchicago.edu/JPE/
Romer PM (1990b) Endogenous technological change. J Polit Econ 98(5, Part 2: The problem of development: a conference of the institute for the study of free enterprise systems):S71–S102

Romer PM (1992) Two strategies for economic development: using ideas and producing ideas. Paper presented at the World Bank Annual Conference on Economic Development. World Bank, Washington.

Rose AK (2000) One money, one market:Estimating the effect of common currencies on trade. Economic Policy 15(30):7–46

Rose AK (2004) Do we really know that the WTO increases trade? Am Econ Rev 94(1):98–114

Rose AK, Lockwood B, Quah D (2000) One money, one market: the effect of common currencies on trade. Econ Policy 15(30):9–45

Sachs JD (1987) Trade and exchange rate policies in growth-oriented adjustment programs. NBER Working Paper Series 2226:1–47

Sachs J (1989) Developing country debt and the economic performance. University of Chicago Press, Chicago, USA

Sachs J, Warner A (1995) Natural resource abundance and economic growth. NBER Working Paper Series (5398)

Sachs JD, Warner A, Åslund A, Fischer S (1995) Economic reform and the process of global integration. Brookings Papers on Economic Activity (1, 25th Anniversary Issue) 1–118

Sala-i-Martin X, Blanke J, Drzeniek Hanouz M, Geiger T, Mia I (2009) The global competitiveness index 2009–2010: Contributing to long-term prosperity amid the global economic crisis. In: Schwab K (ed), The global competitiveness report 2009–2010 (pp. 3–47). Geneva: World Economic Forum

Sala-i-Martin X, Blanke J, Drzeniek Hanouz M, Geiger T, Mia I (2010a) The global competitiveness index 2009–2010: Contributing to long-term prosperity amid the global economic crisis. World Economic Forum, Geneva, pp 1–57

Sala-i-Martin X, Blanke J, Drzeniek Hanouz M, Geiger T, Mia I (2010b) The global competitiveness index 2010–2011: looking beyond the global economic crisis. In: Schwab K (ed) The global competitiveness report 2010–2011. World Economic Forum, Geneva, pp 3–56

Salin D, Mello E (2009) Snapshot of Colombian transportation and infrastructure. Washington D.C.: United States Department of Agriculture - USDA

Savage IR, Deutsch KW (1960) A statistical model of the gross analyisis of transactions flows. Econometrica 28(3):551–572

Sánchez-Páramo C, Schady N (2003) Closing the skills gap: education policies. In: De Ferranti D, Perry G, Gill I, Guasch JL, Maloney W, Sánchez-Páramo C, Schady N (eds) Closing the gap in education and technology (pp. 75–107) World Bank, Washington DC

Sánchez-Páramo C, Schady N (2003) The gaps that matter most. In: De Ferranti D, Perry G, Gill I, Guasch JL, Maloney W, Sánchez-Páramo C, Schady N (eds) Closing the gap in education and technology (pp. 23–47) World Bank, Washington DC

Sánchez-Robles B (1998) Infrastructure investment and growth: some empirical evidence. Contemp Econ Policy XVI:98–108

Schiff M, Wang Y (2003) Regional integration and technology diffusion: the case of the North America Free Trade Agreement. World Bank Policy Research Working Paper, (3132)

Schiff M, Wang Y, Olarreaga M (2002) Trade-related technology diffusion and the dynamics of north-south and south-south integration. World Bank Policy Research Working Paper (2861):1-25. http://www-wds.worldbank.org/servlet/WDSContentServer/WDSP/IB/2002/07/31/000094946_02071204322621/Rendered/PDF/multi0page.pdf

Schwab K (2010) The global competitiveness report 2009–2010. World Economic Forum, Geneva

Schwab K, Sala-i-Martin X (2009) The global competitiveness report 2009–2010. World Economic Forum, Geneva, Switzerland

Segerstrom PS, Anant TCA, Dinopoulos E (1990) A Schumpeterian model of the product life cycle. Am Econ Rev 80(5):1077–1091

Sen S (2005) International trade theory and policy: what is left of the free trade paradigm? Dev Change 36(6):1011–1029

Singer HW, Gray P (1988) Trade policy and growth of developing countries: some new data. World Dev 16(3):395–403. doi:10.1016/0305-750X(88)90006-X

Smith J, Juhn T, Humphrey C (2008) Consumer and small business credit: building blocks of the middle class. In: Haar J, Price J (eds) Can Latin America compete? Confronting the challenges of globalization. Palgrave MacMillan, New York, pp 79–97

Soloaga I, Alan Wintersb L (2001) Regionalism in the nineties: what effect on trade? N Am J Econ Finance 12(1):1–29. doi:10.1016/S1062-9408(01)00042-0

Stanley DL, Bunnag S (2001) A new look at the benefits of diversification: lessons from Central America. Appl Econ 33(11):1369–1383

Subramanian A, Wei S (2007) The WTO promotes trade, strongly but unevenly. J Int Econ 72(1):151–175. doi:10.1016/j.jinteco.2006.07.007

Summers R, Heston A (1991) The penn world table (mark 5): An expanded set of international comparisons, 1950–1988. Quarterly Journal of Economics 106(2):327–368

Suranovic S (2009) International trade theory and policy. Retrieved 14 Dec 2010, from http://internationalecon.com/Trade/tradehome.php

Svensson J (2000) Foreign aid and rent seeking. J Int Econ 51(2):437–461

Taylor L (1988) Economic openness — problems to the century's end. WIDER Working Papers, 1–81

The Economist (2009) Alvaro Uribe's Colombia. The Economist, Print Edition

The Economist (2010) It's only natural: commodities alone are not enough to sustain flourishing economies, Retrieved August/17, 2010, from http://www.economist.com/node/16964094

Thirlwall AP (2000) Trade, trade liberalisation and economic growth: theory and evidence. Economic Research Papers, African Development Bank (63):1-28. http://www.afdb.org/fileadmin/uploads/afdb/Documents/Publications/00157660-FR-ERP-63.PDF

Tiffin S, Bortagaray I (2008) Fostering innovation: technological innovation in urban clusters. In: Haar J, Price J (eds) Can Latin America compete? Confronting the challenges of globalization. Palgrave Macmillan, New York, pp 121–141

Tinbergen J (1962) Shaping the world economy: suggestions for an international economic policy. Twentieth Century Fund, New York

Todaro MP, Smith SC (2006) Economic development, Ninthth edn. Pearson Addison Wesley, Boston

Tomiura E (2006) Is our economy globalized? – the emergence of "new new trade theory" and needs for firm-level empirical analysis. Retrieved 14 Dec 2009, from http://www.rieti.go.jp/en/columns/a01_0202.html

U.S. Department of State (2002) Country reports on human rights practices, Retrieved June/22, 2010, from http://www.state.gov/g/drl/rls/hrrpt/2001/wha/8326.htm

UNCTAD (1995) Recent developments in the diversification of developing countries' commodity exports. Unpublished manuscript

UNCTAD (2010) UNCTAD handbook of statistics 2009. Retrieved 31 Aug 2010, from http://www.unctad.org/Templates/Page.asp?intItemID=1584&lang=1

United Nations Conference on Trade and Development - UNCTAD (2006) Investment policy review: Colombia. UNCTAD, Geneva

United Nations Economic and Social Commission for Asia and the Pacific (ESCAP) (2001) Role of human capital in economic development: some myths and realities. In Development planning in a market economy (LDC series no. 6, 2001), ESCAP

United Nations Economic and Social Commission for Asia and the Pacific (ESCAP) (2004) Export diversification and economic growth: the experience of selected least developed countries, No. 24, United Nations

United Nations Economic and Social Commission for Asia and the Pacific (ESCAP) (2009) Statistical yearbook for asia and the pacific 2009, 2010, from http://www.unescap.org/stat/data/syb2009/15-Research-and-development.asp

United Nations Economic Commission for Africa (UNECA) (2007) Diversification trends in africa. Addis Ababa: United Nations Economic Commission for Africa

United States Department of Labor (2010) International labor comparisons, 2010, from http://www.bls.gov/fls/

Vamvakidis A (1998) Regional integration and economic growth. World Bank Econ Rev 12(2):251–270
Van den Berg H, Lewer JJ (2007) International trade and economic growth. M.E. Sharpe, Armonk, New York
Venables AJ (2003) Winners and losers from regional integration agreements. Econ J 113(490):747–761
Vernon R (1966) International investment and international trade in the product cycle. Q J Econ 80(2):190–207
Von Kirbach F (2010) A country's competitive advantage, 2009, from http://www.tradeforum.org/news/fullstory.php/aid/536/A_Country_92s_Competitive_Advantage.html
Von Kirchbach F (2003) A country's competitive advantage. http://www.tradeforum.org/news/fullstory.php/aid/536/A_Country_92s_Competitive_Advantage.html. Accessed 2009
Wacziarg R (2001) Measuring the dynamic gains from trade. World Bank Econ Rev 15(3):393–429. doi:http://wber.oxfordjournals.org/
Wacziarg R, Welch KH (2003) Trade liberalization and growth: new evidence. NBER Working Paper Series, (10152) http://www.nber.org/papers/w10152
Wälde K, Wood C (2004) The empirics of trade and growth: where are the policy recommendations? Int Econ Econ Policy 1(2–3):275–292
Weil D (2009) Economic growth, 2nd edn. Pearson, New York
Wooldridge JM (2002) Econometric analysis of cross section and panel data. MIT Press, Cambridge, MA
Wooldridge JM (2009) Introductory econometrics: a modern approach, 4th edn. South Western Cengage Learning, Canada
World Bank (2002) Trade frictions and welfare in the gravity model. Retrieved 25 July 2010, from http://info.worldbank.org/etools/BSPAN/PresentationView.asp?PID=416&EID=217
World Bank (2006) Colombia contracting education services. Washington D.C.: World Bank
World Bank (2008) The quality of education in Colombia. Washington D.C.: World Bank
World Bank, International Finance Corporation (2010) Doing business in Colombia 2010. World Bank, Washington, D.C.
World Bank (2010) Colombia, country brief. Retrieved January 2010, from http://web.worldbank.org/WBSITE/EXTERNAL/COUNTRIES/LACEXT/COLOMBIAEXTN/0,contentMDK:22254365~pagePK:1497618~piPK:217854~theSitePK:324946,00.html
World Bank (2010) Doing business: measuring business regulations, from http://www.doingbusiness.org/, Accessed on 4 June 2010
World Bank (2010) Logistics performance index. Retrieved July/7, 2010, from http://info.worldbank.org/etools/tradesurvey/mode1a.asp
World Bank (2010) World development indicators, Retrieved February/3, 2010, from http://databank.worldbank.org/ddp/home.do?Step=12&id=4&CNO=2
World Bank (2004) Colombia: recent economic developments in infrastructure. World Bank, Washington DC
World Bank (2007) Doing business in Colombia 2008. World Bank, Washington DC
World Economic Forum (2010) The global competitiveness report 2008–2009, 2009, from http://www.weforum.org/en/initiatives/gcp/Global%20Competitiveness%20Report/PastReports/index.htm
World Economic Forum (2009) The financial development report. World Economic Forum, Geneva
World Economic Forum (2010) The global competitiveness report 2010–2011. World Economic Forum, Geneva
World Trade Organization (WTO) (2006) Trade policy review, colombia. WTO, Geneva
World Trade Organization (WTO) (2010) Trade policy review. WTO, Geneva
Wright G (2001) Resource-based growth then and now. Unpublished manuscript
Zentrum für Europäische Wirtschaftsforchung (2010) Panelökonometrie: Teil I - grundmodelle, teil II - nichtstationäre paneldaten. Unpublished manuscript

Kolibri 360 GmbH
Ferdinand-Jühlke-Straße 7
99095 Erfurt, Deutschland
produktsicherheit@kolibri360.de